An Illustrated History of the Civil War

An Illustrated History of the Civil War

IMAGES OF AN AMERICAN TRAGEDY

William J. Miller and Brian C. Pohanka

BARNES & NOBLE
NEW YORK

2006 Barnes & Noble

ISBN-13: 978-0-7607-8411-2
ISBN-10: 0-7607-8411-6

Printed and bound in China

10 9 8 7 6 5 4 3

Editorial Director: Morin Bishop

Design Director: Barbara Chilenskas

Project Editor: Mary Arendt

Associate Editor: Ylann Schemm

Photography Editor: Bill Broyles

Managing Editor: Jeannan Pannasch

Researchers: Ward Calhoun, Theresa Deal, Jeff Labrecque

Designers: Jia Baek, Vincent Mejia

Additional writings by Harris Andrews and Phil George

Calligraphy by Mary Lou O'Brian / Inkwell, Inc.

Table of Contents

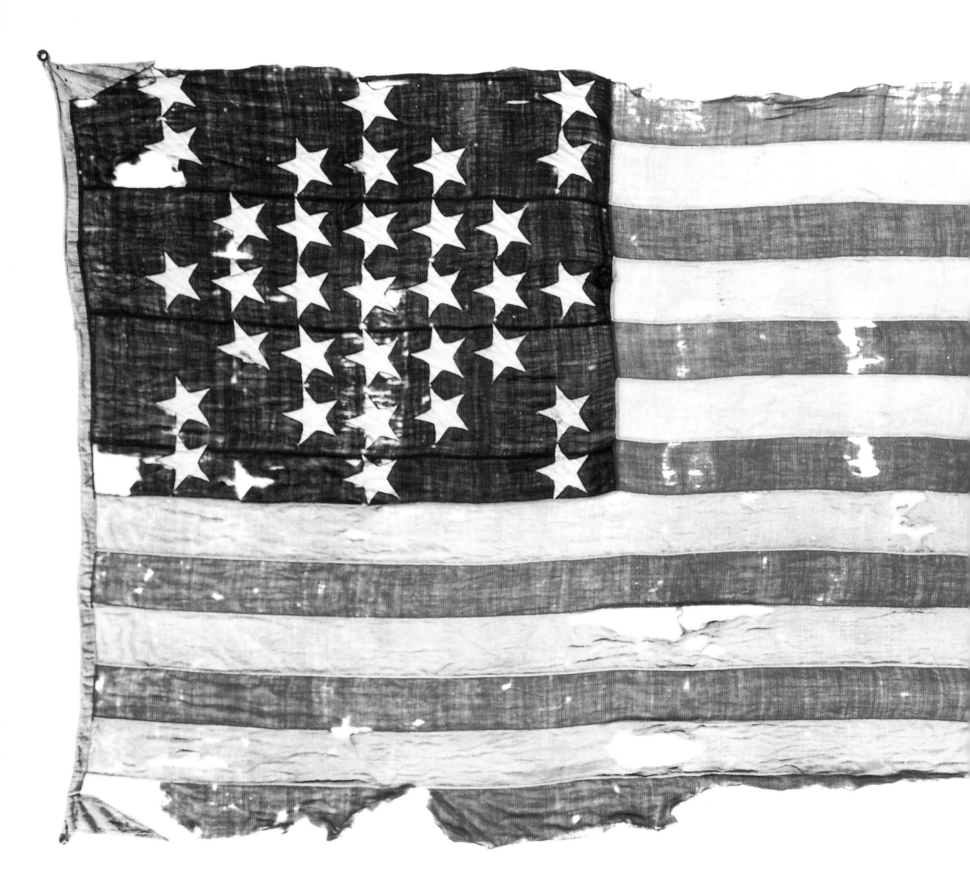

Introduction

NO EVENT IN THE HISTORY of the United States has been as written about, as studied, or as analyzed as the Civil War. Millions fought in the battle. More than 622,000 Americans died, and many more were maimed or left with a life of ruined health. But the scope and cost of the war are not what make it such a fascinating and enduring subject. The Civil War drastically changed American society, and the changes it wrought were so sweeping that the effects are still being felt.

What was behind the conflict? "A storm is rising," Senator William H. Seward of New York wrote in the 1850s, "and such a one as our country has never yet seen." The senator was referring to the upheaval that America experienced in the decade before the war. Though young, prosperous, and growing, the country was in turmoil. Rancorous debate concerning the spread of slavery into the new territories echoed in the halls of the state legislatures and in both houses of Congress. Violence in "bleeding Kansas," a new territory where pro- and antislavery advocates were fighting for control, had for years left countless dead and torn communities apart. Major political parties died or broke up and new ones took their places. New Englanders disparaged Southern slave owners. Westerners decried the far-reaching power of the eastern industrial establishment. Immigrants suffered the prejudice and discrimination of nativists, and Southerners vehemently defended what they believed to be their rights against what they saw as an increasingly intrusive federal government. The major disagreement was over human bondage and its relation to the essential components of American life—liberty, union, self-government—and Seward was among those who saw little hope of a peaceful compromise. The rising storm, he declared, was "an irrepressible conflict between opposing and enduring forces."

The conflict, in short, was inevitable, because it was founded not on differences of opinion but on the very concept of America and how Americans perceived themselves. In the second half of the nineteenth century, Americans believed their creator had endowed them with certain inalienable rights: life, liberty, property, and the pursuit of happiness. The Revolutionary fathers had fought for and won these rights, and Americans before the Civil War strongly believed it was their responsibility to preserve them. They also had not forgotten that the Puritans who founded the Colonies did so believing that God chose them to work His will in the new country and to live godly, moral lives. This sense of America as a land of superior moral character was very much alive in the nineteenth century. So in the 1850s, when Southerners talked seriously of breaking up the Union in order to retain the institution of slavery and maintain control over

their own affairs, they did so because they were convinced that secession was the only way to preserve the ideals of self-government that had been decreed by the Almighty through the Founding Fathers. Unionists, on the other hand, saw secessionists as rebels, madmen bent on destroying God's creation.

By 1861, Northerners and Southerners believed they were more different—ideologically, culturally, and morally—than they were alike. Ralph Waldo Emerson, a Northerner and abolitionist, wrote, "I do not see how a barbarous community and a civilized community can constitute one state. I think we must get rid of slavery, or we must get rid of freedom." A Southerner, even more blunt, wrote, "They are a different people from us . . . and there is no love between us. Why then continue together?"

And so the war came, a result not merely of political and economic issues but of the nature of America and the beliefs and interests of her proud people. In retrospect, the inevitability of the conflict seems plain. And perhaps today we can most fruitfully view the war as a period of reckoning—tortuous and painful but necessary for growth and the preservation of freedom.

Americans began the Civil War as naive idealists. In their rush to the colors, through the early months of the conflict, they rode a wave of patriotic fervor and popular enthusiasm as leaders tried, unsuccessfully, to fight a limited war on a small scale. Indecisive results led the North to attempt to wage organized, systematic war on a grand scale by building an enormous army that would overwhelm the Confederacy from the Atlantic to the Mississippi. But this too failed to produce victory and led instead to enormous battles and unimagined casualties. With the war in its third year, both sides grappled with chaos and destruction. The South found that a string of successes did not equal final victory, and the North that battlefield defeats destroyed national unity. The two sides had no choice but to endure the fighting and confirm their commitment to achieving total victory by digging deeper into their resources of manpower, matériel, and resolve. War with nothing spared or held back resulted in still more slaughter and suffering. The North persevered to victory, but by 1865 rivers of blood had flowed, and innocence had died beside the hundreds of thousands who perished on battlefields and in hospitals and prisons.

Arms may have decided the question of secession and established the primacy of the central government, but more than five generations after the surrender at Appomattox, issues associated with the outcome of the Civil War remain paramount: The rights of the individual, the power of the federal government, the rights of states to control their affairs, the power of majorities and the rights of minorities in a representative democracy, patriotism versus loyalty to higher truths—these are core issues in today's America. To understand that the United States was divided in 1861, and to see how it became vastly transformed in just four years, is to understand much about modern America. What we have been is part of what we are.

William J. Miller
Stone Harbor, New Jersey
June 2000

RUSH TO THE COLORS

A Fire Bell in the Night

AMERICA IN THE 1850s was a place of vast wealth, untrammeled power, and rapid change. In the most literal sense, the country was a land of opportunity, a place where the poor could become rich, the illiterate acquire a free education, and the obscure and the powerless earn fame and rise to influence. In America in the 1850s, the hopeful and the ambitious could find cheap land, boundless rights, and a new life. The country was not yet 80 years old, but already it had become one of the best places in the world in which to live if one were strong, brave, and white.

But if it's true that most Americans in the 1850s couldn't imagine a better place to live, then it's also true that they couldn't imagine the carnage they would cause and that would envelop them a few years later. For four years Americans would kill and maim each other with an efficiency never before witnessed. By the time the last shots were fired in 1865, more than 600,000 young Americans were dead and at least three quarters of a million wounded. The war subjected hundreds of thousands to chronic disease and its consequent lifelong suffering. Meanwhile, uncounted wives, widows, and orphans faced bleak futures.

The American Civil War was more than a century in the making, and many paths—none of them distinct, all of them twisted, intertwined, and interdependent—led to the destruction. Technology, politics, economics, prejudice, greed, and the rapid mixing of cultures and "radical" ideas separated Americans at the time. But the most divisive issue in 1850s America was the system of slavery that had existed for more than 200 years. Many believed the time had come to end slavery; others, recognizing that America's new prosperity was due largely to that "peculiar institution," argued for its protection. Had time not been of the essence, the debate might have been resolved peacefully, but by the end of the 1850s, time was running out.

The United States in the first half of the nineteenth century experienced explosive growth in territory, population, and wealth. With the Louisiana Purchase in 1803, Congress more than doubled the size of the fledgling nation. Forty-five years later, victory in the war with Mexico brought the country nearly a million additional square miles of frontier land. Homesteaders came not only from the eastern states but also from Europe to settle the vast new territory.

In the decade before the Civil War, disputes over slavery in Congress and the western territories often ended bloodily. With the cloth sign above, Republicans mocked the platform of the 1856 Democratic presidential ticket of James Buchanan and John Breckinridge. The cloth's image of slavery riding into the territories on a ram symbolized the violent, proslavery "Border Ruffians."

Ironworkers across the North, like those at New York's West Point Foundry, depicted at left in John Ferguson Weir's *The Gun Foundry*, helped make the United States an industrial giant by 1860. The technological revolution and a booming economy brought a flood of immigrants seeking the good life. The 1857 handbill below lured new Americans west, to a region that was more accessible than ever, thanks to technological wonders like trains and steamboats.

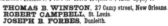

EMIGRATION
UP THE MISSISSIPPI RIVER.

The attention of Emigrants and the Public generally, is called to the now rapidly improving

TERRITORY OF MINNESOTA,

Containing a population of 150,000, and goes into the Union as a State during the present year. According to an act of Congress passed last February, the State is munificently endowed with Lands for Public Schools and State Universities, also granting five per cent. on all sales of U. S. Lands for Internal Improvements. On the 3d March, 1857, grants of Land from Congress was made to the leading Trunk Railroads in Minnesota, so that in a short time the trip from New Orleans to any part of the State will be made in from two and a half to three days. The

CITY OF NININGER,

Situated on the Mississippi River, 35 miles below St. Paul, is now a prominent point for a large Commercial Town, being backed by an extensive Agricultural, Grazing and Farming Country; has fine streams in the interior, well adapted for Milling in all its branches; and Manufacturing **WATER POWER** to any extent.

Mr. JOHN NININGER, (a Gentleman of large means, ideas and liberality, speaking the various languages,) is the principal Proprietor of **Nininger**. He laid it out on such principles as to encourage all **MECHANICS**, Merchants, or Professions of all kinds, on the same equality and footing; the consequence is, the place has gone ahead with such rapidity that it is now an established City, and will annually double in population for years to come.

Persons arriving by Ship or otherwise, can be transferred without expense to Steamers going to Saint Louis; or stop at Cairo and take Railroad to Dunleith (on the Mississippi). Steamboats leave Saint Louis and Dunleith daily for **NININGER**, and make the trip from Dunleith in 36 to 48 hours.

NOTICES.

1. All Railroads and Steamboats giving this card a conspicuous place, or gratuitous insertion in their cards **AIDS THE EMIGRANT**, and forwards their own interest.

2. For authentic documents, reliable information, and all particulars in regard to Occupations, Wages, Preempting Lands in neighborhood. Lumber, Price of Lots, Expenses, &c., apply to

THOMAS B. WINSTON, 27 Camp street, New Orleans.
ROBERT CAMPBELL, St Louis.
JOSEPH B. FORBES, Dunleith.

During the same period, America began to feel the effects of a revolution in technology. Eli Whitney's cotton gin, which extracted seeds from cotton fiber, enabled slaves to pick 20 times more cotton than previously. Thus the invention made cotton a profitable crop and slavery a profitable institution in the South, where the climate suited cotton. Congress ended the African slave trade in 1808, but in the South the slave population continued to grow. In 1790 there were 700,000 slaves in all of America; in 1860 there were 4,000,000—all in the South and the border states. In the North, steam-driven machinery in factories began performing tasks that previously had been done by hand in shops and homes. The textile industry thrived in New England. By the 1850s the South produced three-fourths of all the cotton grown in the world. Cotton made up 80 percent of the trade between the United States and Great Britain; it was by far America's most important export. The slave-driven cotton economy of the South fueled Northern industrial growth and national trade, and slavery continued to flourish because it benefited so many— Northern mill owners and shippers, Southern planters, European merchants. Cotton was king.

Economic gains, bolstered by technology and the growth of slavery, contributed to a population increase of 300 percent in 50 years. The per capita income in the United States doubled in that half century, and the gross national product increased sevenfold. Including free

blacks but excluding slaves, 90 percent of the people in America in 1860 could read—among the highest literacy rates in the world at the time.

Attracted by the burgeoning wealth and almost limitless cheap land, Europeans, mainly from Germany and Ireland, swarmed to America and settled mostly in the North. Crop failures in Ireland and revolutions on the Continent in the 1840s displaced millions. Many of these immigrants were poor and lacked the skills needed to succeed in a runaway industrial economy. In addition, many were Roman Catholics, which in predominantly Protestant America made them unappealing to employers. Some Americans objected to the influx of foreigners, whom they perceived as stealing their jobs, housing, and land. Fueling the resentment, the new arrivals also spoke, acted, and worshiped differently. The situation provoked a strong nativist movement—its followers were called Know-Nothings—and in 1856 its supporters went so far as to nominate a candidate for president. The nativists had no lasting influence on the politics of the time, but their existence in the 1850s confirms the desperation many Americans felt as they tried to retain some control over a country that was hurtling into the future and changing too fast for their liking.

Most Americans adapted to their new neighbors and concerned themselves with their own problems and progress, and for an increasing number that progress was westward. In 1815 Senator John C. Calhoun of South Carolina had urged his colleagues to "bind the nation together, with a perfect system of roads and canals." What followed was nothing less than a transportation revolution. Steamboats, canals, and railroads drove the nation forward by opening new lands and ever more markets. By 1850 more than 3,700 miles of canals connected merchants and consumers, steamboats plied almost every navigable river, and more than 9,000 miles of iron rails linked American cities. No other country in the world came close to matching this internal infrastructure. But this was only the beginning. Between 1850 and 1860, Americans laid another

In the thriving economy of the 1840s and 1850s, America was all about manufacturing, moving, and selling. Sailing and other ships from around the world stopped in New York City and turned the docks at the end of Wall Street (opposite) into a forest of commerce. Factories served by ships and rail lines— America more than tripled its track mileage in the 1850s—made fabulous profits, especially in the Northeast (top), the center of the nation's wealth. The North dominated the nation's commerce, controlling most of the manufacturing, railroads, and shipping. Above, the South's Louisville & Nashville line.

The slavery business was especially profitable for auctioneers who worked for hire at slave markets like the one at top right, in Atlanta, and advertised their services on trade cards (above). Auctioned slaves were issued identification tags (middle). A healthy slave could fetch $2,000 or more by 1860, so owners might sell a troublesome one—or merely punish him by putting him in an iron neck brace with bells (top).

21,000 miles of railroad. The West boomed. In the 1840s a journey from Cincinnati to New York consumed a month and a half. A decade later the trip took five days. Chicago grew almost 400 percent in 10 years.

The country's psychological landscape also changed. Many Americans had been uncomfortable with slavery for decades (it was outlawed north of the Mason-Dixon by 1800) and had sought ways to end it. Through the American Colonization Society, founded in 1816, Northerners and Southerners alike supported a plan to emancipate slaves and send them to other countries. Others rejected the idea. "Tell us no more about colonization," wrote Bostonian David Walker, a free black, "for America is as much our country as it is yours." After the founding of the American Antislavery Society in 1833 and the publication of William Lloyd Garrison's abolitionist newspaper, *The Liberator*, two years earlier, the number of abolitionists grew, and their strong, energetic rhetoric ensured that slavery would never again be accepted merely as an economic reality. Theodore Dwight Weld, a popular and powerful abolitionist orator, declared that slavery was "preeminently a moral question, arresting the conscience of the nation."

J.H.ELLAWELL

Southerners disagreed. To most of them, slavery was not a matter of economics or conscience but of culture. In 1860 only one out of four Southern families owned slaves, and most of those families owned five or fewer, so the great majority did not participate in slavery directly. Still, slaves had always been part of the fabric of Southern society, and to Southerners, destroying slavery meant destroying that society—a thought that roused and incensed Virginians, Louisianans, and everyone in between. "We of the South," Senator Calhoun declared, "will not, cannot, surrender our institutions. To maintain the existing relations between the two races, inhabiting that section of the Union, is indispensable to the peace and happiness of both."

Though Calhoun expressed the sentiments of most Southerners, only a few could relate to what Calhoun himself represented—the economics of slavery. The 40,000 "planter" families that owned 20 or more slaves were a small minority, yet they exerted a disproportionate influence. They dominated politics and their wealth and status gave them access to the national stage, where they defined "Southern interests" and protected them in Congress and the White House. Of the 16 presidential elections held between 1788 and 1848, 12 were won by a Southern slaveholder. These men helped shape the national debate in the 1830s, '40s, and '50s, casting sectional disagreements into debates

Cotton plantations under good management could turn immense profits. Slaves labored in the fields to plant, harvest, and gin the crop, but they also served as skilled workers—producing everything from milled lumber to nails to tanned leather—making large plantations like the one above nearly self-sufficient.

over the rights of states and the power of the federal government, rather than slavery and freedom. When they did address these issues, however, they argued that slavery was not an evil. Declared Calhoun in 1837, "I hold it to be a good, as it has thus far proved itself to be to both [races], and will continue to prove so if not disturbed by the fell spirit of abolition."

In 1845 the country annexed Texas. A few years later, as part of its settlement in the war with Mexico, Congress accepted almost a million more square miles, including California. By 1850 the United States extended from the Atlantic to the Pacific. Ironically, it was these new territories, not the South or North, that brought the slavery issue to a head, lending urgency to the question, Should the nation permit slavery to expand into the new territories?

The nation couldn't answer, and attempts to find a solution only raised new questions. Did Congress have the right to prohibit slavery in any state or territory? Did the states have a right to protect their own interests against decree from Washington? Did the people of a region have the right to decide for themselves what was in their best interests? Leaders on both sides compromised in the hope of avoiding bloodshed. All recognized that the secession of states and open conflict between North and South, once unthinkable, was now a distinct possibility.

On October 16, 1859, John Brown and at least 20 other armed men took over the United States arsenal at Harpers Ferry, Virginia. The intensely religious Brown had dedicated his life to freeing America's slaves, but unlike most abolitionists, he embraced violence as a method. A few years earlier, he and several others had murdered five proslavery men in

Early in his life, John Brown (above) swore his allegiance to the cause of freedom. This earliest known photograph of him was probably taken in 1846 in Massachusetts. Thirteen years later, a bearded Brown led an attack on the United States arsenal on the banks of the Potomac River at Harpers Ferry, Virginia (top left). Colonel Robert E. Lee (inset, as he appeared in the mid-1850s) and a company of U.S. Marines were called in from Washington to manage the incident.

Kansas. To many, Brown was a hero. Wealthy abolitionists supported him financially through the late 1850s as he planned his bold stroke: With the weapons captured at Harpers Ferry, he would escape to the mountains of Virginia and establish a stronghold, revealing the location only to slaves. Once the expected droves of escaped slaves arrived, Brown planned to arm them and lead them to liberate more slaves, adding them to the ranks so that his army of freedom would grow. The scheme was as preposterous as it was grandiose. Most of the Harpers Ferry raiders were killed or, like Brown, wounded. Brown was quickly tried for treason and hanged. Resolved to the end, he declared that he would give up his life joyfully if it led to freedom for the slaves. Just before his death he wrote that "the crimes of this guilty land will never be purged away but with blood."

To Southerners, Brown's raid and his portrayal by abolitionists as a martyr proved what they had long been arguing: Northerners were bent not only on stopping the spread of slavery, but also on eradicating it in the South. Southern leaders argued that Brown's attack was ultimately an attack on the South. The handwriting was on the wall. The killing had begun. Was war inevitable?

When word of Brown's raid spread, militiamen converged on Harpers Ferry (above). Several of Brown's men fell dead in the streets, and the rest barricaded themselves in the fire-engine house of the arsenal. When Brown refused to surrender, the marines stormed the fort and captured Brown and the few of his men who survived.

AMERICA MAKES

By 1860 America was making almost everything in factories, and the work was being done not by skilled human hands but by machines. The North was far ahead of the rest of the country in manufacturing. The 11 Confederate states had about 20,000 factories of all types in 1860, but New York and Pennsylvania each had more than that. New England produced more than 10 times as much cotton cloth as the entire South. Although working conditions were often cramped and unsafe, millions of urban Americans—men, women, and children, including the men at left, at a Vermont chisel and steel-square works—accepted manufacturing jobs. About a third of New England's factory workers were women.

MEN OF IRON

On the brink of war and in the age of railroads, steamships, and ironclad gunboats, any nation that could forge iron possessed an enormous advantage over a foe that could not. The Jackson Pit Iron Mine near Negaunee on Michigan's Upper Peninsula (opposite), and others like it, helped increase production at America's iron foundries by more than 40 percent between 1850 and 1860. In the last year before the war, those foundries made 92 pounds of iron for every man, woman, and child in the country, and 92 percent of that iron came from the North.

AMERICA BOUND

In the 1840s and 1850s America was a magnet for Europeans. Millions of Irish fled the potato famine of the late 1840s; most arrived impoverished and settled in eastern cities. Many Germans who arrived in those decades were fleeing political unrest, and generally they were not as destitute as the Irish. Many of the Dutch—an English corruption of *Deutsche*, or "German"—could afford to travel westward to cheap land in Ohio and beyond. In the illustration at right, immigrants crowd a London medical inspector's office to gain the necessary clean bill of health that would permit them passage to America.

COMMERCE

SOUTHERN IRON

The 10-inch mortar that fired on Fort Sumter, setting off the Civil War, had been cast years earlier at Tredegar Iron Works (right), on the banks of the James River in Richmond, Virginia. Founded in 1836, Tredegar became the Confederacy's most important manufacturer and its main foundry. Before the end of the war, Tredegar produced 1,160 iron and bronze guns, mortars of 49 different types, and about 90 percent of the Confederacy's artillery ammunition, earning the title "Arsenal of the South."

KING COTTON

In the 1850s cotton stood high on docks from Charleston (left) to Galveston, Texas, and it made Americans—and some Europeans—rich. One planter boasted that Southerners were "unquestionably the most prosperous people on earth, realizing ten to twenty percent on their capital with every prospect of doing as well for a long time to come." Because cotton fed national economies on both sides of the Atlantic, Southerners were confident they held vast strength. British and French mill owners, they believed, could not do without cotton and so would pressure their governments to aid the South in any conflict. "Cotton," wrote one Atlanta editor, would bring "wooing princes to the feet of the Confederate States." A Southern senator put it more strongly: "No power on earth dares to make war on cotton. Cotton is King."

GOTHAM CITY

Perhaps no city characterized America's boisterous growth, economic vitality, and urban dynamism better than New York. For bustle, Broadway (left, in 1860) could match any grand thoroughfare in Europe; in fact, British visitors were surprised to find New York thoroughly modern. They marveled at the size and up-to-date appointments of the hotels, the excellence of the restaurants, and the continuous clamor of the streets. With nearly a million inhabitants, and more arriving almost daily from Europe, New York was the largest city in America, five times the size of the South's biggest city, New Orleans.

SLAVE SALE

Abolitionists missed no opportunity to provoke outrage over the cruelties of slavery. Above, a slave mother pleads with her unmoved master to not sell her infant child while an indifferent auctioneer displays the babe to prospective bidders. The sale of slaves, especially away from their spouses and families, was one of the more odious aspects of the institution and it deeply troubled some Americans. Abraham Lincoln recalled a riverboat trip down the Ohio in 1841: On board were "ten or a dozen slaves, shackled together with irons. That sight was a continual torment to me ... and continually exercises the power of making me miserable."

HAPPINESS AND FREEDOM

Depending on where they lived and for whom they labored, the four million slaves in America in 1860 subsisted in greatly varied conditions, and those who debated over the slaves' fate often framed those variations to their side's advantage. In 1857 Virginia lawyer George Fitzhugh wrote with no irony that "The negro slaves of the South are the happiest, and, in some sense, the freest people in the world. The children and the aged and the infirm work not at all, and yet have all the comforts and necessaries of life provided for them. They enjoy liberty, because they are oppressed neither by care nor labor." Abolitionists, however, saw slavery as a crime against the spirit. "Here lies the evil of slavery," thundered Reverend William Ellery Channing, "the extinction of the proper consciousness of a human being with the degradation of a man into a brute."

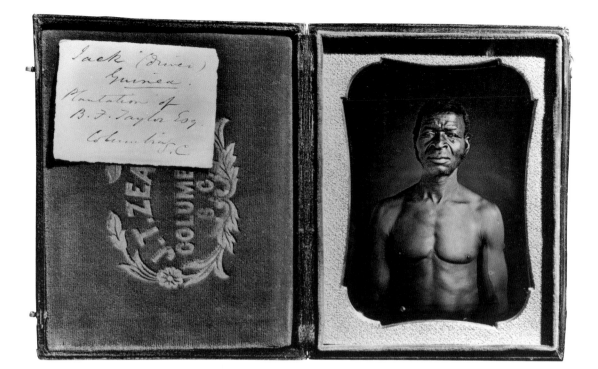

MANHOOD

Jack Guinea, a South Carolina slave, sat for the portrait above in 1850 as part of a scientist's study of racial characteristics. Such pictures of pride and strength inspired abolitionists in their crusade. "We have to undo the accumulated wrongs of two centuries," wrote the poet John Greenleaf Whittier, "to remake the manhood which slavery has well-nigh unmade, to see to it that the long-oppressed colored man has a fair field for development and improvement."

SLAVE BREAKING

The South's slavery-based economy spawned ancillary businesses. An 1855 receipt from Kentucky (below) reveals that a "slave breaker" earned four dollars for whipping eight slaves. The slave above, inconceivably altered by the lash, is believed to have escaped and served in the Union army.

YANKEE INGENUITY

When Eli Whitney, a mechanically inclined Yankee fresh from Yale College, arrived in Savannah, Georgia, in 1794, he learned that slaves could pick and clean only a pound of cotton a day. The trouble was the tiny seeds nestled in the valuable lint. The problem of extracting the seeds intrigued Whitney, and he set to work in a borrowed workshop. His remarkably simple invention, the cotton gin, permitted slaves (opposite) to pick and clean up to 20 pounds per day, thus revolutionizing the Southern economy by making cotton—and slavery—profitable.

Abolitionists

The goals of the abolitionists were simple: in the words of one of their leaders, William Lloyd Garrison, "Let me give the sentiment which has been, and ever will be, the governing passion of my soul: Liberty for each, for all, and forever!"

THE VOICE OF FREEDOM

Born a slave in Maryland, Frederick Douglass (right), escaped at about age 20. Educated and articulate, he settled in Massachusetts, where he became involved in the abolitionist movement. He traveled widely and lectured tirelessly against slavery. "He stood there like an African prince," wrote one woman who heard him speak, "conscious of his dignity and power, grand in his proportions, majestic in his wrath, as with keen wit and satire, and indignation, he portrayed the bitterness of slavery." By the early 1860s, when he was in his early 40s (the period of this photograph), he was known throughout the country and was influential in Northern political circles. He met with Lincoln at least twice, and inspired blacks to serve in the Federal army.

A FREE WOMAN

Sojourner Truth (above) was born Isabella Van Wagener, the daughter of slaves, in New York State in the eighteenth century. She escaped to Canada and freedom in 1827, only a year before the state abolished slavery, then moved to New York City in 1829. She acquired a reputation as a spiritualist, and in 1843 renamed herself Sojourner Truth. For the next 40 years she would be a popular and effective speaker for the abolitionist cause and for women's rights. In 1864 she visited with Abraham Lincoln at the White House.

BEST-SELLING AUTHOR

Harriet Beecher Stowe (right) had been publishing essays for 15 years by the time she began writing *Uncle Tom's Cabin*, the story of a harried slave family and the cruel whites who oppressed them. "I look upon it," she wrote, "as almost a despairing appeal to a civilized humanity." The book was published in 1852 and sold an amazing 300,000 copies in its first year. Stowe had struck a chord in American hearts and minds. Many Northerners came to look at slavery differently, for Southern slaves now had names—Eliza, little Eva, Tom. When she met Lincoln during the war, he shook her hand and said, "So this is the little woman who made this big war."

NERVES OF STEEL

Like Douglass, Harriet Tubman (right) escaped from slavery in Maryland. But where Douglass's trademark in the fight for freedom was eloquence, Tubman's was courage and cunning. She repeatedly returned to Maryland in the 1850s to help escaped slaves, including her sister, make it northward. She is credited with freeing as many as 300 slaves, and slaveholders offered a reward of $40,000 to anyone who caught her. During the war, she spied on Confederate troops in South Carolina and provided valuable intelligence to the Federals.

ABOLITIONISTS FOR SECESSION

William Lloyd Garrison (above, center) was an indefatigable social reformer and an ardent and vocal enemy of slavery. "I am an Abolitionist," he declared in Boston in 1835, "I glory in the name." His newspaper, *The Liberator*, championed freedom and equality for blacks for almost 40 years. With his close collaborators, Wendell Phillips (left) and George Thompson (right), he insisted that the North secede from the proslavery Union. "If your Union does not symbolize universal emancipation," he said, "it brings no Union for me. If your Constitution does not guarantee freedom for all, it is not a Constitution I can ascribe to. If your flag is stained by the blood of a brother held in bondage, I repudiate it in the name of God."

Fate of the Nation

THE OVERCAST SKIES of the morning had cleared, and Abraham Lincoln, the new president of the United States, stepped into bright sunshine and prepared to address his fellow Americans from the portico of the U.S. Capitol. Never in the nation's young life—it was March 1861—had a chief executive's inaugural address been more eagerly awaited, had a new

Among Lincoln's most ardent supporters during his 1860 presidential campaign was a group of young, energetic, vocal Republicans called the Wide-Awakes. Known for their torchlight parades, in which they carried tin lamps (inset), the group grew to be 400,000 strong by Election Day.

president taken his oath amid such strife and chaos: seven Southern states had seceded from the Union and formed a new government—the Confederate States of America. The Confederate president, Jefferson Davis of Mississippi, had declared that his country did not want to fight but was ready for war if it came. Northerners too wished to avoid bloodshed. So from Texas to Maine, Americans were anxious to learn what Lincoln's policy would be. Many believed the fate of the nation was at stake.

Lincoln had followed a long road to Washington, but he rose to power suddenly, hand in hand with the new Republican Party. Born in a Kentucky cabin 52 years earlier and largely self-educated, Lincoln had made himself perhaps the most articulate man of influence in his adopted state of Illinois. He had spent four terms in the state legislature and two years in Congress. When he turned to practicing law, he prospered. The rancorous debates of the mid-1850s drew him into politics again, and he became a champion of the new Republican Party's ideals. Strained allegiances and failing compromises had led to dissatisfaction with the old parties in the early 1850s, and the Republicans, with remarkable swiftness, filled the void. They defined themselves by their opposition to slavery and particularly its extension into the new territories. In 1856 they ran John C. Frémont for president ("Free Soil, Free Speech and Frémont"). Though he lost to Democrat James Buchanan, Frémont made a strong showing. Lincoln labored to refine the Republican message, and in 1858 he ran for U.S. Senate against the powerful Democratic incumbent, Stephen A. Douglas. Though the debates between these two giants of oratory brought Douglas victory at the polls, they won national recognition for Lincoln and his beliefs: Slavery was morally wrong, and though he declared that he would neither judge Southerners for retaining the institution nor advocate the abolition of slavery in the South, he made it clear that he was adamant about stopping slavery's spread.

By the time the nation girded itself for the presidential election of 1860, sectional and partisan animosity was intense. So divisive were the issues that the Democrats found themselves rent by

THE UNION MUST AND SHALL BE PRESERVED

FREE SPEECH.
FREE HOMES.
FREE TERRITORY.

PROTECTION TO AMERICAN INDUSTRY

FOR PRESIDENT
ABRAHAM LINCOLN
OF ILLINOIS

FOR VICE PRESIDENT
HANNIBAL HAMLIN
OF MAINE

internal disputes. The April 1860 Democratic convention in Charleston, South Carolina, was marked by anger and frustration. Secession was openly discussed in the streets and featured in all the newspapers, deeply troubling Northern delegates. Not only could the factions not agree on a candidate, but many delegates could not consent to be in the same room. When the Deep South's representatives demanded but did not receive the support of Northern Democrats, they walked out, vowing to hold their own convention. When they met in Richmond, Virginia, two months later, they settled on Vice President John C. Breckinridge of Kentucky. Most of the rest of the Democrats met in Baltimore and nominated Douglas as their candidate. Still other Democrats, with some former Whigs and other independents, formed the Constitutional Union Party and fielded a compromise candidate, John Bell of Tennessee.

Lincoln took the Republican nomination in Chicago. Though committed to the Union and unyielding in their view that slavery must not spread, the Republicans tried to build a moderate platform, giving space to mundane matters like a transcontinental railroad, naturalization laws, and accountability in government. Despite their strong stance on the controversial issues, Republicans tried to embrace some Southerners by declaring "the right of each state, to order and control its own domestic institutions according to its own judgment." In other words, the Republicans promised to not interfere with slavery in the Southern states.

"I authorize no bargains and will be bound by none," Lincoln told his managers at the "Wigwam" (top), constructed for the 1860 Republican convention in Chicago. He was elected to run with Hannibal Hamlin of Maine (above, right).

31

CHARLESTON
MERCURY
EXTRA:

Passed unanimously at 1.15 o'clock, P. M. December 20th, 1860.

AN ORDINANCE

To dissolve the Union between the State of South Carolina and other States united with her under the compact entitled "The Constitution of the United States of America."

We, the People of the State of South Carolina, in Convention assembled, do declare and ordain, and it is hereby declared and ordained,

That the Ordinance adopted by us in Convention, on the twenty-third day of May, in the year of our Lord one thousand seven hundred and eighty-eight, whereby the Constitution of the United States of America was ratified, and also, all Acts and parts of Acts of the General Assembly of this State, ratifying amendments of the said Constitution, are hereby repealed; and that the union now subsisting between South Carolina and other States, under the name of "The United States of America," is hereby dissolved.

THE
UNION
IS
DISSOLVED!

Barely two months after South Carolina moved to secede, the new Confederacy inaugurated Jefferson Davis as its president in Montgomery, Alabama. About the ceremony (right), he later wrote, "Upon my weary heart were showered smiles, plaudits and flowers, but beyond them I saw troubles and thorns innumerable."

Unmollified, Southern "fire-eaters," as the rabid secessionists came to be known, declared openly that their states would secede if Lincoln were elected. "Let the consequences be what they may," wrote an Atlanta editorialist, "whether the Potomac is crimsoned in human gore, and Pennsylvania Avenue is paved ten fathoms deep with mangled bodies or whether the last vestige of liberty is swept from the face of the American Continent, the South will never submit to such humiliation and degradation as the inauguration of Abraham Lincoln."

In the November 6 election, Lincoln carried almost the entire North. Though he took only 40 percent of the popular vote, he tallied 180 electoral votes. Breck-inridge, his closest competitor, garnered fewer than half that but carried all the Deep South states plus North Carolina, Maryland, and Delaware. Bell carried the border states of Tennessee, Kentucky, and Virginia, and Douglas won only Missouri and part of New Jersey. Lincoln and Douglas, both openly opposed to the extension of slavery, together took 70 percent of all the votes cast, and Northerners had given Republicans a strong majority in Congress. The results confirmed for the South what it already knew, and the Deep South states, true to their word, withdrew from the Union. In December South Carolina seceded, and in January every state along the Gulf of Mexico, from Florida to Texas, withdrew as well.

To the job of molding a new nation, newly elected President of the Confederacy Jefferson Davis (above) from Mississippi brought experience as a soldier, congressman, senator, and U.S. secretary of war. The cockade of palmetto fronds (inset), originally worn by South Carolinians in support of secession, became a symbol of sectional solidarity and was displayed throughout the South.

The seven disunited states moved quickly to form a government and adopt a constitution. On February 18, 1861, Jefferson Davis, the former U.S. secretary of war, stood before his fellow Southerners in Montgomery, Alabama, took the oath of office as provisional president of the Confederate States of America, and sought to explain to the world how the Union had fallen apart. "Through many years of controversy with our late associates," he declared, "we have vainly endeavored to secure tranquillity and to obtain respect for the rights to which we are entitled. As a necessity, not a choice, we have resorted to the remedy of separation." Southerners had been guided by "the American idea that governments rest upon the consent of the governed, and that it is the right of the people to alter or abolish governments whenever they become destructive of the ends for which they were established." The people of the Confederate states wished only to "preserve our own rights and promote our own welfare," and as secession had "been marked by no aggression upon others," he sincerely hoped the United States would let them depart in peace. If not, "a terrible responsibility will rest upon it, and the suffering of millions will bear testimony to the folly and wickedness of our aggressors."

And so the nation, and the world, waited to hear what Lincoln would say in his inaugural address just a fortnight later. He was clear, firm, temperate, and eloquent, and he repeated what he had said many times. "I have no purpose, directly or indirectly, to interfere with the institution

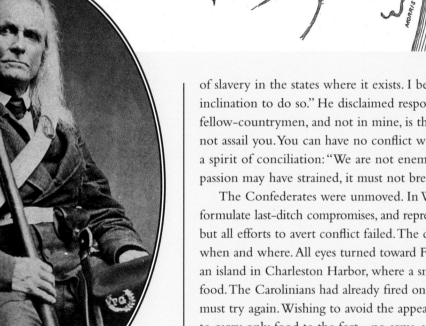

ARMAMENT OF FORT SUMTER, APRIL 12TH &.
BARBETTE TIER: Total number of guns 27 including 11.8 and
Columbiads.
CASEMATE TIER: Total number of gur.
ing 3, 42 pdrs.
Total in both tie:

On the parade (as Mor.
and 1,10in. Columbiads fi
throw shells into Charles
the Batteries at Cummi

2, 32 pdrs. placed to
of gorge
1, 8in. seaco
placed to de

BATTERIES ON SULLIVAN'S ISLAND IN AC
AGAINST FORT SUMTER APRIL 12TH &.
1. Floating Battery. 2, 42-pdrs. 2, 32-pdrs.
2. Dahlgren Battery. 1, 9-in. Dahlgren gun.
3. Enfilade Battery. 2, 32-pdrs. 2, 24-pdrs.
4. Mortar Battery. 2, 10-in. Mortars.
5. Oblique Battery. 2, 24 pdrs.
6. Sumter Battery. 3, 8in. 4, 32-pdrs. 2, 24.
7. Channel Battery. 4, 8in. 6, 32-pdrs. 1, Not
8. Mortar Battery. 2, 10in. Mortars.

BATTERIES ON MORRIS ISLAND
IN ACTION AGAINST FT. SUMTER.
1. Cummings Pt. Battery. 2, 24-pdrs.
3, 10in. Mortars, 1 Rifled 12-pdr.
2. Steven's Battery Iron-clad.
3, 8in. Columbiads.
3 Trapier Battery. 3, 8in Columbiads,
3, 10-in. Mortars.

JAMES ISLAND

SKETCH
OF PART OF THE
HARBOR of CHARLESTON,
SOUTH CAROLINA.
Showing the portion of Batteries
in action against Fort Sumter
April 12th & 13th 1861.

of slavery in the states where it exists. I believe I have no lawful right to do so, and I have no inclination to do so." He disclaimed responsibility for the crisis: "In your hands, my dissatisfied fellow-countrymen, and not in mine, is the momentous issue of civil war. The government will not assail you. You can have no conflict without being yourselves the aggressors." He closed in a spirit of conciliation: "We are not enemies, but friends. We must not be enemies. Though passion may have strained, it must not break our bonds of affection."

The Confederates were unmoved. In Washington, both houses of Congress attempted to formulate last-ditch compromises, and representatives from many states met in a peace convention, but all efforts to avert conflict failed. The question now was not whether war would come, but when and where. All eyes turned toward Florida's Fort Pickens and, especially, Fort Sumter, on an island in Charleston Harbor, where a small garrison of U.S. soldiers was fast running out of food. The Carolinians had already fired on and driven off one supply ship, but Lincoln knew he must try again. Wishing to avoid the appearance of aggression, Lincoln ordered unarmed boats to carry only food to the fort—no arms, ammunition, or reinforcements. He then informed the Confederates that the supplies were on the way. Jefferson Davis now had to decide whether he

would permit the resupply. If he did, he would be admitting his willingness to abide a Federal presence on Southern soil. On April 10 he ordered General P. G. T. Beauregard in Charleston to demand the surrender of Fort Sumter. The fort's commander, Major Robert Anderson, refused. At 4:30 a.m. on April 12, 1861, Beauregard ordered his artillery to open fire. After 33 hours and 4,000 rounds, the Federals officially surrendered on April 14.

Acting swiftly to suppress the insurrection, Lincoln the next day called for 75,000 volunteers to serve 90 days. Each state was to fill a quota based on its population. Necessary though it was from Lincoln's standpoint, the call for troops badly injured the Union cause. He and other Northerners had been working for months to keep the states in the upper South from seceding. His response to the attack on Sumter outraged them, and they declared they would not fill their quotas. The response of Missouri's governor was typical: "Your requisition is illegal, unconstitutional, revolutionary, inhuman. Not one man will the State of Missouri furnish to carry on any such unholy crusade." Within five weeks of Lincoln's proclamation, Virginia, Arkansas, North Carolina, and Tennessee decided to join their "Southern brothers" and secede.

The preliminaries had ended. America was at war.

Fort Sumter's strategic position in Charleston Harbor (opposite) also left it vulnerable to fire from a number of ringing forts. After the secessionist agitator Edmund Ruffin (opposite, inset) supposedly fired the first shot on Sumter from a battery on Cummings Point, "shell followed shell in quick succession; the harbor seemed to be surrounded with miniature volcanoes belching forth fire and smoke," wrote one witness to the ensuing nighttime bombardment (above).

THE CAMPAIGN TRAIL

While tradition held that candidates not actively campaign for the presidency, the campaign might still come to the candidates. Abraham Lincoln, at his Springfield, Illinois, home (above), towers head and shoulders over supporters at a Republican rally in August 1860. Across the nation, partisan parades, cacophonous rallies, sumptuous picnics, and fiery speeches urged the populace to support a candidate. In New England, Lincoln supporters stressed his views on liberty and preservation of the Union. In the Middle Atlantic states, the emphasis was on union and Lincoln's plans for economic growth.

A PLEA FOR PEACE

On March 4, 1861, some 30,000 spectators stand before the unfinished Capitol building (opposite) to witness the inauguration of Abraham Lincoln as the 16th president of the United States. With sharpshooters posted in nearby windows to guard against assassination attempts by Southern sympathizers, Lincoln addressed his Northern audience with words aimed southward: "In your hands, my dissatisfied fellow countrymen, and not in mine, is the momentous issue of civil war. The government will not assail you. You can have no conflict without being yourselves the aggressors. You have no oath registered in heaven to destroy the government, while I shall have the most solemn one to preserve, protect and defend it. We are not enemies, but friends. We must not be enemies. Though passion may have strained, it must not break our bonds of affection."

SECESSION'S BIRTHPLACE

Charleston Harbor and a forest of masts crown the key Southern city (opposite), host to South Carolina's secession convention. At rallies at the Mills House, headquarters for convention dignitaries, impassioned orators whipped up separatist sympathies. After the Ordinance of Secession was signed, firebrand Edmund Ruffin recorded his impressions: "Military companies paraded, salutes were fired . . . bonfires were lighted . . . and innumerable crackers discharged by the boys. As I now write . . . I hear the distant sound of rejoicing, with music of a military band, as if there were no thought of ceasing."

SOUTH CAROLINA'S "ULTIMATUM".

A SUICIDAL ULTIMATUM

An unknown political cartoonist portrays Francis Pickens (right), the governor of recently seceded South Carolina, threatening to fire a cannon labeled "The Peace Maker" if U.S. President James Buchanan (1857–61) does not surrender Fort Sumter. Since the gaping bore of the cannon is pointed at Pickens, the artist seems to suggest that open, armed conflict between the United States and the South would be suicidal for those doing the threatening, rather than tragic for those being threatened.

FINAL CAUSE

A contemporary engraving (left) depicts the Union garrison furtively evacuating Fort Moultrie on Sullivan's Island during the evening of December 26, 1860. Conflicting reports from Washington, coupled with growing hostilities from the surrounding secessionists, led Union Major Robert Anderson to move his command to Fort Sumter, a tiny island in the middle of Charleston Harbor. Southerners perceived Anderson's action as one of aggression, while Northerners acclaimed it for its apparent defiance of Southern disloyalty. Fort Sumter thus became the final cause and first objective of the war.

FIRST ENGAGEMENT

THE OPENING BALL

At 6 a.m. on January 9, 1861, a cannon on Morris Island (left), under the command of gunner George E. Haynsworth, a cadet at the Citadel, fired two poorly aimed shots at the steamer *Star of the West*. This was the first overt act of war. The unarmed vessel was attempting to take reinforcements and supplies to besieged Fort Sumter. Cannon from other batteries soon joined the shelling and the *Star* was forced to withdraw after suffering two minor hits. According to the *Charleston Mercury*, the firing on the Federal ship was "the opening ball of the Revolution."

FORT SUMTER UNDER FIRE

The April 1861 shelling of Fort Sumter (below) by the Confederates lasted 33 hours. From rooftops and elsewhere, residents in Charleston (barely visible in the upper left) cheered and wept as smoke and fire engulfed the Federal bastion. With so much wood and stored ammunition, including 300 barrels of powder near a wooden barracks, fire was the biggest threat. "We came very near being stifled with the dense, livid smoke," a Northern officer later remembered. "The men lay prostrate on the ground [eyes and mouths covered with wet handkerchiefs], gasping for breath."

FRIENDS IN OPPOSITION

Strikingly handsome Confederate General Pierre Gustave Toutant Beauregard (above) and austere Federal Major Robert Anderson (right), opposing commanders in the struggle for Fort Sumter, knew each other before the current unpleasantness. Anderson, a loyal Kentuckian with a Georgian wife, had taught artillery at the U.S. Military Academy at West Point when Beauregard, a Louisianan who finished second in his class of 1838, attended that institution. Both men had been wounded and brevetted in the Mexican War. Learning that Beauregard was in command of Southern forces at Charleston, Anderson warned Washington that his presence would ensure "the exercise of skill and sound judgment in all operations of the South Carolinians."

SUMTER IN SOUTHERN HANDS

As news of the fall of "Sumpter" was being reported in Northern papers (right), Southerners were pouring into the captured fort. On April 15, the day after the Federals surrendered, two Confederate officers and a top-hatted civilian pose near cannon on Sumter's eastern parapet (above). Docked to their right is a steam-powered side-wheeler that shuttled back and forth between Charleston and the fort, transporting Southern soldiers and civilian sightseers to the scene.

"GRIEVOUS WRONG"

As Confederate soldiers man guns on the parade ground of captured Fort Sumter (left), the Stars and Bars snaps in the breeze atop a derrick used to hoist guns to the fort's upper tier. After ceremoniously lowering the Stars and Stripes and leaving the fort to the rebels, Major Anderson wrote, "Our Southern brethren have done grievous wrong. They have rebelled and have attacked their father's house and their loyal brothers. They must be punished and brought back but this necessity breaks my heart."

VOL. X.....NO. 2984.

FORT SUMPTER FALLEN.

PARTICULARS OF THE BOMBARDMENT.

The Fort on Fire and the Garrison Exhausted.

NO ATTEMPT AT REINFORCEMENT.

The Cessation of Firing and the Capitulation.

NO LIVES LOST ON EITHER SIDE.

Major Anderson and his Men Coming to New-York.

THE NORTH AWAKES

Volunteers from the Northern states march in solid, uniformed ranks (above) to the succor of the United States and its Capitol while Fort Sumter burns (center foreground). Earlier national victories like Bunker Hill are remembered in this allegorical work, in which the artist, by completing the Capitol dome—unfinished at the time of the war—suggests the nation's might and right to become and remain whole. Across the country, a blizzard of posters, paintings, and rallies urged men to join the Union cause.

A PLEDGE OF ALLEGIANCE

From rooftops, balconies, and window ledges, citizens of Detroit (opposite) look down on the city's "loyalty demonstration" following the attack on Fort Sumter. As part of the Detroit affair, patriotic spectators watched local civil and military authorities swear an oath of allegiance to the United States and some 3,000 children sing "The Star-Spangled Banner" at City Hall. Similar gatherings took place across the nation.

Secessionists

Hot, cold, or moderate on secession, Southerners debated among themselves the limits of power for state and national governments. Not all were eager to break the bonds of union, but eventually even pro-Union Southerners came to consider Washington too domineering.

ALEXANDER H. STEPHENS

Ardently proslavery *and* pro-Union, Stephens of Georgia was an odd choice for the vice presidency of the new Confederacy. He went to his own state's convention to argue against secession, but ended up signing the ordinance it passed and helping to write a constitution. His strong stance in support of states' rights conflicted with President Davis's attempts to impose centralized authority for the sake of national unity.

LEROY P. WALKER

An active secessionist, jurist, and legislator in his home state of Alabama, Walker was named secretary of war in the Davis cabinet in February 1861. The rigors of the job proved too much for his health and he resigned the following September, accepting an appointment as brigadier general in the Confederate Army. Serving in the Department of Alabama and West Florida, he sought, but never received, an active field command.

JOSEPH E. BROWN

Governor Brown of Georgia had seized two Federal forts in January 1861 and put two infantry regiments in the field before the Confederacy was officially in existence. Allied with Alexander Stephens in the defense of states' rights over national needs, the independent-minded Brown quickly became a thorn in the side of the Confederacy, criticizing Jefferson Davis and his conduct of national affairs and the war.

JOHN C. BRECKINRIDGE

Immensely popular in both the North and South, U.S. Vice President Breckinridge came in second to Abraham Lincoln in the electoral college vote of 1860. The following January he served as senator of Kentucky, where, because he defended the state's claim to neutrality in the sectional conflict, he was branded a traitor. Fearing arrest, he went south and led troops in both the eastern and western theaters. In February 1865 he was named secretary of war.

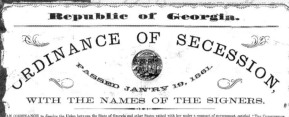

THE UNION IS DISSOLVED

Southern patriots fill Charleston's Institute Hall (left) at seven o'clock in the evening on December 20, 1860, to witness the ceremonial signing of South Carolina's Ordinance of Secession. It read in part, "We, the people of the State of South Carolina, in Convention assembled, do declare and ordain . . . that the union now subsisting between South Carolina and other States under the name of 'The United States of America' is hereby dissolved." The pen and knotted palmetto (opposite, far left) are mementos of the affair taken by one of the ladies in attendance. A month later, on January 19, 1861, another state passed a similar ordinance (above) and heralded itself as "The Republic of Georgia."

Warriors and Patriots

H AD PRAGMATISTS GOVERNED the Southern states in 1861, the Civil War might never have happened. At the time, the 11 states that formed the Confederacy possessed some of the most beautiful and fertile land in America. Southern farms were productive, Southern cities were dynamic and genteel, and members of the Southern elite were educated, articulate, and

Modeled on headgear worn by European armies, the shako (below) was a feature of many American militia volunteer uniforms. This one belonged to a Massachusetts militiaman who served during the Civil War with his state's Fourth Light Artillery regiment.

courageous. But for all its riches, the South was woefully unprepared to wage war against a powerful, industrialized North.

In 1860 America's wealth was centered in the Northeast. Industrialists, manufacturers, and, perhaps most of all, shipping magnates—who had been thriving on maritime trade for decades—controlled most of the nation's money. Despite producing the bulk of the country's most important export—cotton—the 11 states that became the Confederacy together produced less than 8 percent of the country's "value of annual product."

The industrialized North far exceeded the South in production of war materials. Any nation wishing to produce artillery and ammunition—as well as railroad cars, locomotives, and track, and ships, tools, and machinery—had to have iron. In 1860, when the 11 Confederate states produced 26,252 tons of iron, Pennsylvania alone produced 10 times that amount.

Compared with the North, the South lacked a sound transportation network. The North had more turnpikes, surfaced roads, and canals, and a vast advantage in railroads. More than 22,000 miles of track, much of it in good condition and fairly new, linked the Northern states from Boston south to Washington, D.C., and west to Minnesota. The South, meanwhile, had fewer than 9,000 miles of track that varied in quality and gauge, and because different-gauged tracks required different cars, a train couldn't travel from point A to point B without having to stop and unload and reload along the way.

The North also dominated agricultural production. Though the South produced almost all of America's cotton and was ahead of the North in producing rice, peas, sweet potatoes, and some other crops, the Unionists produced more wheat (81 percent of the national total in 1860), more meat (61 percent), more wool (83 percent), and more of almost every other agricultural product that could help win a war.

Of particular importance was the horse and mule population, since at the time almost all cargo was moved at some point by wagon. The North had 66 percent of the total number of

horses and mules, an advantage that would tell heavily later, when the enormous armies used up animals at a prodigious rate—500 horses a day in the North in 1864.

These disadvantages mattered little to Southerners, however; they were confident that courage, determination, and ingenuity would even the odds, especially in a short conflict. Few in the South—or the North, for that matter—expected the war to last longer than several months or a few battles. Editors, politicians, and the throngs of inexperienced military volunteers on both sides confidently proclaimed that one Southern man, or Northern man, was worth 10, 15, even 25, of the enemy. Victory would come quickly and decisively. Most believed that the war would not be one of factories, farms, economics, and naval power, but of men. And the South was more than willing, even eager, to pit its masculine power against the best the North had to offer. Only a lengthy war could tip the scales in the Union's favor.

But even in manpower the South faced what seemed a prohibitive disadvantage. The states and territories that had remained loyal to the Union had a population of more than 20 million, more than double that of the 11 Confederate states. Of the South's nine million, meanwhile, about four million were slaves, which meant a huge disparity in the regions' military populations: Northern armies could draw from 3.5 million white males between the ages of 18 and 45, while only about one million men in that age bracket were available to Confederate recruiters. Neither side was yet considering putting blacks in uniform, a policy that might have favored the South.

A bustling Pennsylvania railroad junction (top) and a Union army corral (inset) reflect the North's superiority in transportation and horseflesh. The South hoped that decisive victories on the battlefield would negate those advantages.

The Confederacy could take some solace in the fact that the North was no closer to fielding an army than the South was. Despite months of saber-rattling about war before the actual outbreak, both sides, especially the North, had to scramble when the time came to rouse manpower. The United States had no plan to mobilize volunteers, and the only method it did have for quickly raising a volunteer force was severely limited. Lincoln had called for 75,000 troops by authority of an eighteenth-century law that decreed that the president could call out the militia for no more than 90 days. Realizing that three months was not enough time to organize, arm, equip, and train citizen soldiers, Congress authorized Lincoln to summon more than 45,000 additional volunteers to serve for three years. But the time it would take to raise and organize those troops would prove costly.

Indeed, Lincoln could only fret about whether the North could bring its men to arms and discipline faster than the Confederates, for he had almost no reserve force upon which to call. In January 1861 the Union army numbered 16,367 officers and troops, and most of the troops

President Lincoln's call for volunteers led to a blizzard of posters and broadsides (opposite). On April 20 more than 100,000 people jammed Manhattan's Union Square in a rally (left) that *The New York Times* called "the largest meeting ever held on this continent." As politicians exhorted the crowd, Major Robert Anderson raised Fort Sumter's flag atop a statue of George Washington. Supervision of the Northern war effort would go to 75-year-old General Winfield Scott (above).

were scattered across the nation, many in garrisons at the 79 frontier posts west of the Mississippi. Their arms were mostly outdated smoothbore muskets. Many of the most senior officers were in their 60s and 70s and had little experience developing strategy or leading large bodies of troops. General in Chief Winfield Scott had led the armies to victory in the Mexican War, but by 1861 he was 75 years old and infirm. Time would soon show that he lacked the vigor to organize the army's war effort.

Even in 1861, when almost everyone, North and South, expected a short war, a conflict that involved thousands of miles of coastline clearly required naval strength. The Northeast's maritime heritage, coupled with its wealth and industrial clout, gave the North a significant advantage in procuring and building vessels and recruiting sailors to man them. The U.S. Navy grew from about 40 steam-driven ships at the start of the war to 260 by the end of 1865, when 100 more, including ironclads, were under construction. The South had no navy to speak of, but Confederate Secretary of the Navy Stephen Mallory worked wonders in acquiring ships,

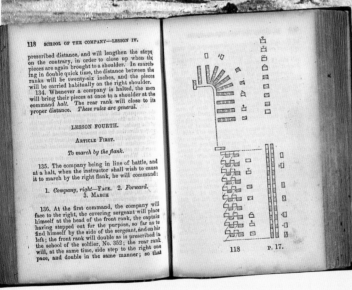

118 SCHOOL OF THE COMPANY—LESSON IV.

prescribed distance, and will lengthen the steps on the contrary, in order to close up when the pieces are again brought to a shoulder. In marching in double quick time, the distance between the ranks will be twenty-six inches, and the pieces will be carried habitually on the right shoulder.

134. Whenever a company is halted, the men will bring their pieces at once to a shoulder at the command *halt*. The rear rank will close to its proper distance. *These rules are general*.

LESSON FOURTH.

ARTICLE FIRST.

To march by the flank.

135. The company being in line of battle, and at a halt, when the instructor shall wish to cause it to march by the right flank, he will command:

1. *Company, right*—FACE. 2. *Forward.*
3. MARCH.

136. At the first command, the company will face to the right, the covering sergeant will place himself at the head of the front rank, the captain having stepped out for the purpose, so far as to find himself by the side of the sergeant, and on his left; the front rank will double as is prescribed in the school of the soldier, No. 352; the rear rank will, at the same time, side step to the right one pace, and double in the same manner; so that

118   P. 17.

Only through constant study and repetitive drill could Civil War units like the Federal company shown at top hope to master the complex choreography of maneuvers prescribed in the tactical manuals (inset).

especially from England. Still, the South would never overcome the disadvantages of fewer ships and scarce manpower.

The volunteers who did come forth in the spring of 1861, however, were game and enthusiastic, whether they joined the army, the navy, or the marines. By the time Lincoln called for 75,000 volunteers in mid-April, the South already had 60,000 men under arms, though they were still imperfectly organized. The basic unit of the armies was the regiment: 1,000 men commanded by a colonel and grouped into 10 companies of 100 men, each commanded by a captain. Most of the volunteer officers won their commissions either by recruiting large numbers of men, by appointment from one of the state governors, or by winning an election among the men of the company. Few of the officers in any regiment had military experience, and those who did very often acquired it not in the regular army but at a military school, such as the U.S. Military Academy at West Point, the Virginia Military Institute, or the Citadel, in South Carolina. These schools produced an excellent cadre of disciplined leaders. The Virginia Military Institute alone sent 1,700 men, mostly as officers, into the Confederate ranks. Such trained leaders were by far the exception, however, and most volunteers, Northern and Southern, were led by men who knew little more about the army than they did.

Enlistment fever was rampant, and as the volunteers came forward they bonded in several ways. Whole neighborhoods or towns would enlist together, with brothers, fathers, cousins, and childhood friends all marching off to fight side by side. A workers' guild might send forth a

Arlington, Washington City P.O.
20 April 1861

Hon.ble Simon Cameron
Sec.y of War

Sir

I have the honor to tender
the resignation of my Commission as Colonel
of the 1st Reg.t of Cavalry

very resp.y your ob.dient

R E Lee
Col 1st Cav.y

U.S. Military Academy cadets, instructed in all branches of the service, demonstrate the intricacies of artillery drill (top). Colonel Robert E. Lee was among the many West Point graduates who resigned their commissions (inset) to join the Confederate forces.

company of glassmakers, canalmen, miners, or firemen. City dwellers often banded together along ethnic lines, producing companies and regiments made up entirely of Irishmen or Germans or a mix of immigrants from several countries. They gave themselves names like the Raccoon Roughs, the Polish Legion, the Schwarze Jäger, the Black Horse Cavalry, and the Grayson Dare Devils. Most of those who enlisted were hopelessly naive about what lay before them: frigid nights with no fires; dysentery and pneumonia; harsh discipline; rain, mud, heat, and dust; unrelenting loneliness and fatigue—incomprehensible carnage.

The secession of the Southern states saw many regular army officers resign their commissions to join the Confederacy. The army lost almost half its officer corps, including some very senior, very highly regarded men, such as Joseph E. Johnston, Albert Sidney Johnston, and Virginia's Robert E. Lee, who had been in the army 32 years. Lee would become the Civil War's most famous soldier. But in April and May 1861, when it came to understanding what lay ahead, neither Lee nor his colleagues had any more advantage than the lowliest private in either army. Every man in uniform in 1861 was a novice, for the world had never seen a war like the one that was brewing.

UNIONIST VIRGINIANS

Only partially armed and without uniforms, a contingent of Virginia volunteers (left) forms ranks in the streets of Morgantown on a hot summer day in 1861. Like many residents of the rugged western region of the Old Dominion, these men remained loyal to the Union. By the end of the year, more than 12,000 Virginians had joined the Northern war effort, and eight Virginia regiments were serving at the front with Federal forces. In 1863, in defiance of the secessionist government at Richmond, the new state of West Virginia was admitted to the Union.

COMRADES IN ARMS

Outfitted in neatly tailored uniforms, and well equipped with knapsacks and U.S. Model 1841 Mississippi rifles, soldiers of the Charleston Zouave Cadets (opposite) were among some two dozen South Carolina militia companies that took part in the siege of Fort Sumter. Established in 1860, the Zouave Cadets became one of the best-drilled and most-disciplined units in the Confederate Army.

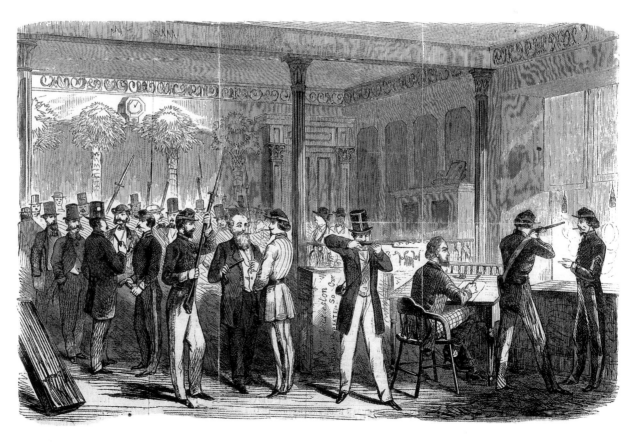

TESTING THE WEAPONS

South Carolina volunteers (right), most of them still in civilian attire, line up to test-fire their muskets at an indoor range in Charleston's Ordnance Armory. Though often issued weapons of varying caliber, most early-war regiments rarely engaged in target practice, since military authorities considered it a waste of ammunition that would be needed on the battlefield.

A SOUTHERN WEST POINT

The fortresslike ramparts of the South Carolina Military Academy (above), popularly known as the Citadel, tower beside the Ashley River near Charleston. Established in 1842 to provide a skilled officer corps for the state militia, the school offered a military curriculum modeled on that of the U.S. Military Academy at West Point. Of the 224 graduates of the Citadel living in 1861, 193 served the Confederacy—four as general officers and 17 as colonels.

THE STUDY OF WAR

With some 20,000 volumes on its shelves and an atmosphere far removed from the realities of battle, West Point's library (right) offered a wide variety of reading material, from military texts, the classics, and biographies of famous commanders to popular literature of the time. In the spring of 1861 the library was the setting for the administration of a newly instituted and mandatory oath of allegiance to the Union—a decree that fueled the exodus of Southern cadets to Confederate ranks.

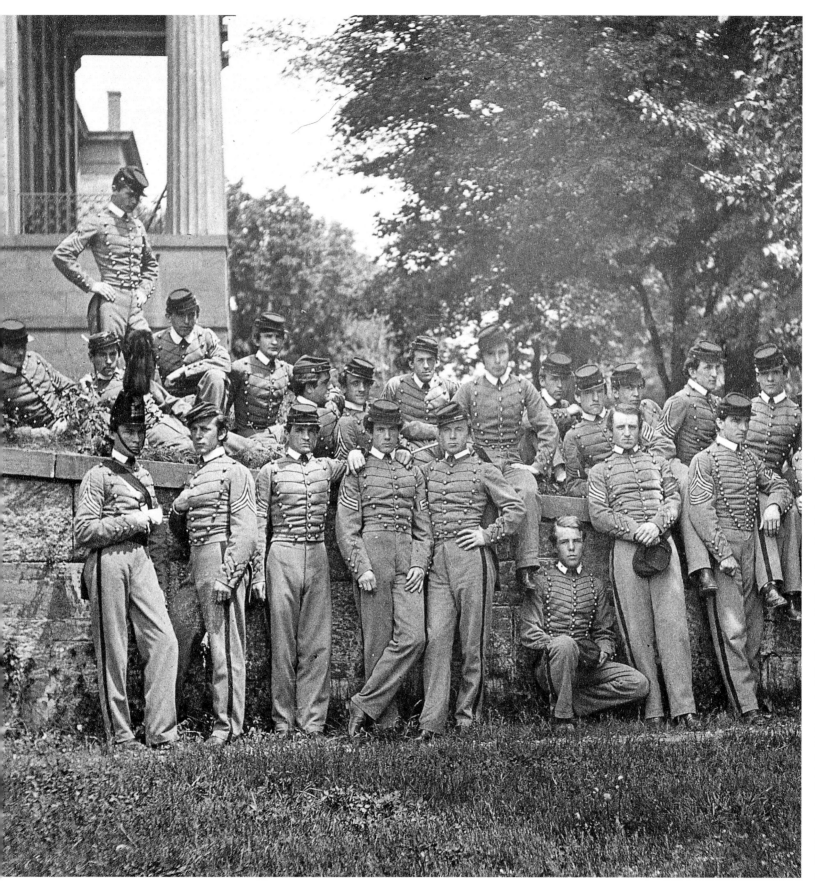

THE THIN GRAY LINE

Because of the national emergency, cadets who would normally have graduated in 1862 were issued their military commissions a year early; thus West Point graduated both a May and a June class in 1861. The members of the class of 1863, shown here shortly before graduation, had entered the academy in 1859 at the height of the sectional crisis. The class was initially 59 strong, but 34 failed to graduate, and of those, at least 17 resigned to join Confederate armies. John R. Meigs—first row, seated to acknowledge his place as first in the class)—was killed by Southern cavalry in October 1864.

EARLY TROOPS

VOLUNTEERS FOR DIXIE

Clad in a mix of civilian attire and hastily manufactured battle shirts, and shouldering muskets brought from home, the men of Company H, Third Arkansas Infantry (above), muster in the streets of Arkadelphia in June 1861. Two months later the regiment sustained 110 casualties in the Battle of Wilson's Creek in Missouri—the heaviest Confederate loss in that engagement. Afterward, the survivors were reassigned to other Southern units.

GUNNERS FROM LOUISIANA

Outfitted in dark-blue uniforms and red caps, or kepis, that were reminiscent of French military attire, the Washington Artillery of New Orleans (right) drew its membership from the Louisiana aristocracy and was considered one of America's finest state-militia units. "For efficiency, drill, and discipline," noted Washington Artillery lieutenant William Miller Owen, "it was not surpassed by any organization of citizen soldiery in the Southern States." Initially a battalion of four companies intended to serve in the war's eastern theater, the artillery later recruited a fifth company for duty in the western campaigns. The gunners shown here were photographed in the battalion's camp near Carrolton, Louisiana, prior to departing for Virginia on May 27, 1861.

SOUTHERN STALWART
Confederate private Edwin Francis Jemison (above), of the Second Louisiana Regiment, typifies the fledgling warriors, North and South. Yanks and Rebs were similar in many ways. Statistics indicate that the typical Civil War soldier was a farmer in his early 20s; had brown hair, blue eyes, and a light complexion; and stood five feet eight and weighed 143 pounds. Most were unfamiliar with the land beyond their native state and had never fired a shot in anger. Private Jemison fought and was killed at the Battle of Malvern Hill in July 1862.

NINETY-DAY WARRIORS

Like many Americans North and South, the high-spirited soldiers of Company D, First Rhode Island Infantry (above), expected the war to be settled quickly, in one decisive battle. That optimistic but ultimately naive assumption was reflected in the fact that, along with thousands of other volunteers, the Rhode Islanders had enlisted for a three-month term of service. Under the command of Colonel Ambrose Burnside, a veteran West Pointer, the regiment went into temporary quarters at Washington, D.C., dubbing their bivouac "Camp Sprague," in honor of Rhode Island's governor. The unit received a harsh introduction to the war in the disastrous first engagement at Bull Run, which left 82 of its number killed, wounded, or missing.

PRESENTING THE COLORS

On May 11, 1861, the 600 troops of the First Michigan Volunteer Infantry (right) march into downtown Detroit from their nearby campground for a ceremonial presentation of regimental colors by the ladies of the city. Accepting the flags on behalf of his soldiers, Colonel Orlando B. Willcox thanked the "beautiful daughters of Michigan" for their "sisterly love and devotion." Following patriotic orations by Detroit's mayor and other dignitaries, Willcox recalled, "the pretty girls stepped forward and pinned a rosette on each warrior's breast and a cockade on each hat amid the cheers of the multitude and martial strains by the regimental band." Two days later the First Michigan departed for Washington and arrived on May 16, the first regiment from west of the Alleghenies to reach the capital.

WORKING THE GUNS

Photographer George S. Cook recorded the image above, of Confederate artillerymen—possibly men of the Third "Palmetto" Battalion of South Carolina Light Artillery—drilling beside an earthen gun emplacement in the defenses of Charleston. Firing a Civil War cannon such as the light 12-pounder shown here was a team effort in which each of the seven-man gun crew had a specific task that he was expected to execute with clockwork precision. Experienced gunners could load and fire a field piece every 30 seconds, even when enemy shells were bursting around them. To compensate for the inevitable casualties, every artillery-man had to learn the duties of each position on the crew.

DEFENDING THE CHIEF EXECUTIVE

Wearing top hats and civilian frock coats, but equipped with muskets and military accouterments, members of the so-called Frontier Guard (right) assemble on the White House lawn in April 1861. Hastily mustered to defend the capital pending the arrival of reinforcements from the North, the Frontier Guard was comprised of local citizens, government clerks, even several members of Congress. Its commander was the notorious Kansas jayhawker, Senator James H. Lane.

Accouterments

In addition to a musket, cartridge box, cap pouch, and bayonet, items the typical early Civil War soldier was expected to carry included eating utensils (left), which he usually brought from home, rations in his haversack, and camping gear. An Indiana volunteer described the lot as "a chaos of straps and buckles."

THE FOOT SOLDIERS

The men in the two ambrotype portraits (opposite)—16-year-old Private Edwin Porter Elrath of the 15th Texas Infantry (far left) and an anonymous Federal infantryman—show typical early-war gear. Each is armed with a musket and wears a knapsack containing blankets, tent basics, and personal items. Ambrotypes were mirror images, thus it should be noted that the Union soldier's haversack, canteen, and bayonet actually would have been worn on the left side, and his cap pouch and cartridge box on the right.

FEDERAL MUSKETS

Though the decade preceding the Civil War saw marked improvement in infantry weapons due to the introduction of muskets with rifled, rather than smoothbore, barrels, many Union volunteers marched to battle in 1861 armed with smoothbore muskets. These had been converted from the antiquated flintlock firing system to percussion—the cartridge powder ignited when the musket's hammer struck a small copper cap placed over the vent cone. Rifled percussion muskets issued to Federal troops included the Colt Special Model 1861 (below, top) and the U.S. Model 1861 Springfield Rifle Musket (second from top).

EARLY-CONFEDERATE ARMS

In modern firearms, the Confederacy was at a distinct disadvantage. Though many flintlock muskets had been converted to percussion in the first year of the war, there were not enough, so some Southern troops were issued antiquated flintlocks like the Nippes Model 1840 Musket (above, third from top), a .69-caliber smoothbore that was less accurate than a rifle though deadly at close range. The South started the war with just 1,881 breechloading carbines. Among the most well made was the .52-caliber Model 1833 (fourth from top); its parts were interchangeable from one gun to another.

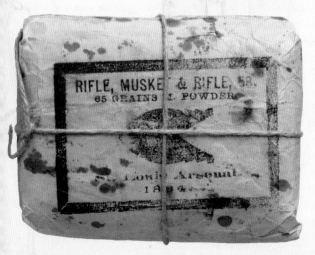

AMMUNITION

Packs of ammunition, like this one (left) of .58-caliber rounds, were carried by the troops—generally 40 rounds in a cartridge box. To load the musket, a soldier tore off the end of the bullet's wrapping with his teeth, exposing the powder. He then poured the powder into the barrel, inserted the conical round, and pushed it down with a ramrod. The powder was ignited by a percussion cap placed over the vent cone of the piece and set off by the hammer when the trigger was pulled.

SIDEARMS

Usually issued to cavalry troopers and sometimes carried by infantry officers, pistols were most effective at very close range. The Smith & Wesson No. 2 Army Revolver (above) was one of dozens of sidearms used by Civil War armies. The Union government of Kentucky purchased 700 of these revolvers from B. Kittredge & Company of Cincinnati and issued them to the Seventh Kentucky Volunteer Cavalry regiment. The No. 2 proved to be a tough, well-constructed handgun.

Sacred Cause

"OH! JOYFUL and ever to be remembered day," wrote a Richmond, Virginia, girl on April 17, 1861. "Virginia has seceded from the abolition government." On that day, Virginians flew a Confederate flag over the state capitol and throngs of Richmonders, the girl among them, ran to see it. "We stayed there in the rain," she wrote giddily,

Soldiers and civilians alike sported colorful kerchiefs, ribbons, and cockades made by loyal seamstresses, North and South. A Southern woman fashioned the child's dress below as an expression of support for the Confederacy. The dress's skirt features an early-pattern Confederate flag while the sash bears emblems associated with South Carolina—a palmetto and crescent.

"jumping and clapping our hands." Two nights later, the heady enthusiasm reached a crescendo. The streets of Richmond teemed with Southern patriots openly declaring their joy in having left the Union. Celebrants packed Main Street from sidewalk to sidewalk. Rockets roared into the night sky, Roman candles showered sparks over the multitudes, and a torchlight parade more than a mile long wound through the city. Bands played the new national airs of the Confederacy and thousands of voices joined in song. It was impossible, wrote one participant, to mistake the source of the crowd's euphoria; it was not mere excitement, but a sense of release, of fulfillment, and of the enjoyment of "real emotion, long cherished." Long cherished and long deferred, according to one Richmond lady: "The fact was, that long before secession, almost every woman in Richmond had in her possession a Confederate flag—ready, at any moment, to run it out from her window."

For months, even years, Americans in the North and South had hoped to avoid war. Though the two sides differed widely in their views on the power of the federal government, states' rights, and slavery—and neither was about to concede those views to the other—most had hoped patience and tolerance would win out over conflict, and most had been willing to compromise in order to preserve peace. Now, peace had flown from its cage, and the people of the divided nation vigorously rejected the spirit of compromise. Decades of rhetoric and appeasements had made them weary of words and eager for battles. Victories alone would satisfy them now. "Come what would," wrote a South Carolina woman, "I wanted them to fight and stop talking."

Northerners and Southerners alike reveled in patriotic displays—they wrote songs and poems, formed parades, gathered for rallies and recruitment meetings—and they couldn't get enough of the exhilaration these displays brought them. By embracing a nationalism that united them with their neighbors, they found they could abandon restraint

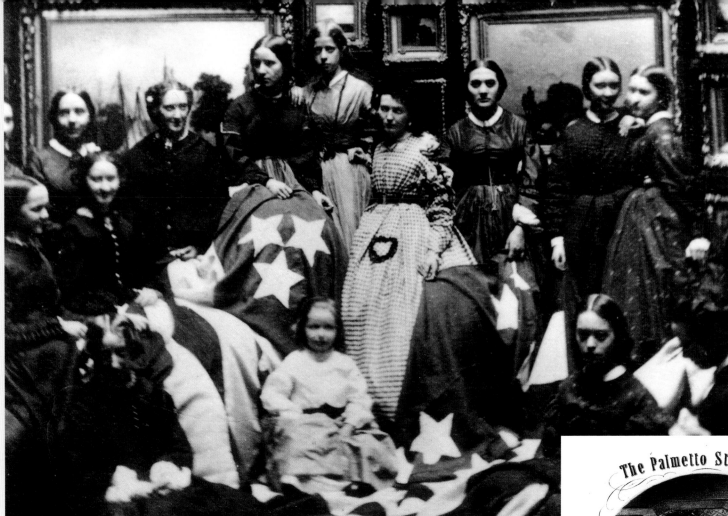

Eager to assist in the Union war effort, a group of Philadelphia women (left) crafts a large American flag at the Pennsylvania Academy of Fine Arts. Hundreds of nationalistic marches and ballads were composed and distributed across the North and South. "The Palmetto State Song" (below) celebrated the signing of the Ordinance of Secession.

and that they loved doing so. By May, Northerners had contributed more than $23 million to the war effort. At the urgings of many, young men flocked to the colors as if on crusade. When Lincoln asked for 14,000 volunteers from Pennsylvania, for example, 25,000 signed up in just 10 days. Other states, North and South, were equally enthusiastic. Each side believed it was fighting in the spirit of the Founding Fathers, and each believed it was doing God's will by defending His chosen people and His instrument—the American Republic—from its enemies.

To Northerners, the Stars and Stripes symbolized the best form of government the world had ever known. The flag, a powerful image for all Unionists, not only represented their independence and their right of self-government; it also represented the courage, sacrifice, and idealism of the Founding Fathers. When Senator Daniel Webster declared in 1830 that the foundation of the American Republic rested on "Liberty and Union, now and forever, one and unseparable!" he had provided the Unionists with a vision of their country and a rallying cry that would endure for decades. A free society in which men governed themselves was the apex of humankind's efforts at government, and since the Founding Fathers had invoked God's will in the creation of the new government, Americans came to think of their country as divinely sanctioned. So when the South Carolinians fired on the flag at Fort Sumter, they galvanized the North by committing

The symbols of the new Confederacy reflected Southerners' conviction that their cause was rooted in the ideals of the American Revolution. George Washington emblazons the Great Seal of the Confederacy (top), while a rendering of the goddess of liberty graces the banner (above) of Virginia's Princess Anne Cavalry.

what amounted to a sacrilegious act: the Southerners had assailed the idea of the Union as God's instrument and insulted not only the North, but also the heroes of the Revolution. "I know how great a debt we owe to those who went before us through the blood and sufferings of the Revolution," a Northern private told his wife. "I am willing—perfectly willing—to lay down all my joys in this life, to help maintain this government, and to pay that debt." The South, a Chicago editor intoned, had "outraged the Constitution, set at defiance all law, and trampled under foot that flag which has been the glorious and consecrated symbol of American Liberty." To Northerners, the campaign to preserve the Union was a sacred cause. Dr. George Junkin, a minister and staunch Unionist despite his long residence in Virginia, declared that "secession is the essence of all immorality" because it neutralizes the citizen's obligation to serve God by preserving the Union. Junkin eventually fled the South for Pennsylvania, leaving behind his daughter and son-in-law, Thomas J. Jackson, soon to be nicknamed "Stonewall."

Even Northerners who viewed the Union cause somewhat differently—the abolitionists, for example—saw it in religious terms. The abolitionists had no doubt that God had willed the war to eliminate slavery. But they hoped the conflict would be fought solely for freedom— freedom for all men. In their eyes, a Northern victory would free white men as well as black, master as well as slave, from the scourge of slavery; it was God's will that his children be free. New Englander Julia Ward Howe captured the idea in her 1861 "Battle Hymn of the Republic":

> In the beauty of the lilies Christ was born across the sea,
> With a glory in his bosom that transfigures you and me;
> As he died to make men holy, let us die to make men free,
> While God is marching on.

Religion played a dominant part in the South's response to the war as well. Many Southerners had been raised to believe that theirs was a nearly perfect society, ordained by God. In their view, the South was an orderly, prosperous place where virtue could flourish and the best in human nature be cultivated. Unfortunately, this was just the sort of thinking that encouraged the South to remain indifferent toward the technological and other changes that swept the North and West in the first half of the century. Many Southerners wanted no part of the turmoil of industrialization and mass immigration, of the radical concepts of Utopianism and, of course, abolitionism, as well as all the other "isms" that convulsed Northern society. Southerners' belief that they were God's chosen people allowed them to think that the war had been ordained by God specifically to help them protect their society and win political independence. On the day Fort Sumter fell, a Virginia minister wrote to his teenaged son that he could consent to his joining the army if "the safety of our country [meaning the Confederacy] requires it," for it would be "clearly the duty of Godly people to meet the issue until death."

Just as the North did, the South drew strength and inspiration from the Revolution. Southerners held that secession had begun the *second* American revolution, which was necessary because the North had abandoned the principles of the first. Southerners too revered George Washington and invoked him as a symbol of their cause. The Seal of the Confederacy featured an image of the general and president, and Jefferson Davis was inaugurated within days of Washington's birthday. As one young Georgian wrote, "The dissolution of this Union cannot silence those consecrated voices of the past. Nor can it rob us of our relationship with and veneration for the virtues and great deeds of the Father of our Country. He was of us."

And so the people of the North and South rose up in righteous indignation and the troops went forward with muskets in their hands, testaments in their breast pockets, and malice in

The elite Seventh New York Militia marches down Broadway (above) as Major Anderson, of Fort Sumter fame, salutes from the pediment of the Astor House Hotel. "I shouted and yelled until I was hoarse," recalled one spectator. "There was something thrilling in the thought that these fine young fellows were going to battle." Julia Ward Howe (inset, right) echoed the devotion of the volunteers in her "Battle Hymn of the Republic."

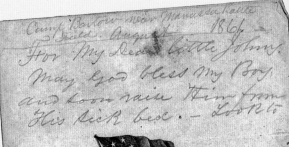

THE LONG ROLL.

FELLOW SOLDIERS,

Amid the quietness of the midnight camp we sometimes hear the hasty steps of our returning scouts, as they report, "The enemy is upon us!"

The long roll is instantly beaten, and we all spring to our arms, feeling that the time for action has come.

We have made great sacrifices for our country's good; we are here fighting for our dearest rights—our most sacred privileges.

We all feel that defeat would be ruin, and that we must have *victory* or *death*.

But, my dear friends, I come to tell you of the approach of a subtle enemy who is stealing upon you unawares. I come to beat the *long roll of alarm* to your souls—your immortal souls.

Americans North and South let the conflict sweep them away. A religious pamphlet for Confederate soldiers (above) bears a note from a regimental chaplain to his ailing son. "Miss Liberty" (right) enjoys herself at a Northern patriotic pageant, one of many such fund-raisers for the Union cause.

their hearts. Some Southern women were especially bellicose. One Arkansas man recalled this about the women in his community: "If every man did not hasten to battle, they vowed they would themselves rush out and meet the Yankee Vandals. In a land where women are worshipped by the men, such language made them war-mad." A Tennessean wrote that every man and woman "was eager for the war, and we were all afraid it would be over and we not be in the fight. . . . Flags made by the ladies were presented to companies, and to hear the young orators tell of how they would protect that flag, and that they would come back with the flag or come back not at all . . . would fairly make our hair stand on end with intense patriotism, and we wanted to march right off and whip twenty Yankees."

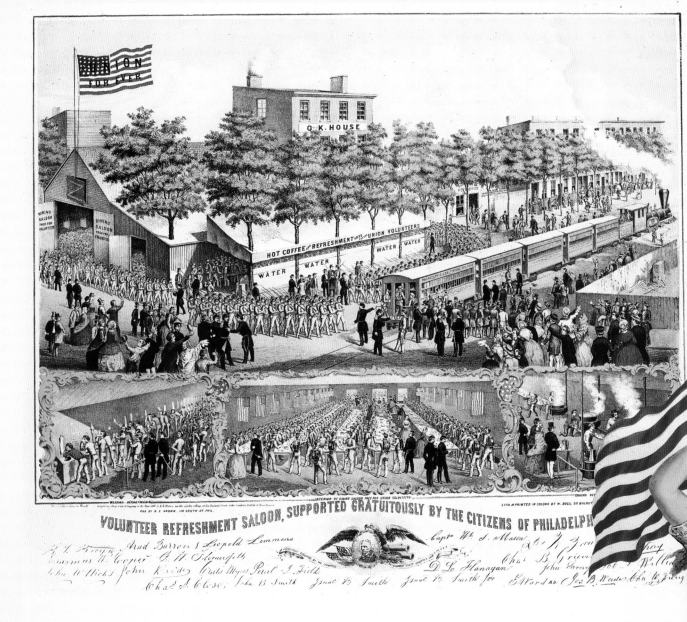

VOLUNTEER REFRESHMENT SALOON, SUPPORTED GRATUITOUSLY BY THE CITIZENS OF PHILADELPHI

At Philadelphia's Volunteer Refreshment Saloon (left), local women dished up bountiful meals to soldiers traveling to the front. The women's initiative and enthusiasm exemplified the "Spirit of '61" (represented below).

While the troops mobilized, so did the citizens. "Volunteer Refreshment Saloons" sought to provide soldiers with clothing and food. Volunteer relief funds raised money to assist the needy families of soldiers. Women carded lint, rolled bandages, and sewed—uniforms, shirts, and flags, tents from sailcloth, and trousers from canvas—until their fingers bled. They knitted socks, undergarments, and scarves. They invited soldiers into their homes for a meal. They met troop trains at dawn to distribute coffee and sandwiches. Religious societies printed thousands of tracts for free distribution in army camps. Even recently arrived immigrants put the needs of their new country above their wish for personal success and rushed to enlist. Everywhere, as the nation fell apart, communities came together in common cause to maintain their idea of the best government on earth.

NEW COUNTRY, NEW SOLDIERS
Recruiters offer cash bounties in an effort to enlist immigrants arriving at Manhattan's Castle Garden (above), while the ethnic composition of the 26th Wisconsin is reflected in a German-language recruiting poster (left). Foreign-born citizens who were indifferent to the issues that divided the Republic opposed military service; others saw a direct connection between soldierly duty and their own aspirations. "Our only guarantee is in the Constitution," wrote Irish-born New Yorker James McKay Rorty, "our only safety is in the Union, one and indivisible."

THE GARIBALDI GUARD
With their regimental colors as a backdrop, soldiers of the 39th New York Infantry (right) flank commanding officers Colonel Frederick D'Utassy and Lieutenant Colonel Alexander Repetti. Their uniforms were styled after those worn by the Italian Army's Bersaglieri. Though the unit was dubbed the "Garibaldi Guard," in honor of the Italian patriot, the regiment actually consisted of at least 15 different nationalities. The *New York Herald* reported that "no regiment that left New York had so much attention given to its spectacular side."

A ROUSING WELCOME

Cheering crowds greet marching Federal troops at Philadelphia's Volunteer Refreshment Saloon (left). A Massachusetts soldier noted that "after a refreshing wash [in the saloon's bathing facility] we were waited upon by a bevy of Christian ladies, overflowing with sympathy and kindness, who served to us the first good, wholesome, clean food since our enlistment."

A BOUNTIFUL REPAST

Enjoying a brief respite from their hectic schedule, waiters prepare to welcome another contingent of hungry soldiers to the mess hall (opposite) of Philadelphia's Volunteer Refreshment Saloon. Established in the war's second month by businessman William Cooper, the saloon occupied a sprawling complex near the terminus of the Camden & Amboy Railroad. A New York officer was pleased by the "substantial and well-cooked food with which the scrupulously clean tables were heavily laden." "At no place were the troops more generously entertained," another volunteer recalled. "A short path to a soldier's heart was by way of his stomach."

CONCERT!

FOR THE BENEFIT OF

The Soldiers.

Greensboro Female College.

A Concert will be held in the
College Chapel
on the night of the 20th inst., for the benefit of our volunteers. Doors open at 6 and a half o'clock. Exercises will commence at 7.

☞ **Price of admission 50 cents. Children 25.**

MUSICAL RELIEF

Despite increasing hardships endured by Southern civilians, fund-raisers were commonplace throughout the war and did much to bolster morale on the home front. A broadside (left) advertises a benefit concert at a North Carolina women's college; the proceeds went to support Confederate troops in the field.

The Zouaves

Dozens of Civil War units marched to war in flamboyant uniforms inspired by the exotic regalia of the French Army's Zouaves. Thomas Southwick, of the Fifth New York Zouaves, wrote, "A more picturesquely unique and fantastical costume could scarcely be conceived."

James E. Taylor

DURYÉE'S ZOUAVES

First Sergeant Henry Vredenburg wore the colorful jacket and sash (above) of the Fifth New York Veteran Volunteer Infantry during the May 1865 "Grand Review" of the Union armies in Washington, D.C. Organized in 1861 by Colonel Abram Duryée, the Fifth New York was considered one of the finest regiments in Federal service.

THE FIRE ZOUAVES

Daring, physically fit, and the heroes of many an urban conflagration, members of Philadelphia's Volunteer Fire Department seemed ideal candidates for military service. Hundreds responded to recruiting poster's like the one above and joined Colonel DeWitt Clinton Baxter's 72nd Pennsylvania Fire Zouaves. New York City's Fire Department, the largest in the nation, fielded two regiments of Fire Zouaves, the 11th and the 73rd New York Volunteer Infantries.

THE NATIONAL ZOUAVES

Twenty-one-year-old James E. Taylor (left) was an aspiring artist when he enlisted for two years in the 10th New York Infantry, the "National Zouaves." (Taylor later joined *Frank Leslie's Illustrated Newspaper* as a sketch artist and war correspondent.) The 10th New York was noted not only for its distinctive variation on the Zouave uniform, but also for establishing in its camp a branch of the Masonic fraternity, the National Zouave Lodge.

A PASSION FOR UNIFORMS

The garb of the famous French Zouaves probably would not have become so popular among Americans had the charismatic young militia officer Elmer Ephraim Ellsworth not emerged in Chicago. In the summer of 1860, in uniforms designed by their commander, Ellsworth's U.S. Zouave Cadets displayed their drill expertise to audiences in 20 cities, winning a prize banner as the country's most proficient militia unit. With many units adopting Zouave attire in emulation of his company, Ellsworth sought to capitalize on the fad by designing uniforms (above) that reflected his passion for European styles.

THE ZOUAVE CRAZE

A Zouave regiment leads a vast column of Union soldiers down Washington's Pennsylvania Avenue in this idealized rendering (left) evoking the "Zouave Craze" that swept the nation on the eve of the war. Due in large part to the success of Elmer Ellsworth's drill exhibitions, the Zouave uniform remained a colorful presence in Federal armies throughout the Civil War.

War, Glorious War

THERE WAS GLORY ENOUGH for everyone in the early weeks of the war. In mid-1861, a Southern soldier wrote to his family, "I am absent in a glorious cause, and glory in being in that cause." Every state had parades, processions, and speeches—people had never seen so much patriotic spirit and expression. But as the conflict intensified, citizens as well as soldiers

Because the war's early uniforms were anything but uniform—Northern and Southern soldiers wore blue, gray, green, or red, regardless of their affiliation—some troops wore special items, like the hat band below, from the Battle of Big Bethel, so their compatriots could identify them.

began to see that war involved more than parades and flag waving, and the novelty of these patriotic displays faded. Northern and Southern leaders, meanwhile—from Presidents Lincoln and Davis down to local drillmasters—were left wrestling with the question of how to turn a mob into an army. The immense outpouring of public energy and enthusiasm was useless unless it could be harnessed.

Most Civil War soldiers went into battle with inadequate training, especially in the beginning, when volunteers—independent, opinionated, and wholly ignorant of war—were the rawest of army material. One West Point–trained officer wrote, "I never saw such a set of grumblers as our volunteers about their food clothing arms &c. and I shall make a Requisition for two wet nurses per soldier, to nurse them in their helpless pitiful condition." A Northern general concurred: "Our men are not good Soldiers—they brag, but don't perform—complain sadly if they don't get everything they want—and a march of a few miles uses them up. It will take a long time to overcome these things." But another Northern officer thought the problem was his peers, not the ranks: "A great many of the officers are worthless & are therefore very angry when anyone tries to oblige them to do their duty. . . . When such thieves & blacklegs are in command how can you expect to have good troops?"

Building armies from this raw material was the responsibility of each side's commander in chief, Jefferson Davis and Abraham Lincoln, and finding leaders was their first priority. But at the time—roughly 80 years after the Revolution—Americans had little experience in war (only 100,000 men fought in the Mexican War in the 1840s, and the cause of death for most of the less than 15,000 who died was disease). What's more, neither the North nor the South had an extensive military system on which its president could draw. Few existing officers possessed significant combat experience; fewer still had worked at developing strategy. Most career officers or graduates of West Point were obscure, young, or middle-aged men who had spent their adult years commanding a few dozen soldiers at a series of frontier outposts. In

THE HERCULES OF THE UNION,
SLAYING THE GREAT DRAGON OF SECESSION.

the absence of a cadre of trained strategists, Davis and Lincoln sought what they thought was the next best thing: intelligent, educated men accustomed to wielding power and influence. Not surprisingly, the presidents looked within their own sphere—politics—to find such men.

Turning political leaders into generals was not a new concept, nor was it necessarily a bad idea. Politicians were good at dealing with large, intricate problems (though not always at solving them), and putting armies in the field was nothing but a succession of difficulties. What mattered most to each president, however, was unifying his country and appeasing the factions in its government. Handing out generalcies helped build alliances and mend fences. With the stroke of a pen, Davis made high-ranking military men out of John B. Floyd and Henry Wise, both former governors of Virginia; former U.S. vice president John C. Breckinridge; and Georgians Robert Toombs and Howell Cobb, whose only previous combat experience had been in the halls of government. Among the many Northerners raised to high command were John C. Frémont and Nathaniel P. Banks, both former presidential candidates and members of Congress. Benjamin

Though General Irvin McDowell (top, fifth from right) commanded Northern forces in the war's first major battle, General Winfield Scott in many respects *was* the U.S. Army. The Duke of Wellington called Scott, a hero of the Mexican War, "the greatest living soldier." Others saw him as the Union's Hercules (above).

Both John C. Frémont (above) and Robert A. Toombs (inset) were born in Georgia. Both also served in the U.S. Senate and both nearly became president—Frémont of the United States and Toombs of the Confederacy. The two were appointed generals in 1861, but neither showed much military ability.

Butler of Massachusetts and John A. McClernand of Illinois, both former congressmen and, more important, Democrats, received stars from the Republican president, as did Lew Wallace, a lawyer from Indiana who after the war went on to write *Ben Hur*. Lincoln, whose constituency included millions of immigrants, hundreds of thousands of whom were of military age, found stars for high-profile Germans Carl Schurz, Franz Sigel, and Louis Blenker, and Irishmen James Shields and Thomas F. Meagher, among others. Of course, the career soldiers, such as Henry Halleck, a West Point graduate who Lincoln would later appoint general in chief, saw little sense in making generals of military neophytes. Wrote Halleck, "It seems but little better than murder to give important commands to such men as Banks, Butler, McClernand, Sigel, and Lew Wallace, and yet it seems impossible to prevent it."

Meanwhile, the conflict's pace quickened. On April 18, Federals were forced to abandon and burn the armory at Harpers Ferry, and Virginia troops occupied it the next morning. On that day, exactly 86 years after Revolutionary patriots fought the British at Lexington and Concord,

pro-Southern mobs attacked the Sixth Massachusetts regiment as it passed through Baltimore. At least 13 soldiers and civilians were killed before the rioting ended. On the night of April 20, Federals, fearing Virginia's encroaching local militiamen, abandoned Gosport Navy Yard at Norfolk, burning and sinking several ships. When the Confederates took possession of the navy yard the next day, they found the Federals had left behind thousands of serviceable cannon tubes, a scarcely damaged dry dock, and a half-burned steam frigate, the USS *Merrimac,* which enterprising Southerners would rebuild into the Confederacy's first ironclad warship, the CSS *Virginia*. In May the Confederate government moved its seat from Montgomery, Alabama, to Richmond, Virginia, thereby placing the capitals of the two warring nations just 100 miles apart, ensuring that the soil of Virginia would be soaked in blood.

As these small incidents—some with large consequences—accumulated in the early weeks of the war, leaders began to emerge. Those who exhibited courage and initiative became instant heroes; others merely died young. On May 24, the day after the state of Virginia officially seceded from the Union, Federal troops marched across Long Bridge over the Potomac River and occupied

Federal soldiers who camped on the Virginia shore of the Potomac River (above, left) drew inspiration from the Washington Monument and the U.S. Capitol, both unfinished but visible across the river. A hundred miles away, in Richmond, Confederates drew strength from another Washington monument—sculptor Thomas Crawford's towering tribute to the first president (above). Standing just outside Richmond's Capitol Building, it became one of the South's most important symbols, reinforcing Confederate lawmakers' beliefs that they were fighting to preserve the nation created by the Founding Fathers.

At the Battle of Bull Run, or Manassas, portrayed above in a painting by Captain James Hope of the Second Vermont, generals on both sides mismanaged the fighting, while the troops displayed surprising determination. Federal general Irvin McDowell (opposite) was as green as the troops he led. Though a military man for 25 years, he had no command experience and approached the battle at Bull Run Creek with doubts about his and his troops' fighting abilities.

the port city of Alexandria, Virginia. Colonel Elmer Ellsworth, the flamboyant leader of New York's colorful First Fire Zouaves, dashed dramatically to the roof of the city's Marshall House hotel and tore down the Confederate flag flying there. While descending the stairs, he met the irate innkeeper, who fatally shot him, giving the Union its first martyr. The officer lay in state at the White House, and Lincoln himself, a friend of Ellsworth's, wrote a letter to the young colonel's parents lamenting the "promised usefulness to one's country, and bright hopes for the future . . . suddenly dashed." It would become a requiem for hundreds of thousands more.

But the North had good news, as well. On June 3, Federals surprised and routed a small Confederate force at Philippi, Virginia, and in mid-July, 2,000 Federals under General William S. Rosecrans won resounding victories in western Virginia at Rich Mountain and Carricks Ford. The South lost more than 600 men. Though small by later standards, these victories were large enough at the time to support the theory that the war would not last long. The *New York Tribune*, an influential abolitionist organ edited by the well-known Horace Greeley, led the growing chorus of "Forward to Richmond!" The Confederate Congress was to meet there for the first time in July, and enthusiastic Northerners wanted to capture the city before the

GEN. Mc DOWELL.

Entered according to Act of Congress, in the year 1861, by D. Appleton & Co., in the Clerk's Office of the United States for the Southern District of New York.

Though General McDowell doubted his soldiers' abilities, they surprised him by coming close to victory at Henry House Hill (top right), only to have the Southern resistance harden, forcing a Union defeat. Private A. P. Hubbard of the Fourth South Carolina was literally saved by the word of God, as his bullet-punctured New Testament (inset) attests.

THE BATTLE OF BULL RUN, 3 P.M. JULY 21, 1861.

lawmakers could convene. General Irvin McDowell, commander of the Federal army around Washington, protested that his untrained men were not ready. Lincoln replied: "You are green, it is true, but they are green, also; you are all green alike." Events would soon prove them both correct.

In April McDowell led 37,000 volunteers from Washington to Manassas, Virginia, on the banks of Bull Run Creek, where they met a combined force of 32,000 Confederates under Generals Joseph Johnston and P. G. T. Beauregard. The Union plan of attack was sound, but far too complicated for novice soldiers. McDowell's men nevertheless fought admirably and effectively, until confusion set in and Southern resistance hardened. After a day of fighting, the Unionists decided they lacked the force to continue. Nearly 2,000 Southerners were killed, wounded, or taken prisoner, but the Federals lost almost 3,000, and the survivors flew the battlefield.

Manassas—or the Battle of Bull Run, as the North called it— remains one of the more dramatic and important events in American history. The Southern victory shocked the North—and the world—and Americans in the Union and the Confederacy began to see war for what it really was. A South Carolinian spoke for many soldiers when he wrote, "For ten long hours it literally rained balls, shells and other missiles of destruction. . . . The sight of the dead, the cries of the wounded, the thundering noise of battle can never be put on paper. The dead, the dying and the wounded, all mixed up together, friend and foe embraced in death; some crying for water; some praying their last prayers; some trying to whisper to a friend their last farewell message to the loved ones at home. It is heartrending. I cannot go any further. Mine eyes are damp with tears."

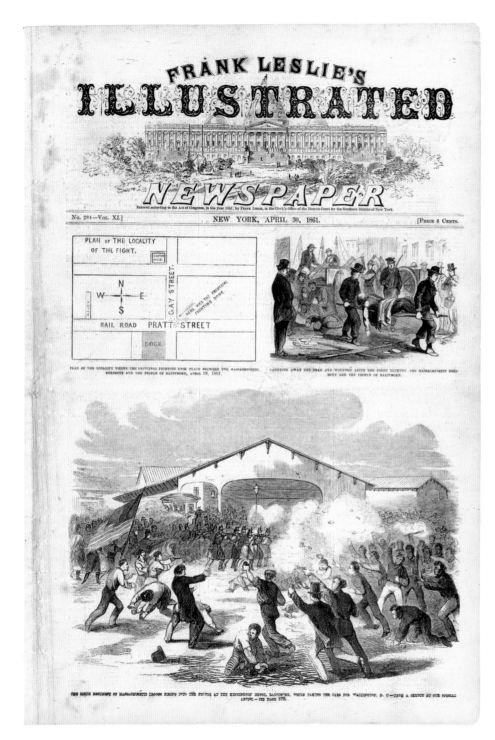

BLOODY PASSAGE

On April 19, 1861, while marching through Baltimore from one train depot to another, three companies of the Sixth Massachusetts, headed for Washington, were met by a pro-Confederate mob hurling
stones and bricks. Colonel Edward Jones ordered his men to ignore them, but when the rowdies fired
pistols, the soldiers shot back. The Federals, said the mayor, fired "wildly, sometimes backward over
their shoulders. [Marching so quickly] they could not stop to take aim." At least 13 soldiers and civilians were killed. The incident made front-page news (above), and afterward Federal troops had to be
rerouted to avoid a hostile Baltimore. This changed in mid-May, when the Federals launched a surprise occupation (right, in a sketch by Frank H. Schell), securing Baltimore for the Union.

Occupation of Baltimore by Gen. Butler.
Union troops passing down Lee St.
May 12th '61

ELMER ELLSWORTH

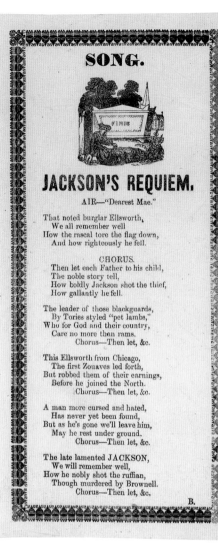

SONG.

JACKSON'S REQUIEM.

AIR—"Dearest Mae."

That noted burglar Ellsworth,
We all remember well
How the rascal tore the flag down,
And how righteously he fell.

CHORUS.
Then let each Father to his child,
The noble story tell,
How boldly Jackson shot the thief,
How gallantly he fell.

The leader of those blackguards,
By Tories styled "pet lambs,"
Who for God and their country,
Care no more than rams.
Chorus—Then let, &c.

This Ellsworth from Chicago,
The first Zouaves led forth,
But robbed them of their earnings,
Before he joined the North.
Chorus—Then let, &c.

A man more cursed and hated,
Has never yet been found,
But as he's gone we'll leave him,
May he rest under ground.
Chorus—Then let, &c.

The late lamented JACKSON,
We will remember well,
How he nobly shot the ruffian,
Though murdered by Brownell.
Chorus—Then let, &c.

B.

SELF-DEFENSE

At daybreak on May 24, 1861, the South got its first martyr in James Jackson (right) of Alexandria, Virginia. An ardent secessionist, Jackson flew a Confederate flag over the Marshall House hotel, where he was manager. When Colonel Elmer Ellsworth tore down the flag, Jackson shot him dead and was immediately killed by Ellsworth's men. Southerners who thought Jackson's stand against Northern invaders symbolized their national dilemma immortalized him in verse (above).

ROMANCE OF WAR

Ellsworth too was lionized. A friend of Lincoln's and the first Northern officer to be killed in the war, Ellsworth lay in state in the East Room of the White House. Thousands filed by to pay tribute. The fancifully illustrated song sheet cover (above) to G. W. Warren's requiem for the fallen colonel—which featured themes of courage, bold action, and heroic self-sacrifice—reflected the popular vision of the struggle ahead.

POWER OF THE FLAG

When Jackson raised his flag over the Marshall House (right) on April 17, 1861, he vowed that if it "ever comes down it will come down over my dead body." The enormous banner stood atop a 30-foot flagpole. Ellsworth, insulted by the flag's billowing taunts, which could be seen from the White House, across the river, mounted the stairs to the attic, climbed out a window, and cut the hated symbol down. Descending the stairs with his trophy, he met the irate Jackson, who fired a shotgun blast into Ellsworth's chest. Corporal Francis Brownell shot and bayoneted Jackson, unknowingly fulfilling Jackson's prophecy.

ORDERLY CHAOS

In meeting the demand for illustrations of great events, Civil War field artists often tinkered with reality, supplying their publishers with orderly and attractive battle scenes. Though troops did fight in long lines, and clouds of gun smoke often obscured both friend and foe, battlefields were intrinsically chaotic. Soldiers from privates to generals knew only what they could see with their own eyes—anything beyond was a mystery. In the painting above, Colonel Ambrose Burnside's brigade of New Englanders and New Yorkers neatly engages Colonel Nathan "Shanks" Evans's brigade near the Matthews House (left foreground) on the hills above Bull Run Creek.

A SOLDIER'S SUNSET

Union general in chief Winfield Scott (left, second from right) had been a superb commander in his prime. His supreme self-confidence made him master of both the art of war and the art of military leadership. "Not even the gorgeously bedizened marshals of Napoleon wore their plumes, sashes and aiguillettes and glittering uniforms with more complacency," wrote one observer. By 1861, however, Scott's age, infirmities, and heft prevented him from mounting a horse. He intended to accompany McDowell's army into the field in a carriage, but even this proved too much for him. In this illustration, Scott, resigned to remaining behind, signs the orders sending McDowell forward. The aged general would retire less than four months later.

ON THE TRAIL OF THE ARMY

A pacific scene at McDowell's headquarters near Manassas belies the intense activity of running an army. Thousands of wagons accompanied the armies on their marches, carrying not only ammunition and food but also baggage for the soldiers and fodder for the horses and mules. Supply problems often paralyzed armies, as they did in the wake of Bull Run.

IN WAR'S PATH

Before the armies came in 1861, Centreville, Virginia (above), resembled thousands of other rural crossroads in America. Its position on high ground on the main road between Washington and the Manassas railroad depot, however, gave Centreville immediate military importance. The Confederates fortified the hills and posted troops around the community. Some of McDowell's army camped at Centreville the night before the advance at nearby Bull Run Creek, and the Federals retreated through the hamlet on July 21. The Union rear guard, assigned to protect the fleeing army from Confederate pursuit, made its stand at Centreville. Most of the buildings in the settlement, including the stone church (center), served as hospitals after the battle.

NEWS FROM AFAR

The *Illustrated London News* brought its readers dispatches as well as evocative illustrations of the rout of the Federals at Bull Run (right). To gain a better perspective, the paper's Frank Vizetelly filed reports from the Northern and the Southern side. Another British correspondent, William Howard Russell of the London *Times*, returned home after Bull Run because the Union army had stopped allowing him in its presence: His dispatches were too disparaging.

ADVANCED POST

Fairfax Court House (left), in Fairfax village, 10 miles from Bull Run, first hosted Federal troops in June 1861. The Unionists considered the crossroads community, about 20 miles from Washington, an ideal advanced post from which to observe Confederate activity in the area. In the village on July 21, officers managed to regain control of many of the troops that had fled the battlefield in panic. Confederates held the village after the victory at Manassas, but the Federals occupied it permanently in 1862.

THE CIVIL WAR IN AMERICA: THE STAMPEDE FROM BULL RUN.—FROM A SKETCH BY OUR SPECIAL ARTIST.—SEE NEXT PAGE.

SENTENCED TO WAIT

The Confederates took about 1,500 Northerners prisoner at
Manassas. Neither side had yet given much thought to caring
for prisoners of war, so captives endured hungry days while
captors figured out how to keep and feed them. Most Union
prisoners from Bull Run were confined in Richmond warehouses; troublesome men were held in more remote sites.
Above, New Yorkers and Michiganders bide their time in the
courtyard of Castle Pinckney in Charleston Harbor; their
undisciplined guards lounge on the parapet above them.

END OF WAR'S GLORY

About 900 men were killed at Bull Run—too
many to be shipped home to places as distant as
Louisiana and Maine. Instead, soldiers' graves
were dug on the battlefield and marked by
crude wooden headboards (right). Bull Run
demonstrated that the young had no advantages in battle. That and the knowledge that a
son or father lay far away in a muddy, shallow
grave dashed once and for all America's romantic notions about the glory of war.

Men of Bull Run

Bull Run—Manassas, to Southerners—was a return to combat for many soldiers who had not heard hostile shots since the Mexican War, almost 15 years earlier. Those who had been junior officers then, in command of a few dozen men, now led thousands as generals.

HERO OF THE SOUTH

Pierre Gustave Toutant Beauregard, a dapper Louisianan, was brilliant as a young engineer on General Scott's staff in Mexico. In 1861, already the hero of Fort Sumter, his performance in command of part of the army at Manassas made him the man of the hour, as evidenced by the cover to a quick-step march (right) composed in his honor.

IN THE LINE OF FIRE

General Joseph E. Johnston (above) arrived late on the battlefield at Manassas, having rushed his troops by rail from the Shenandoah Valley. He took command of the battlefield and helped the South earn the victory. As a colonel of engineers in Mexico, he had fought beside Beauregard and been wounded twice. "Johnston is a great soldier," said Winfield Scott, "but he had an unfortunate knack of getting himself shot in nearly every engagement."

AMBROSE BURNSIDE

West Pointer Ambrose E. Burnside (opposite, center, with his staff after the Battle of Bull Run) fought too late in the Mexican War to distinguish himself, so he began the Civil War as a colonel, but rose to command a brigade at Bull Run. Competent, affable, and politically astute, Burnside was respected by his peers. His star continued to rise until November 1862, when Lincoln appointed him commander of the Army of the Potomac, a role for which he was unsuited and unprepared.

OLD PETE

James Longstreet (above), a stolid Georgian, participated in heavy infantry fighting in Mexico, where he was wounded. At Manassas, his brigade of Virginians guarded a Confederate flank and did not see action, but Longstreet had fought them well three days earlier in a skirmish at Blackburn's Ford. He became known as a soldier's soldier, and his adoring troops called him "Old Pete."

STONEWALL JACKSON

Thomas J. Jackson, shown at left at age 33, when he was a professor at the Virginia Military Institute, had been a lieutenant of artillery in Mexico and so courageous that General Winfield Scott publicly praised him. At Manassas, Jackson commanded five regiments of Virginians, among which were many of his former students. The determined stand of Jackson and his brigade on Henry House Hill earned the men fame and their commander an enduring nickname: "Stonewall."

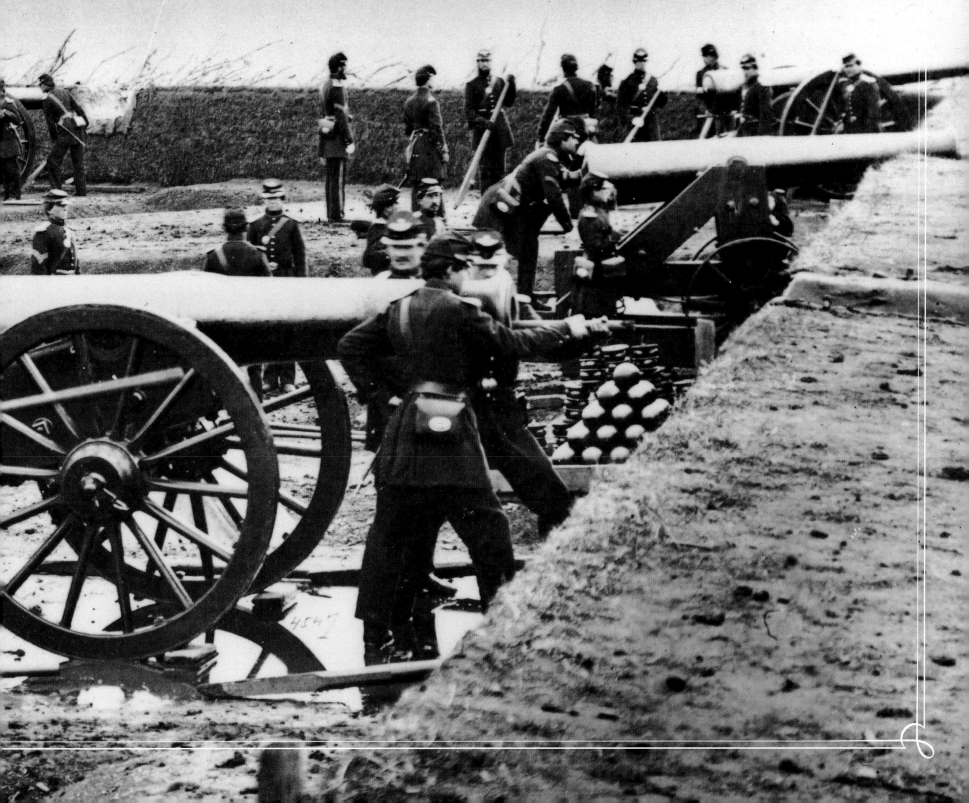

WAR ON A GRAND SCALE

The Young Napoleon

I N THE WAKE of the Union disaster at the Battle of Bull Run, Abraham Lincoln did not stop to consider what went wrong on the battlefield. He acted immediately, replacing his defeated general, Irvin McDowell, with a young man who would radically alter the course of the Union war effort and leave an indelible mark on the history of the conflict.

The 12-pounder howitzer (below), named for the weight of its projectile and shown with a sponge and rammer, for loading and cleaning the gun, could lob shells in long, high arcs. By 1862, thanks to General George McClellan, such artillery was a mainstay of the Federal army.

George Brinton McClellan was just 34 years old when he arrived in Washington in July 1861, five days after Bull Run, but in the estimation of those who knew him, his age counted little alongside his many accomplishments. The son of a renowned Philadelphia surgeon, the handsome and personable McClellan had succeeded at everything he had undertaken. He proved the brilliance of his mind at West Point, where he finished second in his class; he had served in the army's elite Corps of Engineers, earned distinction in the Mexican War, and was the junior member of an official military commission sent to observe and report on the Crimean War. In the business world, just before the war began, he competently administered two railroad companies. McClellan was a man with a large, limitless future, and the widening conflict only made his prospects brighter.

At the beginning of the war, William T. Sherman said of McClellan, "[N]o one commands more universally the confidence of his peers, the officers of our army." The governor of Ohio, William Dennison, Jr., made McClellan a major general, and the appointment soon paid dividends. The young officer proved himself an able planner and administrator in a small campaign in western Virginia that resulted in gains for the Union. Based on that success and McClellan's reputation, and given the debacle at Bull Run, the war department decided to call him to Washington.

What he found on arrival, he later wrote, was not an army, but "a collection of undisciplined, ill-officered, and uninstructed men, much demoralized by the defeat and ready to run at the first shot." McClellan met with General in Chief Winfield Scott, the president, and members of Congress. "All tell me that I am held responsible for the fate of the Nation," he wrote to his wife, "& that all its resources shall be placed at my disposal." The young general had no self-doubts. "It is an immense task that I have on my hands," he wrote, "but I believe I can accomplish it."

McClellan set to work improving supply operations, record-keeping procedures, and discipline. He discharged incompetent officers and tried to implement a course of training for officers and

General George McClellan (below) took command of the Union armies with definite ideas about how to fight the war. He put his faith in the power of artillery and ordered that Washington be surrounded by an elaborate network of more than 60 forts. McClellan deployed trained gunners, like the men of the First Connecticut Heavy Artillery (left), to fortify the capital.

troops alike. Slowly, he brought order out of the chaos on the Potomac, taking steps to make the regiments more efficient—organizing them into brigades and brigades into divisions—all under competent officers who seemed qualified for their duties, who knew their work, and could instruct the troops. He oversaw the building of a series of fortifications to protect the capital, and by the time the job was finished, many months later, Washington was one of the most fortified cities in the world. McClellan devoted much of his attention to forging an army that fit his style of warfare. A careful and intelligent soldier, he loathed gallant, headlong charges that wasted many lives, so he put his faith in engineering and artillery, creating a new battalion of engineers and spending lavishly to build up the army's artillery, which increased in size by more than 900 percent. He would later state, with no little hubris, "I do not know who could have organized the Army of the Potomac as I did." Nor did anyone else.

But McClellan accomplished even more. He not only worked a revolution within the army; he influenced the White House as well. He shared his ideas with the president, and Lincoln—military novice that he was—eagerly listened to the young professional. McClellan attended cabinet meetings. For the president and the secretary of war, he drafted memoranda on military matters and, ultimately, designed and presented a grand strategy for winning the

99

"MASTERLY INACTIVITY," OR SIX MONTHS ON THE POTOMAC.

war. He proposed to raise enormous armies, array them from the Atlantic to the Mississippi, and set them all in motion at the same time, attacking critical points throughout the Confederacy. The Southerners would be so hard pressed at so many points that they would be overwhelmed. General Scott, who had his own plan, disliked McClellan's scheme, and the two quarreled. But the enthusiastic McClellan had impressed Lincoln and the cabinet, so Scott, feeble of body and, increasingly it seemed, of mind, saw that his time had passed. The old warrior resigned, and the president immediately appointed McClellan to replace him as general in chief of all the Federal armies. Lincoln nevertheless wondered whether the young man would find the great weight of responsibility too much, and he expressed his concern to the general in frank terms. McClellan's reply: "I can do it all."

And it appeared that he could. With commanders in both the eastern and western theaters, McClellan worked on strategies for the capture and defense of important points. He planned his Grand Advance of all the armies, and he continued to forge the Army of the Potomac into a splendid fighting machine. That army, in which he took immense pride, would be his principal weapon in the coming campaigns. Well-equipped, well-fed, and well-organized, the men grew to love their commander, and morale soared. McClellan was equally smitten. "I am to watch over you as a parent over his children," he wrote in a widely published address to the entire army, "and you know that your General loves you from the depths of his heart." No other Union general would ever enjoy the measure of love and devotion that the soldiers of 1862 lavished upon the man they called "Little Mac."

McClellan's protracted field preparations inspired a Northern lampoon (top left) of the "Masterly Inactivity" of the general and Confederate P. G. T. Beauregard. Secretary of War Edwin Stanton (inset, top) labored tirelessly to prepare the armies for the field, and Secretary of State William Seward (above) advised Lincoln in 1861 and 1862.

For a time, McClellan had Washington at his feet. He was so articulate, cultured, and eager to please that people found themselves drawn to him. His energy and obvious competence made him seem the very picture of a perfect soldier. The newspapers began calling him the "Young Napoleon," and McClellan became a household name. Some in Washington, however, were unable to appreciate the spirit of professionalism that the young general brought to building the North's war machine, and showed a less enthusiastic response. Congressmen and editors begrudged him the passing weeks—they felt his preparations were taking too long—and urged him to hurry. McClellan stayed his course, however, telling one of his generals that he would "proceed with great caution endeavoring to advance so as never to make a step backward." He knew that making soldiers required time. As one West Pointer said, "Napoleon allowed three years . . . George Washington one year—Here it is expected in nine days and Bull Run is the consequence." So as autumn became winter, the army grew at its own pace and McClellan remained proud of his accomplishments: "Let those who criticise me for delay in creating an army," he wrote, "point out an instance when so much has been done with the same means in so short a time."

President Lincoln appointed McClellan commander of all the U.S. armies in the field in November 1861. General Louis Blenker marked the occasion by leading a brigade of his troops—mostly German immigrants, like their commander—in a torchlight procession (above) through the streets of Washington to McClellan's headquarters. Bands played, the men sang in their rough voices, and fireworks filled the air. A correspondent for the London *Times* declared the event the "prettiest sight" he had seen since crossing the Atlantic.

McClellan (above, sixth from left) formed a cadre of generals that included professional soldiers like Irvin McDowell (fifth from left) and political appointees like Louis Blenker (third from right). In an illustration of a reception in Washington (opposite, top), another political general, Daniel E. Sickles, shakes hands with Secretary of War Edwin Stanton, who, as a trial lawyer years earlier, had successfully defended Sickles against murder charges.

Lincoln, meanwhile, appreciated the importance of building a strong army on a strong foundation, and he saw the wisdom in McClellan's plan. But he also believed that time was of the essence. The war was costing the treasury millions of dollars a day, and politically, with talk of abolition getting stronger in the Republican Party, Lincoln was feeling the pressure. McClellan, a staunch Democrat, would have none of it; he disliked much of what he saw as fanaticism among the Republicans. The tension grew, and McClellan revealed his weaknesses as a general and a man. He openly declared that he "was fighting for my country & the Union, not for abolition and the Republican Party." One of his generals said that "Jeff Davis has not a greater repugnance to, nor less confidence in, Republicans than has McClellan. No Republican can possibly receive justice at his hands. He converses with few, consults none, & trusts none further than he is obliged to." Unfortunately for the Union, the officer had accurately described McClellan's treatment of Lincoln. He viewed Lincoln as both his social and intellectual inferior and, amazingly, treated him as such. In private correspondence, he referred to the president as an idiot and a baboon. On one notable occasion Lincoln and Secretary of

State William Seward arrived at McClellan's home to discuss official matters only to find the general out. The men waited more than an hour, but when McClellan returned, he hastened upstairs, ignoring a servant's plea that the president was waiting. Half an hour later, Lincoln sent the man upstairs to ask if McClellan would come down, but the servant returned to say that the general had gone to bed.

Though Lincoln bore such snubs lightly, the relationship between these two key figures remained strained. Lincoln could only wonder at the paradox that was McClellan. The general had created a superb army and brought vitality and a new professionalism to Washington. He also brought a new sense of military possibility, for from McClellan the administration learned the wisdom of waging organized, systematic war on a grand scale. McClellan had almost single-handedly resurrected the North's war effort. But in late 1861 he had also revealed deep professional—and personal—flaws that would contribute to future Union disasters. Lincoln learned with chagrin that the "Young Napoleon" was a double-edged sword.

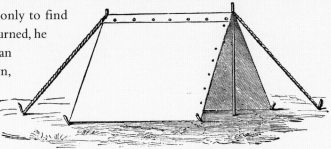

McClellan suggested the army adopt as standard equipment the French *tente d'abri* (above), or "dog tent," as the soldiers called it. Each soldier carried half a tent, buttoning it to another man's half for modest protection from the elements.

RITUAL

Because McClellan insisted on pageantry as a way of instilling pride in his troops, the regiments of the Army of the Potomac formed for dress parade each day while in camp around Washington. Visiting officers often inspected the troops. Left, General Innis Palmer (third from left) poses with men of the Seventh New York Cavalry, also known as the First New York Mounted Rifles. Palmer, a close friend and West Point classmate of McClellan's, was a no-nonsense cavalryman of long experience, the sort of man "Little Mac" relied on to teach raw troops respect for military ritual.

INSPIRATION BEHIND THE SCENES

George McClellan was wholly devoted to his wife, Ellen, and wrote her almost every day when they were apart. "Some one just brought me a bouquet of wild white flowers," he wrote on their anniversary in May 1862. "I clutched it most eagerly, as reminding me of one, who two years ago became my wife. It is on the table in front of me as I write; in a tin tumbler, to be sure, but none the less pure and white." To Ellen, McClellan confided his high opinions of himself and his responsibilities, as well as his unfavorable opinions of those around him. Mathew Brady took the photograph above in 1861 or early '62.

THE VALUE OF ENGINEERS

As a soldier and an engineer, McClellan knew the value of trained engineer troops. When he rebuilt the Federal army in 1861 and 1862, he created a battalion of army-trained engineers as well as a brigade of volunteer engineers, which included the 15th New York. During training in Washington, the unit erected a 300-foot pontoon bridge (above) across the Anacostia River. Under the admiring gaze of visitors, 200 of the New Yorkers needed just 20 minutes to throw the rubber bridge across.

CRACK TROOPS

Well-led and thoroughly trained, the First Connecticut Heavy Artillery, shown below at Fort Richardson, south of the Potomac, became one of the Union army's premier artillery regiments. When McClellan commenced his campaign on Richmond, he took the First Connecticut with him to man the siege train of heavy guns and mortars. The regiment's proficiency earned its men special mention in the commanding general's report on the campaign.

A PERFECT MARCH

McClellan demanded that his subordinates continually drill their commands, and he made it a point to reward those regiments that looked best during reviews. The Fourth Pennsylvania Cavalry's performance on parade, however—no matter how superb—could hardly have matched the fancy of the unknown artist who portrayed its movements as so precise that even the horses were in step (right). The regiment served throughout the war and participated in most of the army's campaigns.

Oct 1861

BARRICADE AT THE CROSSING

At least five strong gun emplacements—some mounting large, 100-pounder Parrott rifles—covered the approaches to the Chain Bridge, but the "Lower," or "Field Gun Battery" (above), consisted of only two old field howitzers. Its location at the mouth of the bridge on the Maryland side ensured its effectiveness against any Confederate force hazarding a dash across the span. Fifty feet above and 200 feet behind this battery, on high bluffs, stood Battery Martin Scott, whose three heavy guns dominated the Virginia approaches to the bridge.

BRIDGING THE DEFENSE

Because the Chain Bridge (left)—originally a suspension bridge supported by chains—spanned the Potomac River just upstream from Washington, where it linked Virginia with Maryland, it was heavily guarded by Union sentries. One Unionist wrote, "Near the centre of the bridge are two large, heavy gates, which completely divide the bridge. The gates are plated with iron, with slits for skirmishers and pickets to fire through, which were dented in several places by bullets and rifle-balls fired by secession pickets."

SHOWING DISCIPLINE

McClellan's emphasis on training and discipline had its effect. In the fall 1861 photograph above, the 17th New York Infantry garrisons Washington's Fort Ellsworth and presents an impressive appearance: The men pass inspection with full packs, white gloves, and well-dressed lines. The regiment's Sibley tents rise up beyond the archways decorated with evergreen boughs.

LOYAL UNDER PENALTY OF DEATH

The distance between the Union and Confederate capitals—just 100 miles—meant it was nearly impossible to restrict the flow of military secrets. The soldiers being checked (opposite) at Analostan Island in the Potomac River, with Washington in the background, had to sign passes that read, in part, "The subscriber accepts this pass on his word of honor that he is and will be ever loyal to the United States; and if hereafter found in arms against the Union, or in any way aiding her enemies, the penalty will be death."

Battle of Ball's Bluff

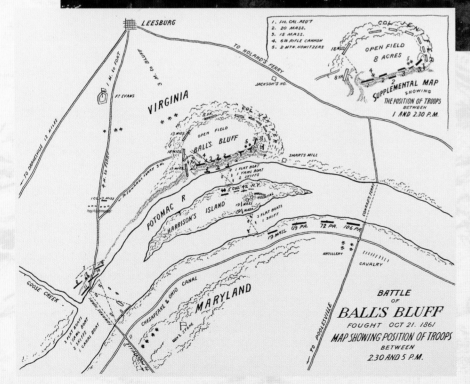

1. 1st CAL. REG'T
2. 20 MASS.
3. 15 MASS.
4. 6th RIFLE CANNON
5. 2 MTN. HOWITZERS

OPEN FIELD
8 ACRES

SUPPLEMENTAL MAP
SHOWING
THE POSITION OF TROOPS
BETWEEN
1 AND 2.30 P.M.

LEESBURG

TO NOLAND'S FERRY

JACKSON'S HO.

VIRGINIA

FT. EVANS

BALL'S BLUFF

OPEN FIELD

SMARTS MILL

POTOMAC R.

HARRISON'S ISLAND

GOOSE CREEK

CHESAPEAKE & OHIO CANAL

MARYLAND

ARTILLERY

CAVALRY

BATTLE
OF
BALL'S BLUFF
FOUGHT OCT 21. 1861
MAP SHOWING POSITION OF TROOPS
BETWEEN
2.30 AND 5 P.M.

Early in the war, what began for the Federals as "a slight demonstration" at Ball's Bluff ended in a humiliating and controversial defeat. The bungled reconnaissance into enemy territory resulted in more than 900 casualties, an angry North, and a congressional investigation.

TESTING THE BATTLE WATERS

While Federal and Confederate troops eyed each other across the Potomac during the early months of the war, artillery duels (top) were common. In October 1861 a small Northern force crossed the swollen river about 30 miles upstream from Washington, near Leesburg, Virginia (left). Overpowered by alert Confederates, the Northerners' only escape route was over the 80-foot-high Ball's Bluff.

HONORED

Colonel Nathan "Shanks" Evans (below) performed so well at the Battle of Manassas, or Bull Run, that he was given independent command near Leesburg and ably commanded the Confederates at Ball's Bluff. The small victory earned him promotion to brigadier general and a gold medal.

RUINED

General Charles P. Stone (left), a West Pointer, commanded the Federals at Ball's Bluff, but his subordinate, Colonel Edward Baker, actually led the troops in the battle. Baker mismanaged the fighting and was largely responsible for the fiasco, but since he died a hero's death atop the bluff, Stone became the scapegoat. A congressional committee recommended that he be arrested and imprisoned. Stone was released a few months later, but his career was ruined.

CIVILIAN RESPONSE

The slaughter at Ball's Bluff inspired heartache as well as anger in the North. "The Vacant Chair," a song of grief written in memory of a Federal officer killed at Ball's Bluff, struck a chord in the hearts of Northerners and Southerners alike. Reprinted widely—this edition (right) is from Richmond—the song remained popular throughout the war.

A DEADLY BLUFF

Confederate Colonel Evans's "bluffing" of General Stone (above) was hardly a game. "Oh such terrible confusion," recalled one Massachusetts man, "men running to and fro, others leaping into the river. The horrid forms of the dead, the last struggles of the dying, the groans of the wounded and the heart-rending cries that would go up from a hundred drowning lips." For days after the battle, bodies washed ashore downstream, even at Washington.

The War at Sea

FROM THE BEGINNING of the conflict, the Lincoln administration was determined to make the North's vast advantage in resources count as much as possible. This meant that Washington, while mobilizing the North's power in the early months of the war, had also to maintain the Union's advantage by making it difficult for the South to secure gains in

A Confederate naval officer's embroidered cap badge (below, top) and a Confederate naval uniform button (bottom)—the latter manufactured by E. M. Lewis of Richmond—bear nautical motifs reminiscent of insignia worn by men in the Federal navy.

areas where it was at a disadvantage. Lincoln aimed to deny the South the aid of its friends.

Though the countries of the Old World officially remained neutral in relation to America's strife, Lincoln knew that many Europeans, especially in Britain and France, sympathized with the Southern cause and so would continue to trade with the Confederate states, sending to the South what it could not produce itself—weapons, ammunition, gunpowder—in exchange for the cotton and forest products that sustained the South's export economy. The importance of this trade to the Southern war effort caused the Confederate government to take steps to expand and protect it; the Union government, meanwhile, wanted to undermine and, ultimately, stop the trading—as swiftly as possible.

On April 19, 1861, a week after the South took Fort Sumter, Lincoln acted on General Winfield Scott's advice and declared a blockade of all Southern ports. Henceforth, all vessels entering or leaving any port between Maryland and Mexico would be subject to arrest, inspection, and seizure by the U.S. Navy. It was a bold step, because the Union also traded with Europe, and the seizure of British merchantmen in Southern waters could well lead to diplomatic difficulties for the North. Washington had to step carefully to avoid giving Britain cause to recognize the Confederacy, but by declaring a blockade, the Union provided the British with a reason to do so, since traditionally a nation dealing with an insurrection merely closed the ports of the rebels. By using the word *blockade*, Lincoln implied that the Confederacy existed as a government, which, in the eyes of the world, meant it had rights as a legitimate belligerent power. And this recognition, of course, is what the Confederacy had always wanted from the Union.

Jefferson Davis chose not to challenge the blockade directly, since international law required nations to recognize a blockade only if it worked, and in Davis's eyes, Lincoln's tiny navy could not possibly effectively limit traffic into and out of the Southern ports. The Confederate president did respond to Lincoln's declaration, though, quickly and offensively. Days after the clash at Fort Sumter, the Confederacy officially suspended its shipments of cotton: Davis and others

At dockside in Bristol, England, the steamship *Old Dominion* (left) undergoes alterations that will transform it into a blockade runner for the South. Because transporting supplies to Southern ports was such a profitable business, many British ships were made into blockade runners or commerce raiders. These vessels supplemented President Davis's small Confederate navy, a subject of ridicule (below) among Northerners who nevertheless could hardly rest assured that the Union dominated the sea.

reasoned that since cotton was so valuable the European powers would be forced to come get it, breaking the blockade in the process. Davis also offered official sanction to ship captains willing to serve the Confederacy as privateers who would prowl the sea for Federal merchant ships in an attempt to capture the vessels, take them to a Southern port, and then sell the ships and their cargoes to the Confederate government for their own profit. The two dozen commanders who accepted privateer rank enjoyed a few months of unrestricted prowling; Davis understood the operation was only a stopgap solution. He and his advisers had grander designs.

Before joining Davis's cabinet as secretary of the navy, Stephen R. Mallory had been a U.S. senator from Florida. Energetic and imaginative, Mallory not only created a Confederate navy out of virtually nothing; he also developed an aggressive plan aimed at negating the Federal advantage in sea power. Mallory urged the South to invest precious funds in building steam-driven ironclad warships that could attack the wooden Federal blockade vessels. More important, Mallory sent an agent to England in June 1861 to commission two new steam cruisers. These ships, eventually named the *Florida* and the *Alabama*, took over where the privateers left off, and between them they captured, sank, or burned more than a hundred Northern ships before being sunk themselves in 1864. These and other commerce raiders played a significant part in the war: They hounded powerful Yankee merchants, who in turn pressured the Lincoln administration,

While opposing naval secretaries Gideon Welles (inset, left), for the North, and Stephen Mallory (right), for the South, prepared their forces for war, Britain's prime minister, Lord Palmerston, moved closer to recognizing the Confederacy, as the *Punch* cartoon above shows. The South gained needed naval supplies when it captured the Union's Pensacola Navy Yard (top, right).

thereby forcing the U.S. Navy to divide its attention between chasing the cruisers and patrolling the waters off the Southern coast.

Once the war began, it would take the North several months to build a strong, unified blockade, because at the time, roughly half its 90 ships were in commission. And though the North had among its 40 steamers five excellent, heavily armed frigates—among the best, most modern ships in the world, in fact—all were out of commission and under overhaul in 1861. The rest of the ships were older and less formidable, but Secretary of the Navy Gideon Welles persevered. One of his assistants, Gustavus V. Fox, scoured the Atlantic coast and purchased almost any vessel that could mount a few guns. The result was an absurd fleet of ferries, whalers, cutters, pleasure craft, ancient barks, and fishing boats. While this odd flotilla went into blockade service, the navy began building new ships, including small, steam-powered gunboats and fast ocean cruisers.

More was required than ships, however. The Confederate coast was immense—3,500 miles from the Chesapeake Bay to the Rio Grande. Eight Confederate states shared the coastline and did business from 10 ports and numerous smaller landings in rivers and inlets. In mid-1861 the Federal navy had but a few dozen ships to patrol this vast area; as a result, nine of every 10 Southern ships eluded capture. The problem for the North was largely logistical: Because it lacked ports in the South, its blockaders could stay on patrol only a few weeks before having to

head north for food, coal, fresh water, and other supplies. It was partly this need for supply bases in the South that led the Federals in 1861 and '62 to undertake joint army-navy operations that allowed the Union to capture several important Southern ports—Hatteras Inlet, Port Royal, and Beaufort in the Carolinas, and Ship Island off the Mississippi—and turn them into supply depots.

Slowly, the U.S. Navy took control of more and more of the coastline. But instead of accepting defeat, Southerners turned to a new type of ship—the blockade runner—built for speed and designed to carry small cargoes. Constructed mainly in British shipyards, blockade runners were faster than most Yankee ships and burned smokeless coal. They were loaded up—with either war matériel or coveted consumer goods—in Bermuda, the Bahamas, or Cuba, and then run hard and fast for Savannah, Georgia, Charleston, South Carolina, or, most often, Wilmington, North

This panoramic view of a bustling shipyard (above), near Liverpool, England, shows one of the two steam cruisers—the *Alabama*, the largest of the three unfinished hulls visible in the dry docks—commissioned by the Confederacy for immediate use. Secretary Mallory believed such ships offered "the greatest chance for success against the enemy's commerce." Before 1864 the *Alabama* helped capture, sink, or burn more than a hundred Federal ships.

"UP A TREE."
Colonel Bull and the Yankee 'Coon.
'Coon. "AIR YOU IN EARNEST, COLONEL?"
Colonel Bull. "I AM."
'Coon. "DON'T FIRE—I'LL COME DOWN."

On November 8, 1861, Captain John Wilkes of the USS *San Jacinto* stopped the British mail steamer the *Trent* and removed Confederate diplomats James Mason and John Slidell. An editorial in *Punch* condemned Wilkes's "impudent conduct," calling it "a violation of all international propriety." The incident outraged the British and worsened already-strained relations between their government and the Union's. Lincoln, meanwhile, as a *Punch* cartoonist showed (above), was as good as treed.

Carolina. The owners, captains, and crews of these blockade runners stood to make enormous profits, for the people of the Confederacy would pay steep prices for goods that could not be obtained domestically. The shippers then filled their holds with cotton and ran back out to the Atlantic and on to Britain, where cotton sold for as much as 10 times its price before the war.

But the profit motive also worked against the blockade runners. Because naval tradition permitted captains and their crews to divide up the goods of any ship they could capture, blockade runners were at greater risk than most for being attacked. The men of the U.S. Navy, aware of the king's ransom aboard a blockade runner, had extra incentive to catch one—a single capture could fix a captain for life or bring the lowliest crewman 10 times his yearly pay. The Northerners developed efficient tactics to cover as much water as possible. Blockaders arrayed themselves in three lines, with small picket boats posted close to shore and larger, faster ships farther out to sea. The ships communicated by signal rocket. When a lookout spotted a

In November 1861, in Beaufort, South Carolina, Confederate soldiers burn cotton (left) to keep it from falling into approaching Union hands. By May 1862 Fort Barrancas (above), in Pensacola Bay, again belonged to the North, and Southern naval officers, who wore blue, not gray, jackets (right), had to fight to maintain control of their threatened ports.

runner, his ship signaled its allies and all would give chase. Captures were rare enough, however, and the greatest enemy of blockaders was boredom. One officer told his family that they could understand his daily routine if they "were to go to the roof on a hot summer day, talk to a half-dozen degenerates, descend to the basement, drink tepid water full of iron rust, climb to the roof again, and repeat the process at intervals until fagged out, then go to bed with everything shut tight."

As the war progressed, the U.S. Navy got better at sealing off Southern ports. By 1865 only half the ships trying to get through the blockade succeeded. Confederate civilians suffered for want of food and clothing, while their armies, already deprived of needed military commodities (chemicals, weapons, lead) went barefoot and hungry as well. Though the U.S. Navy never entirely succeeded in isolating the Confederacy from the rest of the world, the blockade it engineered was effective enough to make the effort an important component in the Northern war effort.

THE STONE FLEET

In July 1861 the Federal government's Blockade Strategy Board suggested that "old vessels laden with ballast" and "sunk in the appropriate places" would prove an effective barrier to Southern trading ships. Secretary Welles agreed and authorized the purchase of some two dozen New England whaling ships, which were then loaded with granite blocks and rigged with pipes and valves so they could be easily flooded. The sinking of the so-called "Stone Fleet" (above), in the main channel leading to Charleston harbor, was supervised the following December by Captain William H. Davis.

A PERILOUS TRADE

Despite the ever-growing Federal naval presence off the Southern coastline, blockade runners managed to ply their perilous trade late into the war. During a two-month period in the spring of 1863, 15 ships successfully made their way into Charleston and 21 departed. The steamer *Georgiana* was not so lucky. On the night of March 19 (rendered opposite by water-colorist David Johnson Kennedy), she was run aground by Yankee warships, abandoned by her crew, and set afire by sailors from the USS *Wissahickon*.

CLOSING FOR THE KILL

The wartime engraving above, of a Federal gun crew preparing to open fire on a blockade runner, captures the drama of pursuit that provided an occasional break in the monotony of blockade duty. One such incident occurred on September 10, 1864, when the blockade runner *A.D. Vance*—en route to England with a cargo of cotton and turpentine—encountered the USS *Santiago de Cuba* off Cape Fear, North Carolina. After a chase of nearly 10 hours, the Yankee vessel closed within range. "At 7:40 p.m. we fired a shot across his stern," Captain O. S. Glisson reported, "and she surrendered without any further resistance."

SHIPSHAPE AND READY

Six officers and some of the 95-man crew of the USS *Pocahontas* stand proudly on the deck of their ship (opposite)—a 700-ton steam sloop that saw its share of blockade action around the Gulf Coast. Armed with six guns and the deck howitzer visible at center, the *Pocahontas* was credited with capturing two enemy blockade runners. On January 6, 1863, she waylaid the British-made *Antona* off Florida, and on March 5 of that year took part in the pursuit and destruction of the *Josephine* in Mobile Bay.

A DERELICT RUNNER

The shattered hulk of a blockade runner (opposite)—its bow, foremast, and paddle wheels visible above the waterline—rests just offshore Sullivans Island, near Charleston. Though the ship in this 1865 photo has been identified as the *Colt*, no ship with that name appears in the Confederate records. It may be the *Flora*, which ran aground near Confederate Battery Rutledge on the morning of October 23, 1864. Fired upon by Federal shore batteries and monitors, the *Flora* was struck by nearly a hundred shells, and as Union General John G. Foster reported, "she now lies a complete wreck."

BATTLING BOREDOM

A lethargic group of Federal infantrymen lounge in a rowboat (above) near Morris Island on a hot summer afternoon during the siege of Charleston. The ship in the background is the USS *Commodore McDonough*, a former New York ferry that had been converted into a blockade gunboat. Purchased by the government in August 1862, the vessel saw extensive service on the Carolina coast from December 1862 to the end of the war, and was often deployed as an escort for army operations. While being towed back to New York on August 23, 1865, the *Commodore McDonough* foundered and was lost.

SUPPLYING AN ARMY

The Federal supply depot at Hilton Head, South Carolina (above), was established soon after Union troops occupied the island in November 1861. Soldiers and former slaves labored side by side to construct commissary and quartermaster warehouses and the quarter-mile-long pier and railroad track seen here. The rail line led to a complex of storage facilities, each with its own sidetrack, enabling dock workers to unload the transport ships quickly and efficiently. From their base at Hilton Head, Federal troops waged a series of campaigns against the Confederate defenders of Savannah and Charleston.

NAVAL REPAIR SHOP

Anchored near Port Royal, South Carolina, a floating machinery and repair shop (right) shows Yankee ingenuity. The hulls of two derelict whaling ships—originally intended for the "Stone Fleet"—were lashed together and planked over and the workrooms constructed on top. The facility was used to fabricate ship-engine parts and to repair damaged armor plating from the Navy's ironclads. The ramshackle structure also contained a brass foundry, smithy, tin, and boiler shops, as well as living quarters for the workmen.

CALM BEFORE THE STORM

English artist Frank Vizetelly, a correspondent with the *Illustrated London News*, sketched the expanse of Charleston Harbor (below) from Fort Johnson, a Confederate earthwork on the eastern end of James Island. At right in the sketch, a Southern transport steams past Fort Sumter. Battery Bee and Fort Moultrie are visible on the shore of Sullivans Island, in the distance at left. On April 7, 1863, this tranquil scene was transformed into what Vizetelly described as "a seething cauldron" when the fortifications opened fire on Rear Admiral Samuel Du Pont's ironclad fleet and repulsed the Yankee incursion.

BETTER THAN THE INFANTRY

The Federal navy drew many experienced sailors as well as inexperienced ones who saw naval service as preferable to the dirt and danger of a foot soldier's life; these men chose to join the navy rather than be drafted into the infantry. The U.S. Navy also drew blacks: At the time of the Civil War, it was the only integrated branch of service, and roughly 8 percent of the 118,000 men who entered the navy during the conflict were black. Remarkably for that time, blacks comprised about a quarter of the crew of the USS *Hunchback* (left), part of the James River fleet.

A PRIZE OFFER

A Navy recruiting poster (left) entices volunteers with an offer that would allow them to enlist for a 12-month tour of duty—two years less than they would have to serve if drafted into the infantry. Equally compelling was the promise of a share in monies captured from Confederate vessels—a potential windfall, given the value of the blockade runners and the high-priced commerce carried in their holds. In fact, though, the total goods captured from all the Rebel ships combined yielded less than one-third of the amount promised in the poster, and few Northern sailors ever received any prize money.

STANDING FOR THE PRESIDENT

On November 16, 1861, sailors of the recently commissioned steamer USS *Pensacola* man the yardarms (above) in honor of President Lincoln's visit to their berth at Alexandria, Virginia. The *Pensacola* departed Alexandria on January 11, 1862, and after running the Confederate batteries on the lower Potomac went on to join Admiral David G. Farragut's West Gulf Blockading Squadron. One of the largest vessels ever to enter the channel of the Mississippi River, the *Pensacola* took part in the battle for New Orleans, and on April 26 members of her crew raised the first U.S. flag over the surrendered Confederate city.

AMPHIBIOUS COMMANDER

Brigadier General Ambrose E. Burnside (above) led the war's first large-scale amphibious operation when he successfully landed more than 10,000 Federal troops on the North Carolina coast in February 1862. His victories at Roanoke Island, New Bern, and Beaufort established a Union foothold in the Carolinas, boosting Northern morale and winning the affable West Pointer promotion to the rank of Major General. Burnside praised his men for their "hearty and cheerful co-operation," noting that the "brave officers and sailors are bound to us by the strongest ties of friendship and companionship in arms."

AN OLD SALT

Flag officer Louis M. Goldsborough (above), commander of the U.S. Navy's North Atlantic Blockading Squadron, transported Burnside's expeditionary force to North Carolina and ably supported the army's coastal operations. Goldsborough began his naval career in 1816 as a 12-year-old midshipman, battled Greek pirates, saw action in the Mexican War, and from 1853 to 1857 served as superintendent of the Naval Academy. Standing six feet four and weighing 300 pounds, the grizzled veteran was nicknamed "Old Guts" by his admiring subordinates.

YANKEE JACK TARS

The 76 men of the USS *Huron*, a schooner-rigged screw steamer launched in September 1861, stand at their posts (left) during a battle drill. Visible in the photograph are the ship's captain, Lieutenant Commander Francis H. Baker (center) and a number of black sailors. While in service with the South Atlantic Blockading Squadron off the coast of the Carolinas, the *Huron* captured five blockade runners and forced two others to run aground.

Shipbuilding

Naval technology during the war underwent profound change, as sail gave way to steam power and wooden warships were rendered obsolete by ironclad vessels. Both the North and the South struggled to meet the challenge of building a modern navy.

NOVELTY IRON WORKS, FOOT OF 12th ST. E.R. **NEW YORK.**

STILLMAN, ALLEN & Cº.

Iron Founders Steam Engine and General Machinery Manufacturers.

CAPTURED IRONCLAD

Before it was destined for scrap, the ironclad *Atlanta* (above, inset) was an English-built blockade runner. Converted into an ironclad ram by the Confederates, the ship saw duty in both navies. In June 1863 the CSS *Atlanta* ran aground in Wassaw Sound, Georgia, while engaging Union monitors. Its crew was forced to surrender and the the captured ironclad was put on Federal blockade duty until the end of the war.

INDUSTRIAL ADVANTAGE

Factories like the Novelty Iron Works (above) gave the North a marked advantage in the race to produce state-of-the-art warships. Employing a thousand workers at its facility in Manhattan, Novelty produced machinery that powered the turret of the soon-to-be-famous USS *Monitor*.

LAUNCHING A MONITOR

A twin-turreted ironclad monitor (above)—most likely the USS *Onondaga*—takes to the water at the Continental Iron Works near Brooklyn, New York. After it produced the hull of the original *Monitor*, Continental continued to serve as one of the North's leading manufacturers of ironclads. Its *Onondaga* was the first of the double-turret vessels. Launched on July 29, 1863, and named for a New York Indian tribe, the ship saw action against Confederate defenses along Virginia's James River.

MAKESHIFT WARSHIP

The USS *Commodore Morse* (above) began as a Staten Island ferry-boat, but, like many civilian vessels, was purchased for use by the Federal navy. Armed with a huge 100-pounder rifled cannon and four smaller howitzers, and refitted with iron bulwarks on the fore and aft decks, the *Commodore Morse* spent the war patrolling the rivers and tributaries of Virginia in support of Union troops. The shallow waters posed no problem for a boat with such a shallow draft

AN IRON GIANT

In a Confederate dry dock at Norfolk, Virginia, the hull of the U.S. frigate *Merrimac* (right) nears completion of its transformation into the 275-foot-long ironclad ram the CSS *Virginia*. Commissioned in February 1862, the ship was destined to confront the Yankees' USS *Monitor* less than a month later in a battle that would cut short her career but forever change the possibilities of naval warfare.

A Killing Blow

IN THE WAR WITH MEXICO in the late 1840s, about 100,000 Americans crossed the border to fight. As was typical of wars fought in the nineteenth century and earlier, the soldiers who did not return (about 13 percent of the total force) died of disease, not in battle. In the early 1860s, Americans who had lived through or during the Mexican War believed they knew what

The heavy casualties sustained in the battles of early 1862 heralded the arrival of a new and brutal type of warfare. Private Frederick Barnhart, Company B, 15th Indiana Infantry, had this bugle (left) shot from his hands at the battle of Shiloh. He later recovered it as a souvenir.

war was: They had endured the death, illness, sorrow, pain, and grief. But they had not learned about slaughter. So when the North and South eyed each other in the late winter of 1862, they could not have imagined what lay ahead. In the months that followed, they would go at each other with a fury that would radically alter their understanding of battle.

Throughout January 1862 Lincoln had tried to prod his armies into action. McClellan was ill and would not divulge his plans for the spring campaign. Frustrated, Lincoln issued General War Order No. 1, declaring February 22—Washington's birthday—"the day for a general movement of the Land and Naval forces of the United States against the insurgent forces." Though Lincoln's order was true to McClellan's principle of delivering a killing blow by overwhelming the Confederacy with simultaneous movements by all the armies, McClellan protested that he could not be ready by the date set. The order stood.

In Cairo, Illinois, meanwhile, an energetic general named Ulysses S. Grant had his eye on two strategically important Confederate forts about 70 miles away, in Tennessee. He thought he could capture them, and received permission to try. Just seven days later, Grant, with the help of U.S. Navy gunboats, forced the surrender of Fort Henry, the gateway to Nashville, on the Tennessee and Cumberland Rivers. He then moved his troops on Fort Donelson, about 10 miles away. The Confederates reinforced the garrison, but Grant, with the help of the gunboats, forced the Southerners to submit. When the Confederate commander asked for surrender terms, Grant replied, "No terms except unconditional and immediate surrender . . . I propose to move immediately upon your works." The fort surrendered on February 16, and Grant became a hero to the North. In gaining Forts Henry and Donelson, the Federals pierced General Albert Sidney Johnston's line of defense and gained control of most of central and western Tennessee. In less than three weeks, Grant had dealt the South a staggering defeat.

Back in Washington, McClellan continued preparing for his campaign with the Army of the Potomac. His plan was to move the army—120,000 strong—down the Chesapeake Bay by boat

Young General George McClellan (below) envisioned an enormous army—an irresistible force—that would overwhelm all opposition. The result was a logistical operation of unprecedented size and complexity. During the drive to capture Richmond in early May 1862, McClellan's officers established a temporary supply base at Virginia's Cumberland Landing (left), on the Pamunkey River, and commenced to feed an army so vast that it was equal in population to the ninth-largest city in America.

to the Virginia peninsula, between the York and James Rivers, then, "by rapid marches," strike about 50 miles inland to capture Richmond. It would be the single grand stroke of the war and the killing blow to the Confederacy. Lincoln disliked the plan because of its complexity, and because it seemed to leave Washington vulnerable to attack. The president authorized the campaign only after McClellan promised to leave behind sufficient force to ensure the capital's security.

As the general and his army lurched into motion in early March (after Lincoln's deadline), a naval battle focused the world's attention on McClellan's destination. In Hampton Roads, where the James River meets the Chesapeake Bay, two ironclad ships—the CSS *Virginia* (built on the ruins of the USS *Merrimac*, which had been salvaged at Norfolk) and the USS *Monitor*— met in battle. Both vessels reflected the genius and dedication of their builders, and neither could best the other in this first fight between ironclads. The *Monitor*'s inability to subdue the

Virginia caused additional qualms in Washington about McClellan's amphibious campaign. Though she seemed to be checked by the *Monitor*, the Confederate ship had already destroyed two wooden Federal warships. What was to stop her from threatening the army's transports and supply vessels and blocking the James River, McClellan's line of approach to Richmond? McClellan's peninsular campaign—so called because it would be waged on the strip of land east of Richmond—went forward anyway.

In the West, the Confederates had been working to reclaim what they could of their lost fortunes. Albert Sidney Johnston, one of the South's senior commanders, had accumulated a force of about 45,000 men, including troops under General P. G. T. Beauregard and Braxton Bragg. Early in April Johnston moved northward from Mississippi, intent on attacking Grant's army of 42,000, camped around Pittsburg Landing, on the Tennessee River. The Southern attack on the morning of April 6 completely surprised Grant. Johnston's brigades tore through the unprepared Federal outposts, driving the Union troops back toward the Tennessee River until the Federals at last regained their balance. The two armies mauled each other with a savagery that the soldiers would have found unimaginable a day earlier. For two days the woods near Pittsburg Landing were filled with the rattle of musketry, the roar of artillery, thick smoke, and soldiers braving it out. Johnston fell mortally wounded and the Confederate assaults weakened. With the help of reinforcements, Grant was able to stem and then turn the tide, forcing the Southerners to retreat again to Mississippi.

The carnage was almost beyond comprehension. The number of Confederates killed in two days—1,700—was more than the Americans had lost in two years in the war with Mexico, and the Federals lost just as many. A total of 16,000 soldiers—the equivalent of a small army—were wounded. The battle was named after a small log church, called Shiloh, near which the fighting began. *Shiloh*, a term taken from the Bible, means "place of peace."

Though Northerners could console themselves with the victory, Americans North and South received the news of Shiloh with shock and disbelief. Confederates saw their fortunes sink lower. The war had not gone well for the South since the victory at Manassas the summer before, and the Federal pressure was mounting. As the dead were being buried at Shiloh, McClellan stood with his enormous army at Yorktown on the Virginia peninsula, just 50 miles from Richmond. The Young Napoleon had found his campaign of "rapid marches"

Across the divided nation, events moved quickly in the spring of 1862. Federal troops crowded the *Aleck Scott* (above), at Cairo, Illinois, in preparation for strategic thrusts down the Mississippi. In Virginia, with the help of the navy, McClellan's army bore down on Yorktown (far left) on the York River. Despite the tightening ring, Confederates clung to their ideals—the flag carried by the 14th Mississippi Infantry featured a painting of Lady Liberty holding a portrait of Jefferson Davis (inset).

While General Joseph E. Johnston (above) defended Virginia, the Federals captured the South's largest city: On April 24, a fleet under Davis G. Farragut subdued two Confederate forts (middle) on the Mississippi, prompting the mayor of New Orleans to surrender the city (opposite, top). General Benjamin Butler's harsh ways during the occupation of the Crescent City earned him the hatred of the Southern people, as the devilish caricature on the *carte de visite* (opposite, bottom) suggests.

mired in bad roads and obstructed by Confederate defenders, but he wasted no time adapting his plans. He decided to lay siege to the fortifications at Yorktown. After capturing them, he would resume his march on Richmond. Lincoln protested the long delay, but McClellan persisted. The general spent a month in siege operations; then, just two days before he was to open fire with his big guns, the Confederates abandoned Yorktown and retreated toward Richmond.

The Federal delays at Yorktown had allowed the Confederates to concentrate most of their troops in Virginia, on the peninsula, where they were consolidated under General Joseph E. Johnston. To the chagrin of President Davis and his cabinet, the Southern commander wished to make his stand closer to Richmond. By mid-May McClellan was within 20 miles of the Confederate capital and still creeping forward. The Confederacy, barely a year old, seemed on the brink of defeat. For months Federal armies had recorded triumph after triumph over the Southerners: Forts Henry and Donelson and the fall of Nashville; the capture of Roanoke Island and coastal regions in North Carolina; the Battle of Pea Ridge, Arkansas, where the Confederates lost control of Missouri and much of the Mississippi River; battles at New Madrid, Missouri, Shiloh, Fort Pulaski in Georgia; the siege of Yorktown and Norfolk, Virginia; and, perhaps most crushing of all, the fall of New Orleans, the South's largest city, which the Federals occupied in late April. All of these reverses had, in Davis's words, "cast the gloomiest of shadows" on Confederate fortunes. To Johnston, Davis wrote, almost in despair, "I hope for you that brilliant result which the drooping cause of our country now so imperatively claims." *The New York Times* soberly declared on May 12, "In no representation of the rebel cause is there a gleam of hope."

Amid such forebodings, Johnston, his army's back to Richmond, attacked. McClellan had divided his army by sending about a third of it across the Chickahominy River north of Richmond. Johnston saw his opportunity and on May 31 he struck hard at the isolated Federals south of the river near a crossroads called Seven Pines. A violent storm had flooded the river, but heroic work by Federal engineers and the boldness of General Edwin V. Sumner—who marched his troops across the bridge, even as the swirling waters rolled over the roadway— kept McClellan's army connected. Though the Confederate attack was badly managed, the

FARRAGUT APRIL 24 1862
J. JOFFRAY P.

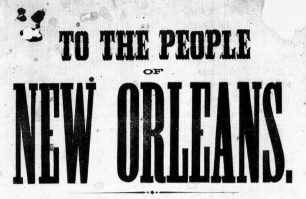

TO THE PEOPLE
OF
NEW ORLEANS.

Mayoralty of New Orleans,
CITY HALL, April 25th, 1862.

After an obstinate and heroic defence by our troops on the river, there appears to be imminent danger that the insolent enemy will succeed in capturing your city. The forts have not fallen; they have not succumbed even beneath the terrors of a bombardment unparalleled in the history of warfare. Their defenders have done all that becomes men fighting for their homes, their country and their liberty; but in spite of their efforts, the ships of the enemy have been able to avoid them, and now threaten the city. In view of this contingency, I call on you to be calm, to meet the enemy, not with submissiveness nor with indecent a[...] but if the military authorities are unable longer to [...] the inevitable m[...] fellow-countrym[...] main among you[...] power or autho[...]

Beast Butler.

Southerners fought with great courage and tenacity, and almost routed the Federals. As at Shiloh, the fighting lasted two days; as in Tennessee, the Confederate commander fell (Johnston was seriously, but not mortally, wounded). And once again, the carnage was beyond belief. More than 5,600 Southerners fell dead or wounded before their commanders pulled them back, beaten again. The North's casualties numbered more than 4,300.

Johnston's attempt to derail the Federals had failed, and Richmond's fate seemed sealed. There would be more fighting, and that, perhaps, was the worst news of all, at least for the soldiers of the ranks. The brutal fighting in the spring of 1862 had set a precedent. In four days at Shiloh and Seven Pines, more Americans had been killed or wounded in combat than in all the 87 years since the Colonists had taken up arms in 1775. These two battles, one in the West and the other in the East, set the standard of bloodletting for the battles to come. Henceforth, commanders would not flinch when they took heavy losses. They would continue to fight even as thousands of their men fell around them.

HISTORY IN THE MAKING

Two unfinished ironclads by James B. Eads lay end to end in the Carondelet Shipyard (left), on the Mississippi near St. Louis. Forty-one-year-old entrepreneur and inventor Eads had lived his entire adult life on the great river and received a contract from the U.S. war department for seven ironclad, steam-driven gunboats in September 1861. Working diligently at Carondelet and the shipyard at Mound City, Illinois, Eads delivered the first vessel by October 12 and produced all seven gunboats within 100 days of signing the contract. Eads built seven more ironclads and converted many more vessels into warships.

POTENCY

Commissioned in January 1862, Eads's ironclad USS *Carondelet* (above), like her sister ships, packed a wallop. She mounted three eight-inch smoothbores in the bow, two 32-pounders in the stern, and 42- and 32-pounders (two each) on the broadsides, plus a mobile 12-pounder howitzer on the main deck. The *Carondelet* became one of the more famous vessels on the western waters, carrying her crew of 251 through long, arduous service on the Mississippi and its tributaries until June 1865.

WATER POWER

A portion of the Federal river fleet lies at anchor (left) near the mouth of the Ohio River above Cairo, Illinois. The stern-wheel paddle boats transported troops under the protection of the gunboats, especially ironclads like the *St. Louis* (center), one of Eads's early creations. At this stage of the war, the river fleet was generally manned and directed by the army. Not until October 1862 did the navy assume control.

THE PRIZE

Fort Henry, built on low ground on the bank of the Tennessee River and mounting 17 guns, was incomplete when Flag Officer Andrew H. Foote's flotilla of seven gunboats arrived on February 6. The Confederates surrendered after Foote's short bombardment. Correspondent Henri Lovie accompanied the Federals, and his sketch (above) reveals a fort badly flooded and in disrepair.

FULL STEAM

Four of Foote's ironclads (right) charge up the Tennessee River toward Fort Henry on February 6, 1862. Foote commanded from his flagship, the *Cincinnati* (left), and the little *Essex* held the right. The artist incorrectly rendered the *Carondelet* and *St. Louis* (center, left to right) as smaller than the *Cincinnati*. All three were 175 feet long by 51 feet wide.

NEW LIFE

In September 1861 the Federal war department bought the five-year-old steamer *New Era* and gave it to Eads to convert into an ironclad gunboat. When she reemerged, she bore five guns, 124 men, and a new name—USS *Essex* (opposite). Her commander, William D. Porter, fought her hard, notably at Fort Henry, where a shot to her boiler crippled the ship and scalded Porter.

PLUNGING FIRE

A week after the victory at Fort Henry, Foote's gunboats, not all of them ironclads, battle the high batteries of Fort Donelson (above) on the Cumberland River. "The excitement on our boat was immense," wrote one soldier, "as we saw the shot and shell from the enemy striking in the water all around the gunboats. Broken pieces of timber, mattresses, and a mangled corpse floated by us." The Confederate gunners in their strong position proved too much for the Federals, and when the flotilla retired, Foote was among the wounded.

A GENTLEMAN

Kentuckian Simon Bolivar Buckner (opposite) was widely liked and respected by his fellow officers in the prewar army, particularly for his strict sense of decorum and his dedication to the principles of honor and integrity. He befriended Grant at West Point—they climbed mountains together in Mexico—and in 1854 Grant, recently resigned from the army, asked his friend for a loan, and got it. The long friendship meant little when the two came together as opposing commanders at Fort Donelson.

Hd Qrs, Army in the Field
Camp near Donelson, Feby 16th 1862

Gen. S. B. Buckner,
Confed. Army,
Sir;

Yours of this date proposing Armistice, and appointment of Commissioners, to settle terms of Capitulation is just received. No terms except an unconditional and immediate surrender can be accepted.

I propose to move immediately upon your works.

I am sir; very respectfully your obt. svt.
U. S. Grant
Brig. Gen.

"UNCONDITIONAL AND IMMEDIATE"

At 3 A.M. on February 16, 1862, a courier under a flag of truce brought Grant a message from Buckner, commander of the garrison in Fort Donelson. Buckner wished an armistice, and asked what terms of surrender the Federal commander would offer. Grant responded at once in his own hand, creating one of the more famous documents in American history. The courtly Buckner was chagrined by his friend's "ungenerous and unchivalrous terms"—"unconditional and immediate surrender"—but accepted them. After the surrender, the two jovially recalled better days.

SHILOH

A RUDE AWAKENING

Federal commanders denied that they had been surprised at Shiloh (above), but many Northerners were still resting in camp when the first attacks came. General William T. Sherman had been warned of the Confederates' approach by a nervous colonel, but had replied that there was no enemy within 20 miles and curtly suggested that the officer "take your damn regiment back to Ohio." The Confederates attacked early the next morning.

COMBAT COMMANDER

Albert Sidney Johnston (left) was one of the Confederacy's highest-ranking generals and among the more respected men in gray. He fell on the first day of battle at Shiloh, after a bullet severed an artery in his leg. He bled to death in minutes. Before the battle, he remarked, "We must this day conquer or perish."

MOTLEY CREW

The British general who called America's Civil War armies "armed mobs" might have seen the men of the 21st Missouri Volunteers (right). Displaying a variety of uniforms and arms, the Federals were apparently as poorly disciplined as they were equipped. Grant considered them a rough bunch: While cruising upriver on a transport, the men kept up "a constant fire all the way" at objects on the riverbank. Even "the citizens on shore were fired at," wrote Grant.

DISHONOR

On April 6, 1862, fearful Federals fled the front at Shiloh and sought refuge in the bluffs on the Tennessee River. Refusing to be rallied, the mobs prevented other troops from reaching the battlefield. One officer leading reinforcements charged into the skulkers shouting, "Damn your souls, if you won't fight get out of the way and let men come here who will!"

ILL AT EASE

A self-conscious-looking Ulysses S. Grant (right) sported a fashionable square-cut beard for this rare portrait in October 1861. According to most observers, one of Grant's more pleasing characteristics was his simplicity—his lack of ostentation and his trusting nature. "He possesses many traits of character that should form a subject of encouragement to others," wrote one associate. "He might not be rated high in any one branch of knowledge or character, but he does his best and leaves the result to the Laws of nature, and then he goes on, with almost the confidence of a child, conscious of his own motives and fearless of results." Within four months of sitting for this photograph, Grant would shed his mantle of obscurity and earn fame at Forts Henry and Donelson.

RAPID TRANSIT

The broad rivers in the West offered vast opportunities for rapid transportation. The Federals made much better use of the waters as thoroughfares than the Southerners did. Stern-wheel steamers (left) carried troops to where they were needed and sometimes played a critical strategic role, as when they ferried reinforcements across the Tennessee River to help turn the battle at Shiloh in favor of the Federals. The *Tigress* (center) served as Grant's headquarters and carried him to the battlefield on the morning of April 6.

CONFEDERATE CHARGE

An artist's rendering of Shiloh (above) accurately portrays the smoke-filled woods, the onward press of the Confederates, and the slaughter. One Southerner later described his feelings in the early attacks at Shiloh: "When the order to charge was given, I got happy. I shouted. It was fun then. Everybody looked happy. Discharge after discharge was poured into the retreating line. The Federal dead and wounded covered the ground."

THE END OF THE LINE

At Shiloh, General Benjamin Prentiss so tenaciously obeyed Grant's strict orders to hold the position below that the Southerners called it the "Hornet's Nest." Prentiss eventually surrendered 2,200 men, but his defense stalled the Confederates, inflicted hundreds of casualties, and possibly saved Grant's army by weakening the Southern forces.

HOOSIER CONFIDENCE

The men of Company H, 44th Indiana Volunteers, exude a calm self-assurance in this portrait (left), but they earned their self-possession the hard way. At Shiloh they ventured into burning woods and fought in dense smoke, suffering 198 casualties. An unusually high percentage of those who fell—12 percent—were killed immediately. Few Union regiments suffered greater loss in the battle.

PENINSULAR CAMPAIGN

OLD FRIENDS

Three Federal generals—(above, from left) Winfield Scott Hancock, William F. Smith, and John Newton—pose together, perhaps in June 1862, when all were on duty with the Sixth Corps on the Virginia peninsula. They had been friends at West Point 20 years earlier, and they remained close. Smith proclaimed Hancock "faithful and gallant, methodical and conscientious, laborious and brilliant." He served as a pallbearer at his friend's funeral in 1886.

MOVING MOUNTAINS

The energetic George McClellan understood that a soldier's life was meant to be one of unremitting toil, and he was good about keeping his men busy. The sketch at right shows some of McClellan's artillerymen loading their battery guns aboard a ship bound for the peninsula. In just three weeks the Federals moved 121,500 men, 14,592 animals, 1,224 wagons and ambulances, and 44 batteries, plus all the necessary equipment and rations to sustain man and beast—the largest strategic movement in American history.

MASSIVE OPERATION
Troops, equipment, and artillery, including small mortars known as coehorns (above, foreground), lay on the beach at Yorktown after the Federals captured the historic riverport in May 1862. The enormous size and scope of McClellan's campaign on the peninsula awed even seasoned military men.

HEAVY METAL
During the siege of Yorktown, McClellan's engineers built Battery Number 4 (left) on Wormley's Creek, 2,500 yards from the Confederate lines. Each of these 13-inch "seacoast" mortars weighed 17,120 pounds and could lob a 200-pound projectile almost two and a half miles. The Confederates evacuated Yorktown before any of these weapons fired a shot.

"SUPERB"

Federal troops spent most of May 5, 1862, advancing through the rain and gloom to attack a strong Confederate rearguard just east of the old colonial capital of Williamsburg. They made little headway, but late in the afternoon, General Winfield Scott Hancock (above, on the brown horse at left) worked his brigade around the flank of the enemy line and unleashed a devastating barrage upon a disjointed Confederate counterattack. After the Southerners abandoned the field, an elated McClellan wrote, "Hancock was superb."

YOUNG LIONS

Service with McClellan's invading army on the peninsula left little time for relaxation, but these junior officers (opposite) found a few moments of repose in camp near Cumberland Landing in May 1862. The dandy fellow with the dog is newly minted Lieutenant George A. Custer, who graduated from West Point less than a year earlier—last in his class. Custer's daring and energy earned him a temporary assignment with the topographical engineers on the peninsula, where his duties included reconnoitering and sketching rough maps.

Dueling Ironclads

MAKING HISTORY

With a previous victim listing over the horizon, the ironclad CSS *Virginia*, nee *Merrimac*, bears down on the frigate USS *Minnesota* and its defender, the USS *Monitor* (above). The March 9, 1862, battle in Hampton Roads, Virginia, the first between ironclads, ended in a draw but marked a new era in naval warfare.

At a time when technology was changing the world, maritime engineers in the 1850s and '60s were far ahead of other innovators, and no two vessels better exemplified the revolutions in power, propulsion, protection, and armament than the USS *Monitor* and CSS *Virginia*.

FERTILE MIND

In a field crowded with brilliant men, Swede John Ericsson (inset, left) was the reigning genius of maritime design in the 1860s. After designing new locomotives and naval guns, he invented the screw propeller, rendering sails and paddle wheels obsolete and changing water travel forever. Ericsson built his design for the ironclad *Monitor* in 101 working days.

TAKING NO PUNISHMENT

The rotating turret of the *Monitor* (above) was more than a match for the *Virginia*'s shot, which dented but couldn't breach the eight inches of armor. The *Monitor*'s twin 11-inch guns with 180-pound projectiles were just as unsuccessful against the sloping sides and 28 inches of pine, oak, and iron protecting the *Virginia*.

IRONCLAD PROFIT

An enterprising merchant in New York capitalized on the public's fascination with the two cutting-edge ships by producing playing cards (left) with an ironclad theme. The caricatures on the face cards bear strong resemblances to prominent figures in the national drama, including Lincoln, McClellan, Ambrose Burnside, and the two first ladies.

NAVY MAN

Franklin Buchanan, a founder of the U.S. Naval Academy before joining the Confederacy, commanded the *Virginia* until March 8, when he was wounded in action with the USS *Congress*. Lt. Catesby Jones succeeded him and battled the *Monitor* the next day.

IN HARM'S WAY

John L. Worden had spent 27 of his 44 years in the navy by the time he was given command of the *Monitor*. He fought the engagement with the *Virginia* boldly, steaming immediately to within a few yards and exchanging fire without flinching.

Deliverance

AS DARKNESS FELL over the battlefield at Seven Pines, and the firing slowed to a sporadic popping of musketry, doctors moved the gravely wounded General Joseph Johnston to a bed in Richmond. If he lived, he would not return to duty anytime soon. President Jefferson Davis had been on the field to watch some of the battle, and now, as he guided his

Confederate General Thomas J. "Stonewall" Jackson, who figured prominently in Robert E. Lee's bold initial battle plans, believed God was using him and his army as instruments of divine will. Jackson prayed several times a day and used the bell at left to summon his men to worship.

horse toward the capital, he bore burdens far heavier than those that had oppressed him in the morning. McClellan's army had not been beaten. His own army was without a commander and disorganized by battle. If McClellan were to attack tomorrow, he might well take Richmond. Oppressed by these thoughts, Davis turned to the man riding beside him, General Robert E. Lee, and asked him to take command of the army in the field. It was May 31, 1862.

Davis had come to know Lee well in the few months that the general had been serving as his chief military adviser, and the two men respected each other. Both were West Point graduates and both were wholly committed to the Confederacy. At 55, Lee could look back on more than 30 years as a military engineer and recall successes in war (as a captain in Mexico) and peace (as supervisor to large engineering projects). Rumor had it that just after the South fired on Fort Sumter Lee was offered—but had declined—command of the Union armies. He disagreed with secession, he said, but he was a Virginian and a Southerner and could not fight against his own people. Lee's grandfather had been one of the state's wealthiest landowners, and his father— General "Light-horse" Harry Lee of Revolutionary War fame—had been governor of Virginia. He was married to a Custis and therefore related to George Washington by marriage.

But résumé and pedigree would not help against an enemy army—the largest in American history to that point—knocking on the gates of Richmond. Even before Seven Pines, the Confederate situation looked so grim that Davis talked about abandoning Richmond and had asked Lee where another defensive line might be established. Lee courteously replied that the next defensible line in Virginia would be about a hundred miles to the southwest, on the Staunton River. Then he added, "But Richmond must not be given up; it shall not be given up!"

When Lee assumed command in early June, renaming his army the Army of Northern Virginia, he was not surprised that the Confederacy was in dire straits. "It is plain we have not suffered enough, laboured enough . . . to deserve success," he wrote to his daughter. "Our people have not been earnest enough, have thought too much of themselves . . . and instead of turning

Robert E. Lee (left) had three sons, and all followed him into Confederate service. Rooney Lee (top, with his father around 1845) became a general, as did older brother Custis (bottom). Lee's youngest son, Robert Jr. (above), served as an enlisted man in the artillery.

Northerners praised the beauty of Virginia's Shenandoah Valley, seen here (above right) from Rockfish Gap in the Blue Ridge Mountains. Stonewall Jackson (above) lived in the region for a decade, and his successful campaign there in 1862 earned him a prominent place in valley lore.

out to be men, have been content to leave the protection of themselves and families to others." Lee would not perpetuate the error; he immediately went to work, determined to invite divine favor. He knew, however, that he did not have much time. He had to do something to derail McClellan's army—and soon. Within two weeks he strengthened and reorganized his troops and developed a plan. Though outnumbered, he would attack.

The crucial column in Lee's plan was still about a hundred miles away, in the Shenandoah Valley, under the command of an eccentric former professor of natural philosophy named Thomas J. Jackson. Many in America now called him "Stonewall" for his performance at Bull Run Creek, where he and his troops stood unmoved against the Federal assaults. Like Lee, Jackson was a Virginian and a West Pointer; he was a classmate of George McClellan's. He had made a name for himself as an aggressive artilleryman in Mexico but left the army in 1851 to take a teaching position at the Virginia Military Institute in Lexington. A devout Presbyterian, Jackson was a deacon in his church and started a Sunday school for black children.

But the war unleashed other sides of Jackson's personality—the soldier committed to duty and the leader determined to get things done. "Old Jack," wrote one general, gives "short, sharp

According to notes on the inside cover of this much-traveled pocket map book (above), it served Jackson's chief of artillery, Colonel Stapleton Crutchfield, before Jackson himself used it in the famous valley campaign. The book was later used by a member of Jackson's staff, Major H. K. Douglas.

commands distinctly, rapidly and decisively, without consultation or explanation, and disregarding suggestions and remonstrances. Being himself absolutely fearless . . . he goes ahead on his own hook, asking no advice and resenting interference. He places no value on human life, caring for nothing so much as fighting, unless it be praying. Illness, wounds and all disabilities he defines as inefficiency and a lack of patriotism. . . . He never praises his men for gallantry, because it is their duty to be gallant and they do not deserve credit for doing their duty." Jackson was as hard on himself as he was on his troops, however, and they grew to love him.

Jackson and his men had been in the Shenandoah Valley for months. Lee corresponded with the wiry officer and found a kindred spirit: Both were energetic, aggressive, and unafraid to take risks. Lee wanted Jackson and his troops to keep the Federals in the valley occupied so that Washington would not send them to reinforce McClellan.

Stonewall Jackson began his remarkable campaign in March, when, with about 3,500 men, he attacked roughly 10,000 Union soldiers at Kernstown. The Southerners were repulsed, but the Federals sat up and took notice. They pursued Jackson for six weeks before deciding he had slipped away to Richmond. Believing the valley to be secure, the Federals prepared to join

McClellan. But Jackson had not gone eastward—he was in the mountains to the west. After building his force to about 6,000, he defeated the enemy at McDowell. Returning to the valley he marched northward, was sent reinforcements from Lee, and went on to lead about 15,000 men to victories at Front Royal and Winchester. Washington dispatched more than 40,000 troops from other operations, including Richmond, to corral the rampant Jackson, but his army eluded the Federals, who were defeated twice more in early June. Fearing more losses, the Federals decided to leave Jackson alone. He had driven his men more than 550 miles to win five out of six battles and dozens of skirmishes—a spectacular success for the forlorn Confederacy.

In mid-June Lee summoned Jackson's army to Richmond and, after learning the position of the Federal flanks, hatched a breathtakingly daring plan to defeat McClellan that violated a chief rule of sound generalship: Never divide your army against a superior force. Lee left about a third of his men to defend Richmond and massed the rest to work against McClellan's weak right flank. Jackson and troops were to arrive secretly, join the army, march around McClellan's flank, and, if possible, into the Union rear. Jackson's turning movement, Lee hoped, would force the Unionists to withdraw from their advanced positions just six miles from Richmond. The risk was that McClellan might use his enormous army to strike at Lee's small force holding Richmond.

Lee could not know that there was almost no chance of McClellan reacting aggressively that week. Convinced he was facing as many as 200,000 Confederates, the Young Napoleon—who seemed so promising a few months earlier—was now feuding with Washington, pleading for reinforcements. He spent weeks just a few miles from Richmond building bridges, roads,

In his drive on Richmond, McClellan put his faith in engineering and artillery. He devoted weeks to building an elaborate infrastructure of roads and bridges (above left) to support his troops, and steadily added field batteries, including Battery C, Third U.S. Artillery (above), to his army.

An artist's view of McClellan's operations around Richmond (above right) shows clouds of smoke billowing skyward from the Battle of Gaines' Mill on June 27, 1862, and swarms of defeated Federals streaming across the Chickahominy River to safety. Richmond, on the James River, is at the center of the print.

and fortifications. Members of Lincoln's cabinet grew weary of the general's delays and the politicking, and wished him removed from command. But Lincoln stood by McClellan.

Lee's offensive began on June 26. Jackson's column moved slowly, and the projected flank march turned into a series of frontal assaults at Beaver Dam Creek. Lee suffered 1,500 casualties, more than four times the Federal loss, but forced the Northerners to withdraw. The next day Lee again found himself waiting for Jackson, and again the Federals were in a strong position. Once Jackson arrived and the Confederate assault began, the carnage was far worse than it had been at Seven Pines. In the forests near Gaines' Mill more than 13,000 men fell in less than six hours. Lee won a resounding victory, but at a steep price. The armies fought three more times in the next four days as McClellan moved his men south to a new supply base on the James River. The bloody climax came at Malvern Hill, where high ground and McClellan's immense advantage in artillery smothered the attacks by Lee's courageous infantrymen. Afterward known as the Seven Days' Battles, the operation was one of the bloodiest of the war. McClellan lost 15,000 men; Lee, 19,000. The long week ended at last when McClellan's army retreated to the James River on July 2.

But if McClellan's army was still alive, so was the Confederacy. Lee had done what had seemed impossible. Many had said the rebellion would be over by Independence Day, but when July 4 dawned, the Southerners held the initiative and the North's greatest army huddled in defeat. Lee had been the engine powering the dramatic reversal, and the months ahead would show that he would not rest on his success. With the emergence of Lee, the war began in earnest.

ON THE SKIRMISH LINE

The men of the 13th Pennsylvania Reserves were so proud of their marksmanship that they made like hunters and wore deer tails on their hats, earning the name the "Bucktails." On June 6, 1862, the riflemen skirmished (above) with Jackson's rearguard, and when the smoke cleared General Turner Ashby, Jackson's cavalry chief and a Southern idol, lay dead.

NATURAL GENERAL

Though he had no previous military experience, Major General Nathaniel Banks was the North's third-highest-ranking general at the start of the war. A former speaker of the U.S. House of Representatives and governor of Massachusetts, Banks was defeated twice by Jackson in the spring and summer of 1862.

TELLING BEGINNINGS

Stonewall Jackson delighted in his first real chance to harm the enemy, which came in 1861, when he and his First Brigade were ordered to destroy all the Baltimore & Ohio Railroad stock it could get its hands on. They torched the B & O's roundhouse and workshops (left), along with 42 locomotives and 305 railroad cars.

COMFORT IN THE FIELD

Federal General Alpheus S. Williams, mounted at far right in the photo above, ably led a division under Nathaniel Banks against Jackson in the Shenandoah Valley. The lawyer from Detroit became a competent military man in part due to his attention to the training and health of his troops. Of his camp in Darnestown, Maryland (above), Williams wrote, "On our hillside are my eight or ten tents, sheltered by the woods in the rear. Just within the wood are our servants' tents. Altogether it is a delightful spot."

FOLLOWING STONEWALL

A SOLDIER'S LIFE

Extraordinarily severe weather plagued Virginia in early 1862, with snow in the Shenandoah Valley well into April and heavy rains into June. Jackson, who believed hard marching saved lives in battle, pushed his men regardless of the weather, and they developed into sturdy marchers who could cover so much ground in so little time that they became known as "Jackson's foot cavalry." A valley woman who saw the weary men trudging past berated the general for pushing them too hard. Jackson's reply was succinct: "Legs are cheaper than heads, madam."

ROAD GANG

McClellan kept his troops constantly occupied, building, expanding, and repairing the small, rustic roads of the Virginia peninsula. Under the supervision of engineer officers, fatigue parties that were hundreds of men strong kept the lines of communication open. Above, workers lay a corduroy road, which called for trimmed logs laid in two layers and covered with brush and packed dirt. Details of 100 or more men armed with shovels moved with every wagon train to repair the road after the passage of the vehicles.

IN THE SWAMPS

In a photograph made from a cracked glass negative, Federal troops on pioneer duty (opposite) add the finishing touches to one of the 11 bridges McClellan had built over the Chickahominy River east of Richmond. Though the stream itself was only several yards wide, the bordering swamps and marshes forced the bridge builders to lay extensive causeways and elevated corduroy roads durable enough to withstand the heavy, constant traffic of supply wagons.

PORT OF CALL

Rocketts Landing (above), on the James River south of Richmond, remained busy as McClellan's legions approached the capital city. Refugees from the peninsula and other Federal-occupied areas flocked to Richmond and then moved on to the relative safety of points inland. The Confederate government too was on the move. The treasury and war departments shipped currency and records southward, and President Jefferson Davis sent his family to the security of friends in North Carolina.

A FAMILIAR SIGHT

A postwar portrait shows Robert E. Lee (left) astride his warhorse Traveller. Lee deeply loved the animal that bore him thousands of miles during the war. During one separation, Lee wrote to a colleague: "How is Traveller? Tell him I miss him dreadfully and have repented our separation but once, and that is the whole time since we parted."

DERRING-DO

Combat artist Alfred Waud shows the downpours (above) that in late May 1862 turned the Chickahominy River into a raging torrent that tore away some of the Federals' bridges. General Edwin V. Sumner nevertheless marched some of his troops to battle across Grapevine Bridge (pictured). The weight of the column held the span together just long enough for the troops to pass. Sumner's men arrived in time to help win the Battle of Fair Oaks.

THE FRONT LINE

The sleepy crossroads hamlet of Mechanicsville (above), six miles northeast of Richmond, consisted of only a few homes and workshops, but it made front-page news when the armies fought there in the spring and summer of 1862. In Mechanicsville on June 26, 1862, Lee began his first offensive.

FIGHTING GENERAL

General Fitz-John Porter, seated on a camp chair (left), poses with his staff for this August 1862 image. As McClellan's confidante and most trusted friend, Porter bore heavy responsibilities. In the Seven Days' Battles, his Fifth Corps troops suffered half of the total Federal casualties.

SOUTHERN CROSS

The 60th Virginia Infantry, raised mainly in the central part of the state, served in General A. P. Hill's division in 1862. Its battle flag (left) tells the story of its involvement in the Seven Days' Battles around Richmond: It fought three major engagements—including fierce hand-to-hand fighting at Frayser's Farm, represented by the crossed bayonets—in five days.

SAVAGE'S STATION
Boxcars, wagons, and tents stand on the plain at Savage's Station, the Army of the Potomac's most important forward supply depot. After McClellan hastily evacuated the area on June 29, he claimed that all the important supplies were removed. Accounts from soldiers, however, suggest that small amounts of rations and equipment were burned.

ABANDONED
Sick and wounded Federals (left), many of them casualties of the Battle of Gaines' Mill, take over the yard at the Savage's Station field hospital. When the army retreated to the James, McClellan abandoned 2,500 of his men at this hospital to the mercy of the enemy, an act that brought him vociferous criticism from editors, the public, and his own troops.

MOBILE FIREPOWER

Lee realized the vital importance of controlling the Richmond & York River Railroad east of the capital city and asked the help of the Confederate navy in developing a railroad gun. The novel weapon (above) saw action in the Battle of Savage's Station—believed to be the first use of rail artillery in history.

SCHOOL OF WAR

The Philadelphians of the 95th Pennsylvania Infantry (right) were initiated into war during the Seven Days' Battles, especially at Gaines' Mill, where in just a few hours 112 of the unit's men were killed, wounded, or missing. After that, recalled one of them, "those bright fresh boyish faces had changed to hard, fierce determined men."

"A CHANGE OF BASE"

Having been outmaneuvered and outfought by Lee, McClellan fled with his men toward the James River. The enormous Army of the Potomac—nearly 120,000 men with 3,000 wagons and perhaps 40,000 horses and mules—struggled over unfamiliar roads and through choke points at bridges and fords, as at Bear Creek (above). Though the movement was plainly a retreat, McClellan sought to save face by styling it as a march to a new base of operations.

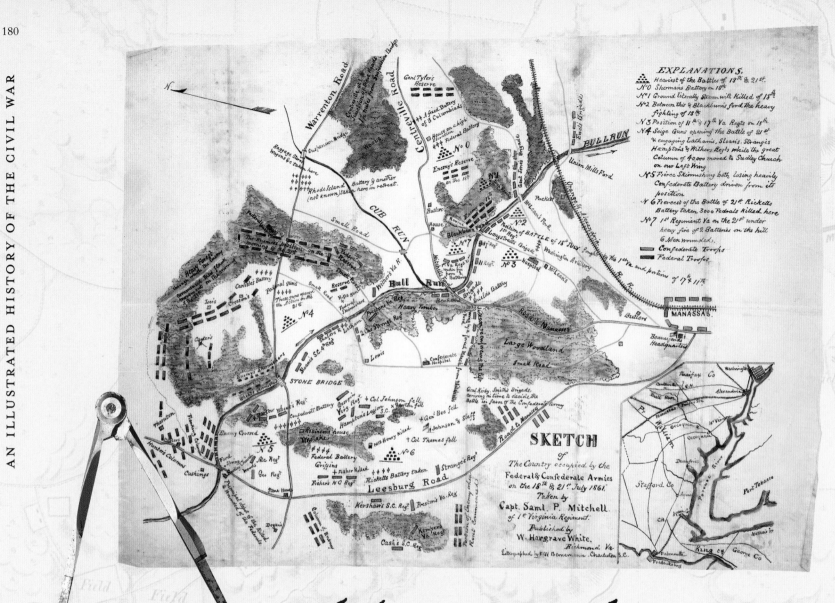

Mapmaking

Maps were scarce in 1861, and those that were available were notoriously inaccurate. Surveyors also were rare, and those who could translate their observations and measurements into useful military maps were in high demand.

SMALL MARGIN FOR ERROR

Cartographers put their protractors (left) to their maps to determine azimuths, or true bearings, and used dividers to measure distance between points. Considering that one degree at Richmond's latitude was equal to about 55 miles, the task required careful work with precision instruments of good quality, usually crafted out of brass or steel.

TOOLS OF THE TRADE

Ambrose Bierce of Indiana used these instruments (right)—four compasses of varying size and a divider for measuring distances on a map—in the field. Educated at the Kentucky Military Institute, Bierce, a Federal, entered the war as a private but became a lieutenant and topographical engineer. After the war, he earned fame as a journalist and author.

HOW HIGH THE HILL?

The leather-bound aneroid barometer at right, complete with shoulder strap, indicated atmospheric pressure, which allowed the surveyor to accurately determine altitude, after making corrections for prevailing weather conditions. This one belonged to Jed Hotchkiss (below, far left); possibly it replaced his original barometer, which was lost with other instruments in a hasty retreat from Rich Mountain, Virginia, in 1861. Hotchkiss had filed a compensation claim with the Confederate government, which gave him a new one.

GOOD, NOT GREAT

Creating maps was prohibitively expensive in peacetime, so once the war began, even crude maps were much sought after as reference tools. Confederate Captain Samuel Mitchell's map of operations around Bull Run in July 1861 (opposite), like most maps of the time, was far more handsome than it was accurate.

SELF-MADE

A New Yorker by birth, Jed Hotchkiss (above) moved alone to Virginia as a teenager. He taught himself surveying and cartography and worked for Stonewall Jackson, Robert E. Lee, and others, becoming the war's most famous topographical engineer.

TIRELESS

William Henry Paine (above), an engineer from New Hampshire, went to work for a railroad in Wisconsin. He assisted several generals during the war, including Joseph Hooker and George G. Meade, and gained a reputation for indefatigable dedication.

INHERITED GENIUS

Washington Roebling (above), an engineer and son of the brilliant builder John A. Roebling, served under Hooker, Meade, and Grant. After the war, with his father, he supervised construction of the greatest engineering project of the age: the Brooklyn Bridge.

GEORGIA VICTOR

Ohioan Orlando Metcalfe Poe (above) finished sixth in the class of 1856 at the U.S. Military Academy and made a name for himself as a topographical engineer. He served as Sherman's chief engineer in the demanding 1864 Atlanta campaign.

Forced to Gamble

PRING VICTORIES in Virginia—in the Shenandoah Valley and around Richmond—brought the Confederates time but not repose, for the Federals continued to press in upon them. Lincoln knew that a hard road lay ahead for the Union, too, because McClellan, who had said, "I can do it all," had so far proved that he could not. In the summer and

After engaging in the bloody battles of the peninsular campaign, the 52nd New York Infantry, whose flag is pictured above, took part in the assault on "Bloody Lane" at Antietam. The unit, one of the war's many predominantly immigrant regiments, called itself the German Rangers.

autumn of 1862, neither side could afford to act conservatively; the war's shifting circumstances pushed men to take desperate chances.

Lincoln received the news of McClellan's disastrous performance in the Seven Days' Battles with calm resignation. "Save your army at all events," he told the young general. "If you have had a drawn battle, or a repulse, it is the price we pay for the enemy not being in Washington." That the president could see the absence of Confederate troops in Washington as a sort of victory—after a year of war, after fielding the largest army the nation had ever seen, after a string of significant victories, and after his main army had been within six miles of the enemy capital only to be repulsed—suggests how disarrayed the Union was in its war effort and that Lincoln knew more could not be expected from McClellan. The president, seeing that circumstances called for significant changes, began to alter the military situation in Virginia by bringing in General John Pope, who had recently succeeded in taking a Confederate stronghold on the Mississippi River. Pope would form an additional army, the Army of Virginia, from Federal troops scattered in the northern part of the state. Recognizing that he needed more military expertise in his counsel chambers, Lincoln also brought General Henry W. Halleck to Washington and appointed him general in chief. But even this, the president knew, was not enough to get the army to "strike more vigorous blows," as he put it. "The Administration must set an example," he said, "and strike at the heart of the rebellion." He began to write, and on July 22 he surprised members of his cabinet by reading them a draft of a presidential proclamation that would emancipate the slaves.

Robert E. Lee, meanwhile, after the losses of the Seven Days' Battles, patched up his army, reorganizing his officer corps, and looked for the chance to do more damage to the Federals. From Richmond in July and August, he watched McClellan's army, still camped at Harrisons Landing on the James River. Lee doubted McClellan would attack Richmond again anytime soon; still, before he could get on with his own plans, Lee had to see what the Federals would do.

McClellan met with the president and Halleck and told them he could still take Richmond if they gave him more men. They had no more men to give him—or at least not as many as he wanted. Lincoln remarked that if by some magic he could send 100,000 men tomorrow, McClellan would say that he could not advance until he had 400,000. In August an exasperated Lincoln directed the young general to put his army back on its boats and return to northern Virginia.

Which is precisely what Lee had been waiting for. Once he was certain that McClellan could not threaten Richmond, Lee swung his army out into central Virginia and prepared to head northward to meet John Pope's Army of Virginia, which was much smaller than McClellan's. Lee planned to attack it in much the same way he had defeated the Army of the Potomac: through a series of punishing frontal assaults. In late August Lee sent Jackson on a sweeping flank march deep into Pope's rear army. After covering more than 50 miles in two days of broiling heat, Stonewall and his men destroyed Pope's supply depot at Manassas

Two or three days after the Battle of Antietam, Federal troops (top) rest near a headboard marking the grave of Private John Marshall of the 28th Pennsylvania. Second Lieutenant Franklin Weaver (inset, left), seated with comrades from the Fourth North Carolina, also died at Antietam.

Federal General John Pope was an aggressive commander with an abrasive style that won him few friends in the ranks. Writing home two days after the second Union defeat at Bull Run, a Massachusetts officer noted, "I've heard twice as much abuse of Pope whom we all hate, as of any rebel." In the collapse of Pope's left flank on August 30, the 73rd Ohio Infantry (right, headed for the war in January 1862) suffered 148 casualties—including 40 killed or mortally wounded—out of 312 engaged.

Junction. Pope followed Jackson, Lee followed Pope, and all came together on the old Bull Run battlefield. Pope, badly mismanaging the battle that ensued, allowed Lee to deliver a crushing defeat, routing the Federals and again sending them fleeing past the banks of Bull Run for the safety of Washington. Lincoln despaired. Lee, unwilling as ever to waste time, decided to press onward and take the war into the North. He prepared to invade Maryland.

Another bold move by a Confederate was taking shape in the West, where the Southern army was struggling to counter relentless Union advances at Corinth, an important railroad hub in Mississippi. The town had fallen to the Federals, who were now moving eastward to threaten Chattanooga, Tennessee, another critical railroad town. General Braxton Bragg, the new commander of the principal Confederate army in the West, decided to upset Union plans by advancing two columns through Tennessee and into Kentucky, a neutral state and buffer between Confederate Tennessee and Unionist Ohio. Lincoln considered the Bluegrass State necessary to success: "I hope to have God on my side," he said, "but I must have Kentucky."

Bragg's men struck deep into the state, but encountered trouble at Perryville on October 8. There, a Federal army under General Don Carlos Buell intercepted part of Bragg's army and a daylong battle followed. Bragg, having lost about 20 percent of his army, was forced to retire. His gambit had failed. The Federals controlled Kentucky.

In Maryland, Lee was gambling as well. With a small, poorly clothed and badly fed army, he hoped to create panic in the North by moving the theater of war from a ravaged northern Virginia to Pennsylvania, where his troops could subsist on the fruits of the coming harvest.

To the Lincoln administration, a Confederate army rampant in Maryland equaled disaster. The president roused the defeated Federal army, now huddled in camps around Washington, by bypassing Pope and turning again to the man who had transformed the army a year earlier. McClellan took command—even of troops that had been Pope's—and set off after Lee. For 10 days he groped blindly westward, finally arriving at Frederick. It was there that he enjoyed a spectacular stroke of luck.

While setting up camp, a soldier of the 27th Indiana found three cigars wrapped in paper lying in the grass. The paper proved to be a copy of Lee's plan. It quickly made its way to headquarters, and McClellan, for once, acted immediately, moving his army in pursuit. On September 14 he met the Confederates at South Mountain and fought a hard battle. Two days later he was on the banks of Antietam Creek peering across at Lee's troops, preparing for battle.

At the second Battle of Bull Run, soldier-artist Henry Berckhoff of the Eighth New York recorded his brigade's assault on Stonewall Jackson's line (top)—a formidable position along the embankments of an unfinished railroad. The postwar photo above captures the daunting expanse.

Lieutenant William H. Willcox, topographical engineer on the staff of Federal General Abner Doubleday, prepared the map above showing the positions of the opposing forces at the start of the Battle of Antietam. Doubleday's division took part in the costly and ultimately unsuccessful effort to crush the left flank of Lee's army north of Sharpsburg.

The Southern commander had once again taken a risk and divided his army—Jackson and his men were to capture Harpers Ferry, and D. H. Hill and troops were to hold the gaps in South Mountain. The armies were to unite at Hagerstown for the move into Pennsylvania. But delays and the unexpected rapid march of McClellan's Army of the Potomac forced Lee to make his stand at Sharpsburg, on the hills above Antietam Creek, instead. When his scattered troops joined him, they numbered fewer than 40,000. McClellan had about 75,000 men.

The firing began on the evening of September 16 and resumed early the next morning. Despite enormous assaults, the Federals made little headway against the stubborn but desperately thin Confederate line. Lee shifted troops to meet threats and breakthroughs and managed to hold on. In the afternoon, attacks by fresh Union brigades came very near to smashing the Confederate rear and cutting off the Southerners' escape route. The timely arrival of gray-clad reinforcements from Harpers Ferry stemmed the tide, however, and darkness ended the fighting with the Confederates maintaining a tenuous hold on the field. McClellan, though, believed he had won a resounding

victory, because the Rebels were forced back to Virginia. But the victory was hardly clear-cut: With a vast advantage in manpower, McClellan had failed to exploit the best chance he would ever have to destroy Lee's army. The bigger story at Antietam was the horrible loss of life. More than 22,000 of the 113,000 who fought that day became casualties. It remains the bloodiest day in American history.

Because the South's invasion had been halted, the North claimed victory at Antietam. Lincoln, considering the moment right for his bold stroke, just five days after the battle issued the Emancipation Proclamation, which freed slaves in the rebellious states. Some Northerners responded with joy; many seemed indifferent or angry. "I am not in favor of freeing negroes and leaving them to run free among us," wrote one Illinois man. Senator Lyman Trumbull, also of Illinois, declared, "Our people want nothing to do with the negro." But whatever the feelings of the public, by redefining the goals of the war, Lincoln had taken a chance. No longer simply a struggle to defend the Constitution, enforce the laws, and restore the Union, the war was now also a crusade to end slavery. Would the people of the North support it?

Many Northerners doubted the value of the Emancipation Proclamation, but abolitionists hailed it as a triumph, claiming it infused the war effort with the righteousness of a moral crusade. A painting (center) and transcription (above) of the proclamation reflect such idealistic hopes.

ON THE MARCH

Tramping northward from Nashville to confront the Confederate offensive in Kentucky, a column of General Buell's Federal troops (left)—some of the men marching in their shirt-sleeves—crosses a bridge spanning the Big Barren River near Bowling Green. Union engineers had recently repaired the damaged structure with pontoons, so infantry companies had to cross at intervals to lessen the weight on the fragile construction.

AN UNPOPULAR LEADER

A grizzled veteran noted for his valor in the Mexican War, General Braxton Bragg (right) appeared older than his 45 years. President Davis had unwavering confidence in Bragg, but the general's irascible temper and tendency to be overly strict with his men made him unpopular on the battlefield. "He loved to crush the spirit of his men," Tennessean Sam Watkins recalled. "Not a single soldier in the whole army ever loved or respected him."

CLASH IN KENTUCKY

The 21st Wisconsin confronts charging Rebel troops in a cornfield (above) during the Battle of Perryville. The regiment's stand blunted the attack of Southerners under General George Maney and prevented the Confederates from flanking the Federal left. Though the October 8, 1862, engagement was a tactical draw, Bragg yielded the strategic initiative to Buell and his superior Union numbers.

CAUGHT IN THE CROSSFIRE

Four days after the Battle of Antietam, photographer Alexander Gardner recorded this view of Sharpsburg (above), looking west along Main Street. General Lee established his command post in the woods beyond the steeple of Saint Paul's Church, visible on the horizon. When it became clear that their town was likely to be caught in the crossfire of the contending armies, many of Sharpsburg's 1,300 residents fled their homes.

TIMELY REINFORCEMENTS

General Ambrose Powell Hill (right) was considered one of the finest division commanders in Lee's army. His performance on the afternoon of September 17 bolstered the Confederates' attempt to maintain their beleaguered position at Sharpsburg. Left behind at Harpers Ferry to patrol thousands of Yankee prisoners captured during Jackson's successful siege, Hill subsequently marched northward, arriving on the battlefield in time to blunt General Ambrose Burnside's Federal advance on the Confederate right.

THE BLOODIEST DAY

With colors flying in the vanguard and soldiers bearing their muskets, a Federal regiment (above), maintaining its formation through a storm of shot and shell, charges toward a Rebel position near Dunker Church. After a morning of unprecedented carnage, the wing of McClellan's army under General Joseph Hooker managed to get near the battered church, but the Yankee offensive stalled in the face of desperate Confederate resistance.

A TERRIBLE PRICE

In one of a series of photographs taken in the days after the Battle of Antietam, Alexander Gardner inveighs against the war with this image (above) of men in General William Starke's Louisiana brigade sprawled in death along a rail fence bordering the Hagerstown Pike. Even veteran soldiers were shocked by the carnage. "I have heard of the dead 'lying in heaps,'" Union Captain Emory Upton wrote, "but never saw it till this battle. Whole ranks fell together."

SCARS OF BATTLE

The Lutheran church (left) on Sharpsburg's eastern edge testifies to the destruction that Union artillery fire inflicted on the town—few buildings escaped the barrage. Nearly a century old at the time of the battle, the church served as a Confederate signal station, and following the fight became a hospital for Federal wounded. Structural damage to the church was so extensive that the congregation eventually tore it down.

THE GENERAL'S GUARD

President Lincoln's visit to McClellan following the bloodbath at Antietam brought photographer Alexander Gardner to the general's headquarters. His image of the 93rd New York, which at the time served as Headquarter's Guard for the Army of the Potomac, is at left. Because the New Yorkers held the guard position under four successive commanders, they did not see battle until 1864.

AN UNEASY MEETING

On October 4, 1862, Alexander Gardner photographed President Lincoln conferring with McClellan (above) in the general's headquarters tent near Sharpsburg. Though the meeting appeared cordial—McClellan described the president as "affable" and "kindly"—the outcome suggested tension. Wrote McClellan to his wife, "I incline to think that the real purpose of his visit is to push me into a premature advance into Virginia." He did not move for another three weeks.

WORKING ON THE RAILROAD
Northern construction crews in occupied Virginia
(above) serve under the brilliant civil engineer Herman
Haupt, head of the transportation and construction
bureau of the U.S. Military Railroads. In recognition of his
energy, diligence, and technical expertise, Haupt, whose
name appears on the locomotive in this image, was
promoted to brigadier general in September 1862.

REPAIRING THE DAMAGE
U.S. Military Railroad personnel (right) pause for soldier-photographer
Andrew J. Russell before righting a locomotive derailed by Confederate
raiders on Virginia's Manassas Gap Railroad. Working closely with
General Haupt, Captain Russell took dozens of photographs that were
intended to serve as illustrations in instruction manuals issued to
Northern railroad corps.

RAILROADS

EFFICIENT ENGINEERING

Prefabricated bridge trusses of Haupt's design (above), stockpiled near the Military Railroad wharves at Alexandria, Virginia, await transport down the Potomac to frontline construction crews. The men called the 60-foot-span trusses, which could support 108,000 pounds, "shad bellies," for their fishlike shape. The massive supply effort undertaken by the U.S. Military Railroads gave the North a decided edge in the mobilization and concentration of men, arms, and matériel.

INVENTOR IN UNIFORM

General Haupt (left) paddles a miniature pontoon that he designed for inspecting the underlying structure and support of U.S. Military Railroad bridges. President Lincoln was impressed with the general's energy and talent for invention. Haupt's secretary, John Hay, described him as "one man who seems thoroughly to reflect and satisfy [Lincoln] in everything he undertakes."

SPANNING BULL RUN

A locomotive and boxcar of the U.S. Military Railroad (right) pauses atop the recently repaired bridge over Bull Run at Union Mills, Virginia. In the course of the war, the span, one of many bridges along the strategically vital Orange & Alexandria Railroad line, was destroyed by Confederate troops and rebuilt by Federal work crews six times.

CONSTRUCTION SUPPLIES

New rails from the abundant supply depot at Alexandria (above) are loaded atop flatcars for shipment to repair crews in the field. The U.S. Military Railroad employed hundreds of workers at its bustling base of operations in the rail yards just west of Alexandria, where photographer A. J. Russell maintained a studio. The officer leaning against the pile of rails is believed to be Captain Russell.

HAUPT'S MEN

U.S. Military Railroad agents (right) rest beside a pile of boxed rations intended for soldiers of the Army of the Potomac. The photograph was probably taken at Aquia Creek, a tributary of the Potomac River where the Union maintained a rail line and supply base for matériel shipped aboard barges from Alexandria. "The railroad is entirely under your control," Haupt told his civilian employees. "No military officer has any right to interfere with it."

Espionage

Spying, smuggling, sabotage—all were aspects of the Civil War. Each side in the conflict had its version of the Secret Service, and both made use of undercover operatives. Modern-day concepts of intelligence gathering and espionage, however, had yet to develop.

CODES AND CIPHERS

A brass cipher disk (top), issued to the Confederate Secret Service, could encode messages sent by signal flag or telegraph, or in writing. Letters of a message were encoded by aligning a designated key letter on the inner wheel with the letter A on the outer wheel, providing each message letter on the outer wheel with a corresponding code letter. While Federal signalmen liked to brag about their ability to break the Southern cipher, they were not always successful, as the decoded message above shows: The third word has been incorrectly translated—it should read *Canton*, not *caution*.

SECRET AGENT

A former employee of the Pinkerton detective agency, Timothy Webster (above) infiltrated pro-Confederate factions in the North and ventured deep behind Southern lines, gathering information on Rebel numbers and troop movements. But Webster's luck ran out when he was arrested during his fourth mission to the Confederate capital at Richmond. Tried and condemned to death, the intrepid Yankee spy was hanged on April 29, 1862.

SOUTHERN BELLE

Belle Boyd, shown above in a photograph taken a decade after the exploits that made her famous, was the most celebrated female spy of the Civil War. The spirited teenaged daughter of a Shenandoah Valley farmer, Belle smuggled messages and medicine through Yankee lines, provided details of enemy operations to Stonewall Jackson, and delighted in her status as "the Rebel Joan of Arc."

CRAZY BET

Born to a prominent Richmond family with deep roots in the Old Dominion, Elizabeth Van Lew (above) was nonetheless an abolitionist and a staunch supporter of the Union. Determined to assist the Northern war effort, "Crazy Bet" cleverly played upon her reputation as an eccentric, adopting a disheveled appearance that made her seem harmless but masked her real purpose: gathering intelligence for the Federal army.

THE ACTRESS SPY

A native of New Orleans, actress Pauline Cushman (below) impressed Southern audiences as a fervent supporter of the Confederate cause. But actually she was a spy for the North, passing information on to Union General William Rosecrans. Discovered and sentenced to death, she escaped execution when retreating Rebel forces left her behind. Cushman relished her consequent celebrity status and returned to the stage wearing a Federal officer's uniform.

CHIEF OF SPIES

Spymaster Allan Pinkerton (above, left) meets with Abraham Lincoln and General John McClernand in October 1862. A Scottish immigrant, Pinkerton served as a policeman and sheriff and established his own detective agency in 1850. His business prospered, and in February 1861 Pinkerton agents thwarted an attempt to assassinate President-elect Lincoln. Pinkerton's success at ferreting out Southern spies led General McClellan to rely heavily on him for military information. But Pinkerton's tendency to exaggerate Confederate numbers fueled the general's tendency to overestimate the strength of his foe.

THROUGH ENEMY LINES

Southern civilians had several ingenious ways of smuggling documents and medicine through Yankee lines. The hollow head and body of the doll at right—named "Nina" by its young owner—transported desperately needed quinine and morphine from the North to Confederate medical personnel. A ring (far right) worn by a South Carolina woman contained a specially constructed recess for coded messages written on onionskin paper. Such seemingly harmless items, carried by women and children, rarely aroused suspicion at Federal army checkpoints.

Compassion's Crusade

W HEN THE PEOPLE of the "disunited" states went to war, they carried not only arms, but also medicine, blankets, bandages, and soup. Countless volunteers, North and South, joined the war effort by working to save the lives and preserve the health of the soldiers. Their task, which in the spring of 1861 began simply enough, soon became daunting.

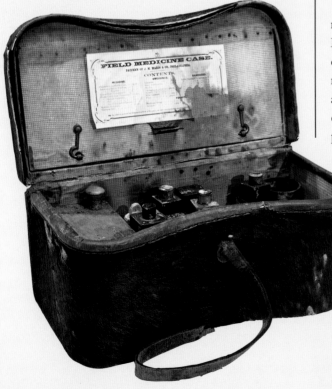

Not until 1863 did the Surgeon's Field Companion (below) replace the bulky and inconvenient hospital knapsack. The 13-by-6-inch leather case, based on British design, had shoulder and waist straps and contained an assortment of medicines and bandages.

For by 1862 it was clear that the technology that had galvanized America in the first half of the century, revolutionizing its industry, commerce, and transportation, had radically—shockingly—changed the nature of war, as well. The change came so rapidly and resulted in such casualties that neither generals nor surgeons could adapt, and men died by the thousands. For every man lost in combat, two died of disease; pneumonia, blood poisoning, and measles were among the biggest killers.

Just days after the war began, a group of educated, wealthy, and well-connected women met in New York City to discuss how they could contribute most effectively to the war effort. Especially concerned with the health of the troops, they formed the Women's Central Association of Relief and planned to organize on a broad scale local efforts to collect and distribute medical supplies and other necessities that would promote health and healing in the Northern armies. Dr. Henry W. Bellows, a Unitarian minister in New York, joined the women in their endeavor and encouraged other prominent men to get involved and expand the association's plans into a Union-wide campaign. In May 1861 Bellows and others traveled to Washington seeking the sanction of President Lincoln and the war department. Though Lincoln said he could not see the need for a national organization devoted to relief efforts, he gave his consent, as did the secretary of war, and a month later the U.S. Sanitary Commission was born. It would become the most powerful and effective of the many humanitarian organizations formed during the war.

The commission had two goals: to improve sanitation and hygiene in the army camps, and care for the ill and wounded. Vigorous fund-raising brought millions of dollars into the commission's coffers, allowing it to purchase not only supplies, but also horses, wagons, warehouses, even ships. When the Union armies entered the field in the spring of 1862, the Sanitary Commission went with them. Military doctors, claiming they could care for the wounded and perform surgery without help, at first rejected the group's assistance as well

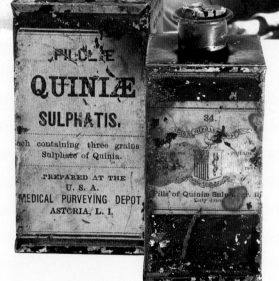

as that of other volunteers. But the big battles of 1862—Shiloh, Second Bull Run, Antietam, Fredericksburg—proved them disastrously wrong (total casualties at Antietam alone numbered more than 22,000). The war had given weapons makers the opportunity to test new theories and refine their inventions, and the slaughter that resulted was on a scale that no one—not even the weapons makers—could have imagined.

The American Civil War was the world's first conflict fought with a conoidal bullet—a projectile pointed at one end—invented a decade earlier by French military officer Claude E. Minié. Muskets, which fired round balls, were highly inaccurate—the balls dipped and wobbled as they sailed through the air, missing their mark half the time. Most attempts to improve the gun focused on the barrel, and the principal change involved lining the inside of the cylinder with grooves, or rifling, that spun the ball as it was fired. Captain Minié redesigned the ball.

Minié's ball was not round but pointed at one end and hollow at the other. The bullet was rammed down the barrel in the usual way, but when the trigger was pulled and the powder exploded, the resulting gases caused the hollow end of the bullet to expand into the grooves. The tight fit gave the bullet more spin and speed as it left the gun, and the pointed nose helped it bore through the air in a relatively straight line. Statistics indicate that the "minnie ball," as soldiers called it, made infantry fire about twice as effective as it had been.

Compared with the field hospitals, Washington's Armory Square Hospital (top), with fresh linen and airy wards, was luxurious. A Federal army surgeon's standard medical kit included quinine (above), for treating malaria. Like other prepared drugs, it was packaged in tin.

A wagon of the U.S. Sanitary Commission (top) leaves Washington, D.C., loaded with medical supplies and comfort items for the troops in the field. Author Louisa May Alcott (above) served as a volunteer nurse in a Washington military hospital. She recorded her experiences in *Hospital Sketches*, published in 1863.

There were other significant weapons inventions. British army officer Henry Shrapnel unveiled an artillery projectile, 20 years in the making, that exploded and hurled small balls and jagged pieces of metal in a broad arc at killing speeds. American Robert Parrott developed a cannon that could fire such projectiles farther and more accurately than almost any field gun then in use. Christopher Spencer invented a repeating carbine that allowed a soldier to fire seven shots without reloading, and B. Tyler Henry built a repeating rifle that could fire 15 bullets in as many seconds. General Gabriel Rains of North Carolina designed land mines. There were exploding bullets, even "machine guns," like Dr. Richard Gatling and Mr. Ager's "Coffee Mill Gun."

The gap between the technology of killing and the science of healing was abysmal. Doctors, who had never seen flesh ripped or bones splintered so severely, had to improvise new methods of treatment. And generals, who had never seen lines of infantry dissolve under enemy fire, hastened to try new tactics that might save their troops from annihilation.

As men fell by the thousands, women were quick to come forward and do what they could. Many volunteered as nurses. Some served in city hospitals. Some who couldn't volunteer opened their homes to the wounded and to surgeons needing a place to operate. Courageous women went to the front with the army or one of the many commissions or aid societies, or simply

Appointed executive secretary of the Sanitary Commission in 1861, landscape architect Frederick Law Olmsted (inset) transformed the organization into a vital medical effort. Olmsted's tasks included chartering transport and hospital ships such as the steamer above, shown in 1862 at White House Landing, Virginia.

on their own. Initially, despite the hospital and army-camp settings, the country's Victorian mores caused both the men and the women tending them to feel uncomfortable. Frederick Law Olmsted, secretary of the U.S. Sanitary Commission, commented in 1861 that only nuns, like those of the Sisters of Charity, should be allowed in the wards because "the odour of sanctity might . . . preserve [them] from scandal." He believed there was "not a woman in all the hospitals of Washington, unless she be of the Sisters, who is not constantly watched for evidences of favor to individuals and for grounds of scandalous suspicion and talked of and probably often talked to, with a double meaning."

Fortunately, the number of women involved helped make their work among the troops less shocking and more respectable. Thirty-year-old author Louisa May Alcott, tired of reading about the activity of war, wished to "do something" for the war effort. "I love nursing, and must let out my pent up energy in some way," she wrote. "I want new experiences, and am sure to get them if I go." In 1862 she left her home in Concord, Massachusetts, and traveled to Washington to

Dorothea Dix (top), was the Union army's superintendent of female nurses. Phoebe Pember (middle), a Richmond widow, was an administrator at the city's vast Chimborazo Hospital. And Clara Barton (above) was one of the few female nurses who served on the battlefield. Sanitary Commission nurses who cared for the casualties of a battle like Fredericksburg witnessed tremendous suffering (top right).

work in a hospital. Phoebe Pember of Richmond was, by her own admission, "used to all the comforts of luxurious life," yet she chose to become superintendent of a Richmond hospital. Pember wrote that many believed that "such a life would be injurious to the delicacy and refinement of a lady—that her nature would become deteriorated and her sensibilities blunted." But Pember found the opposite. Good women— the very best ladies—very willingly adapted to the terrible scenes and harsh conditions. "If the ordeal does not chasten and purify her nature," she wrote, "if the contemplation of suffering and endurance does not make her wiser and better, and if the daily fire through which she passes does not draw from her nature the sweet fragrance of benevolence, charity, and love— then, indeed, a hospital has been no fit place for her!"

Dorothea Dix turned hospitals into places for thousands of nurses. Soon after the clash at Fort Sumter, the 59-year-old former crusader for the destitute and mentally ill volunteered her services to the war department and was appointed superintendent of army nurses. She

recruited only women who were over 30, "plain," and unstylish in dress. Clara Barton, who after the war helped found the American branch of the International Red Cross, came forward at the first shots. Preferring to work as a free agent and with a single wagon filled with food and supplies, she followed the troops to their battlefields, sometimes tending the wounded so close to the firing line that bullets tore her clothing. Mary "Mother" Bickerdyke, remarkably efficient and tireless in the field, became so well known among the Union army that General William T. Sherman asked that she be assigned to his troops.

Like millions of other volunteers, these women worked selflessly. "Let no one pity or praise us," wrote one Rhode Islander, "no one can tell how sweet it is to be the drop of comfort to so much agony." Their altruism was unparalleled, but something else—the pure excitement of being involved in great events—sustained them. Katharine Wormeley, a nurse with the Sanitary Commission, loved the work intensely: "We all know in our hearts that it is thorough enjoyment to be here—it is life, in short; and we wouldn't be anywhere else for anything in the world."

The severity and extent of battle wounds and diseases encountered by Civil War surgeons like those of the First Division of the Federal IX Corps (above) forced doctors to discover their own methods of treatment. Poet Walt Whitman (inset) worked as a government clerk in Washington so he could tend patients in military hospitals there.

LAUNDRY DAY IN NASHVILLE

Volunteers and former slaves work together in the courtyard (left) of Union Army Hospital Number 19 in Nashville, Tennessee. The hospital sparked controversy and elicited criticism when Federal army medical authorities, following an outbreak of venereal disease among troops occupying the city, designated a ward in Hospital 19 to treat prostitutes. The project succeeded in slowing the spread of the disease.

ROAD TO RECOVERY

Wounded Rhode Islanders (right) gather on the porch of an army convalescent hospital in 1864. Wounded men were transferred from general hospitals to convalescent camps—another magnet for volunteers—until they were well enough to return to their regiments. Those unable to serve were honorably discharged and sent home.

UNITED HOME FRONT

When New York City women formed the Women's Central Association of Relief early in the war, they started a trend that led to the establishment of the U.S. Sanitary Commission, sanctioned by Lincoln in June 1861. The New York women, shown at their Cooper Union headquarters (left), collected and distributed medical supplies.

THE GREAT FAIR
Visitors examine some of the thousands of items for sale in nearly two miles of exhibits at the Sanitary Commission's Great Central Fair (left) in Philadelphia in June 1864. Many such fairs—part bazaar, part carnival—were held throughout the North and raised more than $4 million for the commission.

AT WORK IN THE FIELD
Sanitary Commission workers assisted in field hospitals that had often been hastily established; the workers' headquarters, such as this one at Fredericksburg (above), were nearby. In May 1864, the time of this photo, Fredericksburg commission workers saw scores of wounded come off the Wilderness and Spotsylvania battlefields, where the fighting, under Generals Grant and Lee, was particularly horrendous.

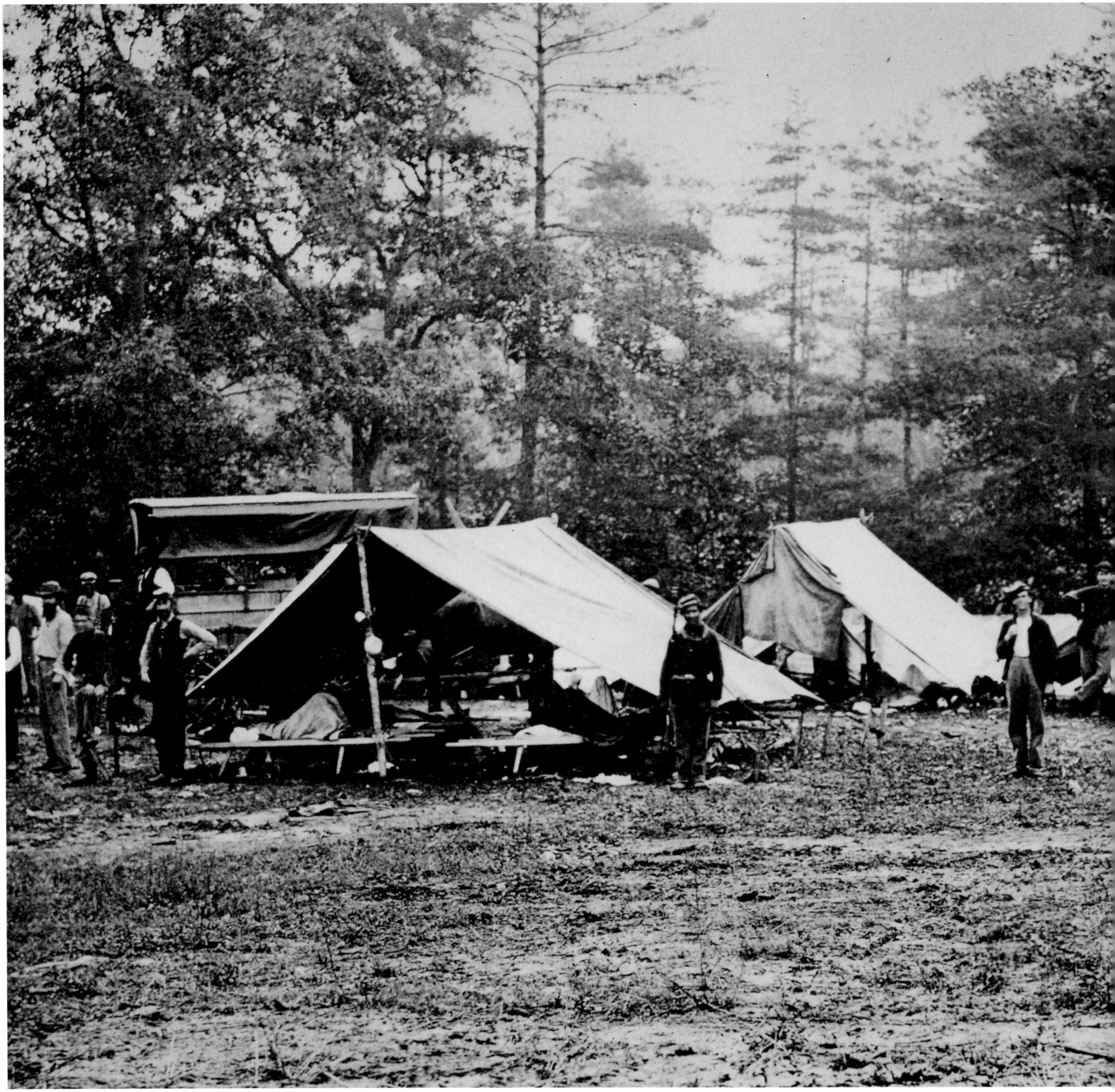

WOUNDED IN THE CAPITAL

A shortage of hospital space led to the use of tents for convalescents. In mid-1863, Washington, D.C., and nearby Georgetown had 30 temporary hospitals capable of treating 21,000 patients. The tents on the grounds of Washington's Douglas Hospital (above) had raised floors and wood stoves for heating. By late 1864 medical authorities had enlarged and improved the permanent hospitals so that only 19 temporary hospitals were needed.

SUFFERING AT GETTYSBURG

In a field hospital (left) near Gettysburg, Pennsylvania, wounded soldiers, possibly members of the Federal II Corps, rest on litters under makeshift shelters. Many of the battle's 26,000 Federal and Confederate casualties were housed in barns, houses, and public buildings. An observer recalled seeing wounded in the courthouse "lying on the bare floor, covered with blood and dirt."

HOSPITALS

BREWERY AND SOAP FACTORY ON PREMISES

Some of the 150 wooden wards at Chimborazo Hospital, near Richmond, take over a hilltop (above) and provide space for more than 8,000 patients. Sharing the grounds were a bakery that could turn out 10,000 loaves a day, a brewery, a soap factory, and five icehouses.

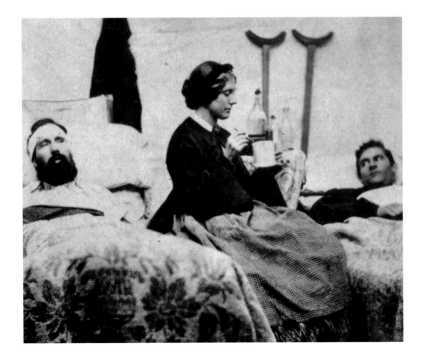

SUSTENANCE

Two recuperating soldiers (left) in a general hospital in Union-occupied Nashville, Tennessee, receive sustenance from Anne Bell. To help nurses and other volunteers feed the wounded, the Sanitary Commission published guides on hospital diets.

NEW AND BETTER ROOMS

A newly constructed wing at Washington's Harewood General Hospital (right), where patients could attend lectures, plays, and concerts, could accommodate 40 to 60 convalescent soldiers. The voracious, disease-carrying mosquitoes that flourished in the city's numerous swamps and marshes made netting over the beds essential.

READY FOR EVACUATION

Wounded Federals (above) wait near the field hospital at Savage's Station, Virginia, in June 1862. Casualties of the fighting during the Seven Days' Battles, the men were evacuated by rail to the Union supply base at White House Landing.

AMBULANCE DRILL

Ambulance corpsmen, probably bandsmen of the 114th Pennsylvania Zouaves detailed to that assignment, load "wounded" comrades (left) into an army ambulance during a staged drill near Petersburg, Virginia, in 1864. The ambulance, a late-war "Rucker" type, could hold four patients on litters.

HOSPITAL ON RAILS

In the wood print at right, a Federal hospital steward watches over wounded men on a train to Nashville in 1864. The special cars, designed by Dr. Elisha Harris of the Sanitary Commission, featured litters fixed with rubber straps that prevented painful jostling during the ride.

MEDICAL WORKHORSE

With their canvas covers stretched carefully into place, Federal ambulances (above) wait
in a park near a Federal hospital complex, possibly around Washington, D.C. Experience
dictated the design of the light, four-wheeled wagons drawn by two horses or mules.
When not used to transport wounded, the ambulances served as general-purpose vehicles.

THE AMBULANCE CORPS

Officers and enlisted men of the Federal Ambulance Corps assigned to
the IX Corps, Army of the Potomac (right), rest at their headquarters near
Petersburg, Virginia. During the first year of the war, most regiments
formed their own ambulance detachments, but by August 1862 the Army
of the Potomac maintained a designated ambulance corps whose personnel wore distinctive green bands around their caps. It wasn't until 1864
that Congress created an ambulance corps for the entire Union army.

Field Surgeons

Regimental surgeons established the field hospitals, evaluated soldiers' wounds, and applied the appropriate treatment; assistant surgeons managed the stretcher bearers and orderlies. Despite widespread infection and crude surgical conditions in the field, a wounded man had a good chance of survival.

HOME REMEDIES

Denied imported drugs by the Federal blockade, Confederate doctors were often forced to compound their own medicines using a simple cast-iron mortar and pestle (above) and locally obtained ingredients. As shortages became severe, the Confederate medical service distributed regular bulletins that discussed various home remedies.

LIFESAVING TOOLS

Since three out of four battlefield operations were amputations, field-surgery tools (right) were designed to allow quick removal of a mangled limb (the procedure generally took about 15 minutes). A Confederate doctor noted that early experience taught that, when bones were splintered, "amputation was the only means of saving life."

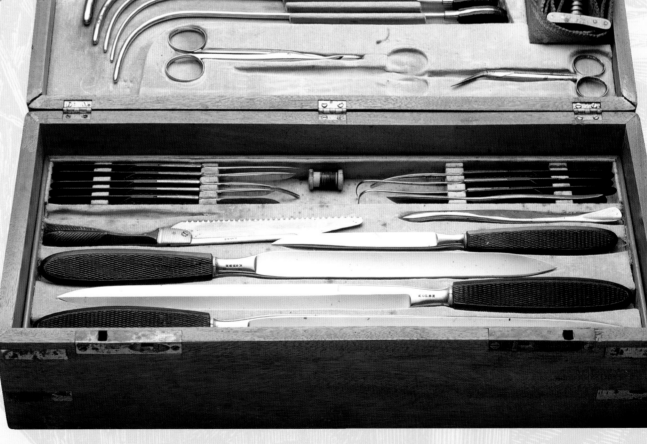

FIELD OPERATION

In a rare photograph (left), Federal surgeon John J. Craven prepares to operate on a soldier in his field-hospital tent on Morris Island, South Carolina. The orderly at the head of the table holds a chloroform-soaked rag over the patient's face while Craven examines his leg. The surgeons usually administered a general anesthetic—chloroform or ether—to soldiers undergoing complex surgery. Ether's extreme flammability made chloroform the first choice.

PREPARATION FOR SURGERY

Surgeon Rufus Gilbert of the Fifth New York Zouaves holds an amputation knife (left) while assistant surgeon B. Ellis Martin prepares to use a bone saw on a wounded patient. Because the medical men are in uniform and the patient still wears his Zouave fez, the procedure—at Camp Hamilton, near Fortress Monroe, Virginia—is believed to be staged.

FIRST FEMALE SURGEON

In a military-style Bloomer dress, Dr. Mary Edwards Walker (right) proudly wears the Congressional Medal of Honor that she was awarded in 1865 for "meritorious service" during the war. A native of New York, Walker was a graduate of Syracuse Medical College and an early proponent of women's rights. Denied a regular commission in the U.S. Medical Service, she volunteered as an acting assistant surgeon—the first female surgeon in the U.S. Army. After serving in both the eastern and western theaters, Walker was appointed assistant surgeon of the 52nd Ohio Infantry in September 1863.

The Cresting Wave

VICTORIES at Antietam and Perryville in September and early October 1862 gave the North reason to be optimistic about the war. Despite a summer made difficult by a bold and aggressive Lee in the Seven Days' Battles, the Federal armies had managed to repel two invasions in autumn 1862, which, coupled with the Emancipation Proclamation, restored some

A regimental musician of the 28th Massachusetts Infantry, whose men came mainly from Boston's Irish community, carried the drum below. In November 1862 the regiment was assigned to the Army of the Potomac's Irish Brigade, and on December 13 took part in the bloody assault on Marye's Heights at Fredericksburg.

of the Union's prestige abroad and lessened the likelihood that foreign countries would intervene on behalf of the Confederacy. Still, the Lincoln administration could hardly rest easy. Less than four months earlier, the North appeared to be on the brink of victory outside Richmond. Now, the Confederate army in Virginia was mobile and dangerous, and the North was really no closer to victory than it had been a year earlier. Lincoln regretted the lost opportunities, and the coming months would not boost his spirits.

Despite the carnage and the Confederate army's escape at Antietam, George McClellan was delighted with the results. "Those in whose judgment I rely," he immodestly wrote to his wife, "tell me that I fought the battle splendidly & that it was a masterpiece of art." The general was content to see Lee return to Virginia, but Lincoln and others urged him to use the favorable autumn weather to follow Lee. "Little Mac" replied that the army could not possibly pursue the Confederates until he rested and reorganized his men after so grueling a battle. Lincoln, deciding the armies did not need the break, relieved McClellan, who, he said, "has the slows."

The new commander, Ambrose E. Burnside, was a capable, amiable, West Point graduate who recently led 80 ships and 13,000 troops in the capture of several key Southern ports, including Roanoke Island and New Berne. He had absolutely no confidence in his ability to command the army, however, and Burnside himself told Lincoln that he was not the man for the job. But the president insisted. Burnside knew why McClellan had been relieved and he knew that Washington expected action. He moved quickly and, with his first step, confidently: He decided to shift part of his army eastward in order to cross the Rappahannock River at Fredericksburg, on the direct route to Richmond. The Federals fooled Lee and easily beat his Confederates to the crossing, but, unfortunately for Burnside, the bridge materials were late. By the time the Northerners could span the river, Lee had reacted and installed his divisions on the hills behind Fredericksburg. Even in the very face of the enemy, however, Burnside persisted in his plan to cross the river and issued orders for an attack.

The Battle of Fredericksburg was a frigid nightmare for the men who fought it on December 13, 1862. Burnside sent his men across a windswept plain directly into the Confederate fire. Though the Union commander had 120,000 men, the advantage in numbers (Lee had 78,000) meant nothing in a strategy that called for throwing wave after wave of troops against a strong defensive position. All afternoon, brigade after brigade of Federals marched in well-dressed lines across the plain—flags flying, drums tapping, bayonets glinting in the winter sun—only to dissolve under the relentless Confederate fire. When the sun went down and the temperature dropped, countless wounded men froze to death on the plain. The North's casualties at Fredericksburg—more than 12,000—far outnumbered the South's approximately 5,000.

When he heard the news, Lincoln said, "If there is a worse place than Hell, I am in it." After the Seven Days' Battles, Second Manassas, and the slaughter at Antietam, Fredericksburg was a blow almost beyond bearing. "We are now on the brink of destruction," the despondent president told a friend. "It appears to me that the Almighty is against us." The North and its army were outraged at the administration that had put Burnside in command. The people, declared *Harper's Weekly*, "have borne, silently and grimly, imbecility, treachery, failure, privation, loss of friends, but they cannot be expected to suffer that such massacres as this at Fredericksburg shall be repeated."

Bearing the flag, Colonel Charles Collis leads his 114th Pennsylvania Zouaves in a charge at Fredericksburg (top). In the same battle, Lieutenant Colonel Elbert Bland of the Seventh South Carolina escaped death when his binoculars (above) stopped a Yankee bullet.

General Ambrose Burnside (top, fifth from right), stands with subordinates after taking command of the Army of the Potomac in December 1863. Popular with the soldiers, Burnside seemed the perfect successor to McClellan, but events would prove otherwise.

There was ire in the South, as well. The Confederate Army of Tennessee, under General Braxton Bragg, was rife with dissension. Bragg, an ill-tempered West Pointer of long experience, had alienated so many of his officers that they began to conspire against him. Edmund Kirby Smith, a senior general, stated that he would rather take a subordinate position in any other army than maintain his rank and serve under Bragg. President Jefferson Davis, however, who was a friend of the general's, decided that despite his flaws Bragg was able, and he supported him.

Bragg was near Murfreesboro, Tennessee, late in December with his army of about 34,000 when Federal General William S. Rosecrans moved 41,000 men from Nashville toward the Confederates. Rosecrans, another West Pointer and a brave and headstrong commander (he was nicknamed "Old Rosy"), advanced on Murfreesboro, determined to push Bragg out of Tennessee. The two armies skirmished at Stones River until December 31. Both commanders planned an early-morning attack that day, but Bragg struck first. Hard-fighting Southerners bent one wing of Rosecrans's army back and almost managed to seize the Federal retreat route, but Rosecrans threw together a defense and held on. The contest was marked by great bravery on both sides—some Mississippians joined the battle armed only with sticks—but the Confederates could not break the makeshift Union line. Still, Bragg felt he had won a victory. He was certain the battered Federals would withdraw and be gone the next morning, New Year's Day. But the sun came up to reveal that the scrappy Rosecrans had stood his ground. The Confederates attacked again on January 2, but were repulsed. Bragg saw that his army was worn out and hungry. The

weather was bad, and Rosecrans had been reinforced. Reluctantly, Bragg retreated. His initial tactical success had turned into a strategic defeat. The armies lost about 13,000 men each, making Stones River one of the war's fiercest battles.

Coming soon after Fredericksburg, the Tennessee battle made Lincoln grateful to Rosecrans: "God bless you, and all with you," he wrote. "I can never forget you gave us a hard earned victory which had there been a defeat instead, the nation could hardly have lived over." Meanwhile, among Bragg's army, the defeat intensified the rancor that the soldiers felt toward their general. He offered to step down, but Davis refused. "My confidence in General Bragg is unshaken," said the president. The decision to allow the feuding and disaffection to continue in the Army of Tennessee was perhaps Davis's most costly as commander in chief.

When spring came to Virginia, the Army of the Potomac had another new commander, Joseph Hooker, known as "Fighting Joe." Hooker had attended the military academy and endured long service in the prewar army, and already in the war he was known for his ambition, aggressiveness, and cunning. At Antietam, he and his troops led the initial advance. He had

In January 1863, a month after the costly Federal defeat at Fredericksburg, General Burnside attempted to outflank Lee's army with an offensive across the Rappahannock, just west of the Confederate stronghold. But the effort came to grief when torrential rains stalled the Northern troops in the mud. Wrote one Massachusetts soldier: "[M]en floundered up to their knees in the liquid filth." The attempt, like the painting above, became known as the "Mud March," and the dismal failure of Burnside's winter campaign moved Lincoln to replace him with "Fighting Joe" Hooker. The decision was ridiculed in a Southern cartoon (opposite).

In a May 1863 photograph by A. J. Russell (top), soldiers of the 15th New York Engineers wait for their ration of stew at a campfire on the Confederate side of the Rappahannock. The men had just finished building pontoon bridges for General John Sedgwick's VI Corps. The young Zouave above served with the 19th Illinois at Murfreesboro.

powerful friends in Washington and was not above using them. Lincoln knew about his politicking, but would overlook it if Hooker gave him victories.

The new commander acted energetically. Dividing his army near Fredericksburg and marching several miles up the Rappahannock, Hooker planned to cross the river and fall on Lee's left flank. But Lee met boldness with boldness. After Hooker placed his army on Lee's flank, Lee divided his army into two and hastened to meet Hooker's force near a crossroads called Chancellorsville. When the surprised Federal commander hesitated, Lee divided his army yet again and sent Stonewall Jackson on a sweeping march around Hooker's flank on May 2. The attack was brilliantly successful, marred only by the accidental wounding of Jackson by his own men. The Confederates, now with the momentum, attacked again the next morning and slowly forced the Federals back toward the Rappahannock. Hooker, already confused by the failure of his plan and the audacity of the Southerners, was further stunned when artillery shots caused bricks from a house to fall on his head. With their commander out of action and the army disorganized by the chaotic fighting in the dense forest, the Federals retreated. Hooker's abortive foray had resulted in 17,000 Federal casualties and another embarrassing defeat. Lee suffered nearly 13,000 casualties, the most damaging of which was Jackson. Doctors amputated Stonewall's wounded left arm, and he died eight days later. "It is a terrible loss," wrote Lee. "I do not know how to replace him."

Ten of the 16 36th Illinois Infantrymen depicted in these miniature photographic portraits, called "gemtypes," were wounded at Murfreesboro—or Stones River, as the battle was known in the North. Shortly before the Chancellorsville campaign, Confederate Mississippians at Fredericksburg permitted Northern photographer A. J. Russell to take their picture (left) from the Union side of the Rappahannock.

Noah Brooks, a friend of President Lincoln's, was with him when he received the news of Chancellorsville. Lincoln's face turned gray, recalled Brooks: "Never, as long as I knew him, did he seem to be so broken, so dispirited, and so ghostlike." The president stared and said, "My God! My God! What will the country say?" In Richmond, meanwhile, except for the loss of Jackson, Confederate morale and hopes had never been higher. The Army of Northern Virginia's several victories over a succession of enemy commanders gave it an aura of invincibility, and Lee felt sure that the North could not sustain many more defeats. "If we can baffle them in their various designs this year," he wrote to his wife, "I think our success will be certain. If successful this year, next fall there will be a great change in public opinion about the North. The Republicans will be destroyed & I think the friends of peace will become so strong as that the next administration will go in on that basis. We have only therefore to resist manfully."

CROSSING UNDER FIRE

On December 11, 1862, men of the Seventh Michigan and 19th and 20th Massachusetts launch an amphibious assault over the Rappahannock (above) to dislodge Confederate sharpshooters at Fredericksburg. A fierce bombardment from the Federal guns had ravaged the town but failed to dislodge the determined Rebel defenders whose fire prevented the Union engineers from completing their pontoon bridges. Once ashore, the Yankees waged a grim house-to-house battle and finally cleared the way for the rest of Burnside's army.

WAR'S DESOLATION

The Gothic Revival mansion of Alexander Phillips (left)—General Burnside's headquarters during the Battle of Fredericksburg—stood atop a bluff overlooking the Rappahannock and was one of the few structures in the area equipped with indoor plumbing. Though the house provides stark testimony to the desolation wrought by the armies there, it actually survived the battle undamaged and became a hospital. In February 1863, fuel spilled from a stove on the second story and caused a fire that quickly consumed the interior.

BATTLE VIEW

A view from the Federal position along the Rappahannock's east bank (above) shows Fredericksburg and smoke-shrouded Marye's Heights on the horizon. The photograph was taken five months after General Burnside's defeat, during a second Union attempt—this one successful—to capture the heights west of the town.

IMPREGNABLE POSITION

A postwar photograph (left) depicts the lane and stout stone wall that provided a readymade fortress for Confederates at the foot of Marye's Heights. On December 13, Burnside's Federals, with parade-ground precision, advanced on the site from the outskirts of Fredericksburg. "We waited until they got within about 200 yards of us," a Georgian recalled, "rose to our feet & poured volley after volley into their ranks."

CHARGING THE HEIGHTS

The lithograph above, based on period photographs and official reports, gives an accurate aerial perspective of the initial Federal assault on Marye's Heights, which is crowned by the white-pillared mansion in the background. Spearheading the attack is General Nathan Kimball's brigade. At far left, skirmishers of the Fourth and Eighth Ohio fire from a prone position, while in the center the 24th and 28th New Jersey regiments charge through exploding artillery shells to a nearby fence. On the far right, columns of reinforcements move up Hanover Street to support Kimball's depleted formations.

VETERANS OF STONES RIVER

On December 31, 1862, the first day of the Battle of Stones River, the 21st Michigan Infantry,
shown above at their regimental campsite in the spring of 1863, waged a desperate fighting
retreat in the face of the Confederate onslaught. The unit lost more than 140 men.

POPULAR COMMANDER

The painting above, by artist William Travis, shows Federal Major General William Starke Rosecrans riding a favorite dappled gray; with him are high-ranking officers of his Army of the Cumberland. Rosecrans, who delighted in galloping along the lines and encouraging his troops, was immensely popular with the enlisted men. "Every time I see him I like him the more," an Illinois corporal wrote. "He has a word for every one of his boys and likes to talk with them." A Wisconsin soldier noted, "We love to hear Old Starkey's thunder-voice; it stirs our souls."

ECCENTRIC LEADER

General Rosecrans (right) was a study in contradictions. Though a brilliant strategist, he was sometimes overly cautious. Known for his profanity, he was also a devout Catholic who arranged to have Mass said in the field. He could be hot-tempered and impatient, but in battle showed uncommon bravery and stoicism. At Stones River, when his chief of staff was decapitated by a cannon ball in front of the men, Rosecrans calmly remarked to his rattled subordinates, "Brave men die in battle. Let us push on."

IN THE WAKE OF BATTLE

The Rutherford County Courthouse in Murfreesboro (above) reflects the
aristocratic veneer of the Tennessee town in which, as one observer noted, "the
poor whites are as poor as rot, and the rich are very rich." Because it was behind
Confederate lines during the bloody three-day clash at Stones River, the town
suffered little actual damage. But after General Bragg's Southern forces retreated
from the battlefield, virtually every building in Murfreesboro became a makeshift
hospital where stricken Yanks and Rebs battled for survival.

AT THE SCENE

A correspondent for *Frank Leslie's Illustrated Newspaper* sketched the scene at
right as it was occuring. The view is looking southward down Stones River. Ohio
and Illinois troops ford the rapidly flowing stream and form up along the east
bank. At left, Confederate ammunition wagons scramble to withdraw, and an
officer prepares to shoot his wounded horse.

FIGHTING JOE HOOKER

While he professed to dislike the nickname "Fighting Joe," Major General Joseph Hooker did have a reputation for courage and aggressiveness that seemed to offset his more negative traits—political scheming and a fondness for drink. In taking command of the Army of the Potomac from the hapless General Burnside, Hooker brought an energetic style of leadership and considerable administrative skills, making sure, for example, that his troops were well fed and supplied through the winter encampment of 1862–63. With morale restored, the soldiers and their leader sallied forth confident that a brilliantly conceived campaign to flank and destroy Lee's army would succeed. Above, Hooker (seated second from right) poses with his staff for photographer Timothy O'Sullivan. The senior officers seated in front are, from left, Colonel Henry F. Clarke (chief commissary), General Henry J. Hunt (chief of artillery), Colonel Rufus Ingalls (chief quartermaster), and General Daniel Butterfield (chief of staff).

A DARING PLAN

Robert E. Lee and Stonewall Jackson (right) discuss strategy in the woods near Chancellorsville. On May 1, 1863, Hooker's Army of the Potomac, having swung around the Confederates and taken position at Chancellorsville, had gone on the defensive. The Federals' right flank was exposed, and Jackson suggested that Lee divide his army and march 26,000 men across the enemy front to strike where the Yankees least expected it.

SPRING MARCH

In a sketch by Edwin Forbes (below), Federal regiments—among them, Zouaves of the Fifth New York—march from their former winter quarters to battle at Chancellorsville. The men of the Army of the Potomac completed the first stage of Hooker's plan to interpose his force on the flank and rear of Lee's position by covering more than 50 miles in four days. On April 30, an order from Hooker that was read to the soldiers assured them that the Rebels would "either have to fly ingloriously or come out from their breastworks, where destruction was certain."

BROTHER CONFEDERATES

In 1861, siblings Daniel, John, and Pleasant Chitwood (left) signed up with a Georgia militia company called the Bartow County Yankee Killers, which became Company A of the 23rd Georgia Infantry. In October 1862 Pleasant Chitwood succumbed to chronic diarrhea in a Richmond hospital, and on May 2, 1863, during the fighting at Chancellorsville, Daniel and John were captured when Federal troops from General Daniel Sickles's III Corps lashed out at the Confederate column marching to strike the Union flank.

SECOND FREDERICKSBURG

On May 3, 1863, General Sedgwick's VI Corps attempted to do what Burnside's army failed to accomplish the previous December—take Marye's Heights by storm. This time, the defenders were stretched thin and the Yankees broke through the Confederate lines, forcing General Jubal Early and his men to retreat toward the rest of Lee's army at Chancellorsville. On May 4, A. J. Russell photographed U.S. Military Railroad chief Herman Haupt (right, jacket over one arm) examining dead horses and a wrecked caisson abandoned by the Confederates' Washington Artillery in their retreat from Fredericksburg.

A YANKEE COMPANY

The soldiers of Company C, 110th Pennsylvania Infantry, stand at shoulder arms in this photograph (right) by A. J. Russell taken at the unit's winter camp near Stoneman's Switch. On May 3, during the final stage of the Battle of Chancellorsville, the 110th was nearly surrounded but refused to surrender; only half the unit escaped death or capture. General Sickles reported, "These troops behaved with the utmost gallantry, maintaining their ground to the last."

TROJAN HOMECOMING

After the Union defeat at Chancellorsville, a welcoming crowd prepares to greet the Second New York Volunteer Infantry on the unit's return to Troy in May 1863 (left). The regiment was one of many Federal units whose two-year term of enlistment expired after the Battle of Chancellorsville.

THE PRICE OF VICTORY

The loss of Stonewall Jackson (right), who died on May 10 from pneumonia and the effects of his wound, dashed Southern spirits, despite the resounding Confederate victory at Chancellorsville. Jackson sat for this photograph just days before his last and greatest battle. His wife, Mary Anna, recalled, "I never saw him look so handsome and noble."

HONORING THEIR OWN

Cadets of the Virginia Military Institute class of 1868 pay homage to former VMI professor Stonewall Jackson at the general's grave in Lexington, Virginia (above). The announcement of Jackson's death "fell like a pall upon the school," noted John Wise, a VMI cadet who was part of the honor guard at the general's funeral. "Men and women wept over his bier as if his death was a personal affliction. We buried him with the pomp of woe, the cadets his escort of honor."

Stonewall Jackson

Thomas J. "Stonewall" Jackson achieved remarkable success in his two years in Confederate uniform, yet took none of the credit for himself. A devout Presbyterian, Jackson saw the Almighty's hand in all things. If the Confederacy saw itself as fighting for a holy cause, then Jackson was the ideal Southern Christian warrior.

HEAVEN–SENT

Jackson's first wife, Elinor, died in childbirth in 1854, as did the infant. Jackson's grief was deep, but he found love again with 25-year-old Mary Anna Morrison (right, in a postwar portrait) and married her in July 1857. He called her "a gift from our Heavenly Father," and declared it "a great satisfaction to feel that God has manifestly ordered our union."

VICTORY

Though powerfully ambitious, Jackson craved humility. "If you desire to be more heavenly minded," he wrote in his notebook of inspirational maxims, "think more of the things of Heaven and less of the things of Earth." Jackson's self-effacement can be seen in his note to his wife (right) informing her of God's latest blessing after the battle at McDowell.

LEGENDS

The postwar tribute to Jackson and his men, "Halt of the Stonewall Brigade" (opposite), shows the general surrounded by his staff and footsore troops. Convinced that hard marching saved blood on the battlefield, Jackson pushed his soldiers to their limit and achieved exceptional results. In May 1862 they marched almost 340 miles in 24 days and fought three battles and countless skirmishes. The inset photo is of Jackson in November 1862, age 38.

A SOLDIER'S GUIDE

Before the war, Jackson and his wife spent quiet evenings memorizing Presbyterian catechism. On campaign, he carried this prayer book (left), and read from it daily. He rated chaplains as among the more important men in the army and actively recruited them. Jackson frequently walked through his army's camps, distributing religious tracts to his men, and frankly admitted that he wished his troops to be "an army of the living God."

CHAOS AND DESTRUCTION

The Enemy at Home

"THESE ARE DARK HOURS," wrote Massachusetts senator Charles Sumner in early 1863. "There are senators full of despair." A string of Federal defeats in the field—most recently at Fredericksburg and Chancellorsville—had fostered dissent and outrage across the North, causing President Lincoln to confess to Sumner, a Radical Republican, that he feared what he called

In Wilmington, Delaware, the names of draft-eligible men were spun inside this 24-inch lottery wheel. Officials selected the soldiers who would fill Lincoln's call for additional troops by drawing the names through a small trap door.

"the fire in the rear" more than the Confederate army. The Union, Lincoln sadly believed, might be destroyed from within.

Like all presidents, but especially those who govern in times of crisis, Lincoln endured much criticism; in fact, it became a hallmark of his presidency. As the war intensified, Democrats and Republicans alike complained vociferously and in greater numbers. Emancipation was illegal, some claimed, while others thought Lincoln and his generals criminally negligent in their handling of the war. Many argued that the president lacked leadership, governing haphazardly and doing merely what he thought the people wanted him to. Lincoln's administration was "milk-livered," wrote one New Englander; "slowness, indecision, and waste of money" were its prominent features. Abolitionist Wendell Phillips called the president "a first-rate second-rate man," and declared, "As long as you keep the present turtle at the head of affairs, you make a pit with one hand and fill it with the other." Pundit Adam Gurowski wrote that as a president "Mr. Lincoln represents nothing beyond the unavoidable constitutional formula. For all other purposes, as an acting, directing, inspiring, or combining power or agency, Mr. Lincoln becomes a myth." Some critics thought Lincoln weak, others saw him as overbearing, but almost all the president's opponents portrayed his administration as adrift and ineffectual. Lincoln responded by clearly articulating his goals: "My paramount object in this struggle is to save the Union, and is not either to save or to destroy slavery. If I could save the Union without freeing any slave I would do it, and if I could save it by freeing all the slaves I would do it; and if I could save it by freeing some and leaving others alone I would also do that. What I do about slavery, and the colored race, I do because I believe it helps to save the Union; and what I forbear, I forbear because I do not believe it would help to save the Union." But as defeats on the battlefield increased, the clamor resounded. There was even talk of impeachment.

The strongest attacks on the Republican administration came, naturally, from the Democrats. Clement Vallandigham, a 42-year-old Democratic congressman from Ohio in 1862, protested

GREAT AMERICAN TRAGEDIANS, COMEDIANS, CLOWNS AND ROPE DANZERS IN THEIR FAVORITE CHARACTERS.

By early 1863, Southerners were not the only ones portraying Lincoln as a ludicrous yet sinister jester manipulating his puppets (above). Lincoln critics in the North included the so-called Peace Democrats. Led by men like Ohio congressman Clement Vallandigham (inset), the group opposed the war and argued vociferously for a negotiated peace. Vallandigham's arrest, conviction and jailing for treason, and eventual banishment to the Confederacy fueled claims that Lincoln was a tyrant.

most vehemently. Though a staunch Unionist, he sympathized with the political views of the South and detested the growing power of the government in Washington. "It is the desire of my heart," he said, "to restore . . . the Federal Union as it was forty years ago." Vallandigham grew ever more strident in his criticisms of abolitionism and emancipation, claiming that Lincoln's management of the war was a crime worse than any committed by a Southern slaveholder: "I see more of barbarism and sin, a thousand times, in the continuance of this war . . . and the enslavement of the white race by debt and taxes and arbitrary power." Though defeated in a bid for reelection in 1862, Vallandigham continued to oppose the administration as "one of the worst despotisms on earth." He blamed New England for the war and called for an armistice and a peace conference. His conditions were clear: "In considering terms of settlement we [should] look only to the welfare, peace, and safety of the white race, without reference to the effect that settlement may have on the African."

Vallandigham found many supporters in Ohio and other northwestern states. The Indiana and Illinois legislatures passed resolutions calling for an armistice and demanded a retraction of the Emancipation Proclamation. Democratic editors from New York City to the Mississippi River, inflamed by Vallandigham's rhetoric, filled their newspapers with antiwar polemics and urged soldiers to desert, rather than participate in an "illegal and unholy" war.

In May 1863 Federal troops arrested Vallandigham in a midnight raid on his home in Dayton, Ohio. A few days later he was convicted of treason and imprisoned. But because the incident brought Lincoln more criticism and lent credence to claims that he was a despot, the president decided the Union was better off with Vallandigham out of prison and banished from the United States. The army escorted the Ohioan to Confederate lines, and he became an exile.

But Vallandigham was as persistent as he was angry. He crossed the Confederacy to the coast, rode a blockade runner to Canada, and there campaigned in absentia for the governorship of Ohio. Though he won the Democratic nomination, he failed to carry the general election, mainly because of Union successes at Gettysburg and Vicksburg in the summer of 1863. Nevertheless, "Peace Democrats" like Vallandigham continued to gain strength and influence, greatly troubling Lincoln's councils as well as the army. "Every reverse we have will make the 'peace party' stronger," wrote one soldier. "I am afraid our government will be persuaded to come to terms with the Rebels; I would rather stay here all my life than see that."

Northerners were further riled when Congress decided to address the issue of declining voluntary enlistments by passing a national conscription law in spring 1863; the first military draft was held the following July. (The Confederate Congress had passed a similar law in

In response to the Confederate food shortage, desperate antiwar Southerners looted stores and warehouses in Richmond, Virginia (above), and other Southern cities during Holy Week 1863.

1862.) In language that echoed the 1861 secessionists, Midwestern Democrats declared, "We will not render support to the present Administration in its wicked Abolition crusade. We will resist to the death all attempts to draft any of our citizens into the army." New York governor Horatio Seymour sounded like a Southern states' rightist when he pledged to "maintain and defend the sovereignty" of the Empire State against the usurpations of the Washington government.

Roused by Democratic rhetoric and convinced that the conflict had become a rich man's war and a poor man's fight, men in New York City took violent action. Mobs, estimated to be about two-thirds Irish, attacked recruiting officers, blacks (who were viewed as the cause of the war), and anyone who looked wealthy. For four days in July 1863 the rioters burned, looted, and lynched. The police were overwhelmed, and not until Federal troops arrived and fired into the mobs did peace return. More than 100 people died in the New York draft riots, but

Dissident, antiwar Southerners were often roughly handled by active Confederate troops (opposite, top). In rural areas, wealthy, generous planters sometimes shared surpluses with hard-pressed neighbors. Above, women and children gather at the Mississippi plantation of Joseph Davis, Jefferson Davis's brother, to receive much-needed supplies.

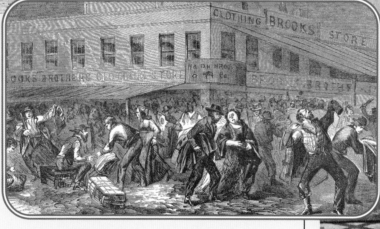

the government was undeterred; the draft was on again a month later.

In the coal fields of Pennsylvania, miners threatened to shut down the mines if not given better pay and housing. The miners, many of them Irish immigrants, presented a thorny problem: The North needed coal—to power its navy's ships, its gun foundries and woolen mills, and the locomotives that hauled its troops and munitions—and its most important supplier was Pennsylvania (the state produced almost as much coal as the Northern and Southern states combined). The Irishmen began agitating against their employers and sabotaging the mines. They revived a secret society, the Sons of Molly Maguire, formed decades earlier in Ireland to fight English oppression. In Pennsylvania the group would fight the mine bosses and the U.S. government. The society did not participate in the draft and would not allow others to be drafted against their will. Working covertly in small bands, they attacked soldiers, mine managers, and almost anyone who did not cooperate with them. The army sent troops to the region, but ultimately the Molly Maguires won their small war. President Lincoln himself signaled his surrender by authorizing the forgery of documents that showed that the most troublesome areas of Pennsylvania had fulfilled their draft quotas.

In New York City, Colonel Cleveland Winslow (above), formerly of the Fifth New York Zouaves, rounded up a volunteer force, mostly of discharged soldiers, to battle the rioting mobs that burned and plundered the Orphan Asylum for Colored Children (top, left) and looted other establishments, like the well-known Brooks Brothers clothing store (inset).

Around the same time, along the Missouri-Kansas border, proslavery bushwhackers and abolitionist jayhawkers were taking matters into their own hands. Under Colonel Charles "Doc" Jennison, the Kansas jayhawkers resorted to such violence and depredation, laying waste to the Missouri countryside and burning entire hamlets, that many in Missouri who had previously favored the Union switched allegiances. Said General Henry W. Halleck: "The conduct of these forces has done more for the enemy in this state than could have been accomplished by 20,000 of his own army. . . . [The jayhawkers] are driving good Union men into the ranks of the secession army." The bushwhackers were no better: A summer 1863 raid on Lawrence, Kansas, led by the ruthless William Quantrill, ended in a four-hour massacre and widespread devastation.

Unrest troubled the South, too. Food was in chronically short supply by 1863, and disruption of the railroads made moving what food there was more difficult. Inflation made everything expensive. The result was genuine famine in some areas. Desertions among the Confederate army mounted as men went home to care for their suffering families. Conscription increased the public's anger, as it had in the North, and the new taxes that the Confederate Congress levied further incensed Southerners. Women throughout the South rebelled by looting bakeries and grocery shops. The worst "bread riot" was in Richmond, where President Jefferson Davis himself had to disperse the mob of starving women and children.

By mid-1863 Lincoln and Davis both had made powerful, vocal enemies within their own camps, and the people of the North and the South were feeling the effects of unrelenting hardship and suffering. How long would they support a conflict whose cost was poverty, hunger, death, and despair? The war had become a test of wills: Which side could endure the agony the longest?

Men of the Seventh New York (top) patrol the city following the draft riots. Part of an elite unit, they detested the rioters and likely agreed with the Massachusetts poster above, which lampooned military-service evaders by announcing a "Grand Procession" of "Toothless Gummers," "Varicose Cadets," and other "Exempts."

JENNISON'S JAYHAWKERS

Diminutive Charles Jennison (above), who once practiced medicine, liked to wear a tall fur hat to give the illusion of height. An ardent abolitionist, "Doc" Jennison rose to prominence in antislavery Kansas and formed a band that became notorious for thievery and vigilante justice. To better control the group, Federal authorities made Jennison a colonel and accepted "Jennison's Jayhawkers" into the Union cavalry. Depredations continued, however, and Jennison was ordered west in 1862 to fight Apaches. He resigned, instead.

THE GRIM CHIEFTAIN

After struggling to see Kansas accepted into the Union, James H. Lane (above) became one of the new free state's senators in 1861. A brigadier general in the state militia and known as the jayhawkers' "Grim Chieftain," he continued to fight against slavery by encouraging violent acts. In September 1861 he led 1,500 jayhawkers in a rampage across proslavery Missouri. He ordered that "everything disloyal . . . must be cleaned out." Even the ruthless bushwhacker William Quantrill called Lane "the worst man that was ever born."

LAWRENCE LAID TO WASTE

William Quantrill and some 450 bushwhackers run rampant through Lawrence, Kansas (left), on August 21, 1863. The attack was in retaliation for depredations committed in Missouri by jayhawkers under Charles Jennison and James Lane. Lawrence was Lane's hometown and, according to Quantrill, the place where the raiders could "get more revenge and more money than anywhere else." After a four-hour spree, about 150 men lay dead around the burning town. Among the escapees was Lane, who fled in his nightshirt to a nearby cornfield.

THE TURNCOAT QUANTRILL

William Clarke Quantrill (above) was an abolitionist at the time of this photograph, taken in Lawrence, Kansas, in 1860. When jayhawking along the border, he wore out his welcome by raiding not only in proslavery Missouri, but also among his Kansas neighbors. To elude capture by Union sympathizers, he shamelessly changed sides and entered Missouri's bushwhacking community, eventually forming his own band, which included Frank and Jesse James, Bloody Bill Anderson, and Cole and Jim Younger. In 1863 Quantrill returned to Lawrence—this time to destroy it.

BLUNT'S BAND

Members of an ill-fated military band (right) lounge near Union General James Blunt's headquarters. When William Quantrill's raiders struck Blunt's troops at Baxter Springs, Kansas, in October 1863, the band was there and all 14 of its members were killed. Blunt, commander of the Union's District of the Frontier and a staunch abolitionist who had associated with John Brown before the war, escaped the onslaught. One observer described the attack's aftermath as "a fearful sight: some 85 bodies nearly all shot through the head, most shot from 5 to 7 times each, horribly mangled, charred and blackened by fire."

BÚSH-WHACKERS, BEWARE!

HEAD QUARTERS DIST. OF THE FRONTIER,
Fort Smith, Ark., Nov. 17, 1863.

The organized forces of the enemy having been driven out of the country in our rear, and there being none on our lines of Telegraphic and Mail Communications, except that common foe of mankind—the guerrilla and bush-whacker—and the cutting of telegraph wires being now the act of these men alone—men who have no claim to be treated as soldiers, and are entitled to none of the rights accorded by the laws of war to honorable belligerents, it is hereby ordered that, hereafter, in every instance, the cutting of the telegraph wire shall be considered the deed of bush-whackers, and for every such act some bush-whacking prisoner shall have withdrawn from him that mercy which induced the holding of him as a prisoner, and he shall be hung at the post where the wire is cut; and as many bush-whackers shall be so hung as there are places where the wire is cut.

The nearest house to the place where the wire is cut, if the property of a disloyal man, and within ten miles, shall be burned.

BY COMMAND OF BRIG. GEN'L JOHN McNEIL.

JOS. T. TATUM,
Act'g Ass't Adj't General.

THE MAD HATTER

A poster (above) hung in Union-held Arkansas spells out the steps that Federal occupiers will take in the event that telegraph lines are sabotaged. Not only is one "bushwhacking prisoner" to be hung for every cut in the line, but "The nearest house to the place where the wire is cut . . . shall be burned." The man who issued the order, Brigadier General John McNeil, originally from Nova Scotia, had been in the hat business for more than 20 years, briefly in Boston and then in St. Louis. By November 1863 he had already cleared most of the Southern-leaning guerrillas out of Missouri.

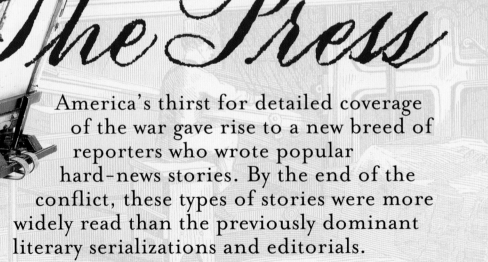

The Press

America's thirst for detailed coverage of the war gave rise to a new breed of reporters who wrote popular hard-news stories. By the end of the conflict, these types of stories were more widely read than the previously dominant literary serializations and editorials.

SINGLE-SHEET PRESS
In 1861 most of the country's newspapers were printed on hand-fed single-sheet presses (left). As demand for news increased, higher-capacity power presses became more common in the North, but the South, with manpower and paper shortages, had to rely on the simpler machines.

POWERFUL PRESSES

Frank Leslie's Illustrated Newspaper of July 20, 1861, ran this engraving (opposite) of a *New York Tribune* composing room with a tri-level rotary press—one of three used by the *Tribune* at the time. By the beginning of the war, even though many newspapers were still printed on single-sheet hand presses, new power presses capable of printing more than 20,000 sheets an hour had begun to revolutionize the business.

FIELD DUTY

Correspondents for the *New York Herald* gather around their paper's ever-moving field headquarters (left) in August 1863; the men had probably covered the Battle of Gettysburg. Like the armies they followed, war correspondents endured extreme weather, poor food, forced marches, even enemy fire. But their dispatches helped readers at home better understand the course of the conflict.

WALLPAPER PAPERS

As stocks of newsprint disappeared in the Confederacy, many Southern editors published sporadic editions on the back of wallpaper. James W. Swords, editor of Vicksburg's *Daily Citizen* (above), believed such editions helped bring some normalcy to the besieged town and provide the troops at the front lines with a diversion from the drudgery of trench life.

GREELEY AND THE "TRIB"

Horace Greeley (above) owned and edited the powerful *New York Tribune*. Read by more than a million Americans each week, the "Trib" was so influential that Lincoln claimed that its support, along with Greeley's, was worth 100,000 men.

THE BOHEMIAN BRIGADE

For photographer Mathew Brady, Alfred R. Waud (above) poses in work clothes with sketch pads and other tools of his trade. A sketch artist for *Harper's Weekly*, Waud was among the most respected of the Northern war correspondents who camped and traveled with the Union armies in the field. Because of their itinerant and freewheeling lifestyle, they called themselves the "Bohemian Brigade."

"Let Him Fight"

BECAUSE MEN in the North and South had all but ceased to volunteer to fight by early 1863, both the Union and Confederate armies faced a manpower crisis less than halfway through the war. Though the Confederate Congress in spring 1862 passed a conscription act that, in effect, had pressured men to volunteer, and the Federal Congress was about to enact

Once black volunteers were accepted into the Union army, they were generally issued regulation Federal uniforms like the infantry private's frock coat below.

its own conscription law, the drafts alone could not bring in the numbers of men needed. Forced to look for additional sources of troops, the war departments turned to the largest untapped pool of potential fighters: black men of military age.

Blacks had fought as volunteer soldiers in the Revolutionary War and the War of 1812, and for most of America's history they had served in integrated crews on U.S. Navy ships. They had been excluded from service in the Regular Army, however, and by the time of the Civil War, most whites believed that a black man could not be made into an effective soldier. This was the view in the South until quite late in the war, but in the North, with hundreds of thousands of healthy, military-age blacks available, the abolitionist wing of the Republican Party began to pressure President Lincoln in early 1863 to enlist them. Not only would it help win the war, they said; it would help in the effort to win equality for blacks.

But Lincoln was against it. When a group of U.S. senators urged him to form black regiments, he replied, "Gentlemen, I can't do it. I can't see it as you do." To the president, the issue was fraught with political danger: "I have put thousands of muskets into the hands of loyal citizens of Tennessee, Kentucky, and Western Northern Carolina. They have said they could defend themselves if they had guns. I have given them the guns. Now these men do not believe in mustering in the Negro. If I do it, these thousands of muskets will be turned against us. We should lose more than we should gain." Such remarks led abolitionist Wendell Phillips to declare, "Lincoln is not a leader. . . . Like an Indian trapper on the prairie, his keen ear listens to know what twenty million people want him to do."

Lincoln was correct, however, about there being opposition to putting blacks in uniform. "I can tell you it will ruin the army," wrote a volunteer soldier from New Jersey. "If a negro regiment were to come and camp near an old regiment out here, the men would kill half of them." A Pennsylvanian wrote, "Though composed almost entirely of republicans, we would charge and drive back a [black regiment] with more delight than they would the rebels. . . .

260

Before going off to war, a soldier of the United States Colored Troops, established in May 1863, poses for a photograph with his family (left). An abolitionist and a staunch advocate of black troops, Massachusetts governor John Andrew (inset) sponsored the first African-American regiment to be recruited in the North: the 54th Massachusetts Volunteer Infantry.

You have no idea how greatly the common soldiers are prejudiced against the negro." Some white troops were more pragmatic. "Let him fight," wrote one Federal, "or make him fight; he ought to fight. He has as much or more at stake in this war than any one else."

But with Union fortunes sagging in the spring of 1863, and the burden of losses at the Battle of Fredericksburg and, especially, Chancellorsville weighing on the president, Lincoln reversed himself in May and approved the establishment of the Bureau for Colored Troops. "The bare sight of fifty thousand armed and drilled black soldiers on the banks of the Mississippi," he wrote in earnest, "would end the rebellion at once."

In fact, though, blacks were already involved in the war effort. In July 1862 the Federal Congress had authorized black militia troops, and in the autumn of that year enterprising Federal generals in Union-occupied areas of the South took it upon themselves to raise

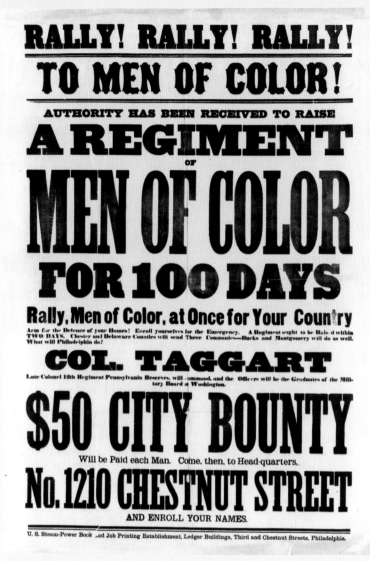

RALLY! RALLY! RALLY!
TO MEN OF COLOR!
AUTHORITY HAS BEEN RECEIVED TO RAISE
A REGIMENT
OF
MEN OF COLOR
FOR 100 DAYS
Rally, Men of Color, at Once for Your Country
Arm for the Defence of your Homes! Enroll yourselves for the Emergency. A Regiment ought to be Raised within TWO DAYS. Chester and Delaware Counties will send Three Companies—Bucks and Montgomery will do as well. What will Philadelphia do?
COL. TAGGART
Late Colonel 12th Regiment Pennsylvania Reserves, will command, and the Officers will be the Graduates of the Military Board at Washington.
$50 CITY BOUNTY
Will be Paid each Man. Come, then, to Head-quarters,
No. 1210 CHESTNUT STREET
AND ENROLL YOUR NAMES.
U. S. Steam-Power Book and Job Printing Establishment, Ledger Buildings, Third and Chestnut Streets, Philadelphia.

By mid-1863, Northern losses and President Lincoln's Emancipation Proclamation combined to bring about the active recruitment of black volunteers, as the Pennsylvania poster above shows. Thousands of blacks—many of them runaway, or "contraband," slaves—served the Union war effort in support roles, which included dock work at a Federal supply depot in Alexandria, Virginia (center).

regiments of free blacks and escaped slaves. In Louisiana, South Carolina, Mississippi, and Kansas, residents saw black men in blue uniforms for the first time. The men of these regiments "of African Descent," like all black soldiers who served in the Union armies, were led by white officers and paid less than white soldiers. The troops were not intended for combat, however. Though trained to handle weapons, they generally worked as laborers on fortifications and roads. Nevertheless, some of these men—members of the Ninth and 11th Louisiana Infantries of African Descent, for example—were among the first black Federals to die for freedom and the Union.

Along with several white regiments, the Ninth and 11th Louisiana Infantries were stationed at a Federal supply depot on the Mississippi River at Milliken's Bend, Louisiana, when it was attacked by Confederate troops on June 7, 1863. When the Southerners saw the black troops, they shouted, "No quarter!" (meaning they would take no prisoners), and charged. Many of the blacks, however, stood firm. According to General Henry McCulloch, who commanded the Confederates, the charge "was resisted by the negro portion of the enemy's force with

considerable obstinacy, while the white, or true Yankee portion ran like whipped curs." The Federals finally repelled the attack, but lost more than 600 men, three times the Confederate loss. In a letter from the battlefield, a white officer wrote of his fallen men, "I never more wish to hear the expression 'niggers won't fight.' Come with me 100 yards from where I sit, and I can show you the wounds that cover the bodies of 16 as brave, loyal, and patriotic soldiers as ever drew bead on a Rebel."

The small fight at remote Milliken's Bend removed any doubts about blacks' ability to become effective soldiers, and by the following December, 50,000 blacks were under arms. One officer engaged in raising a black regiment wrote, "Now that it is decided that coloured troops shall be raised, people seem to look upon it as a matter of course, and I have seen no one who has not expressed the kindest wishes for the success of the project." Even Lincoln, after changing his mind and adopting an enthusiastic attitude about black troops, admitted surprise at the results. There appeared to be, he said, "no loss by it in our foreign relations, none in our home popular

When commissioned a major in the Federal army in February 1865, 52-year-old Martin R. Delany (above) became the Union's highest-ranking black officer. Physician, editor of antislavery journals, charismatic orator, and passionate advocate of black nationalism, Delany displayed a remarkable ability to fire the enthusiasm of black volunteers. As a recruiting agent for the United States Colored Troops, he tirelessly canvassed the North, drumming up support for the black regiments. "The hero and the warrior," he stated, "have long been estimated the favorite sons of a favored people."

sentiment, none in our white military force, no loss by it anyhow or anywhere." By the end of the war, nearly 190,000 blacks would wear the Federal uniform.

In the South, the idea of Negroes carrying arms terrified most Southerners. For generations they feared a Haiti-style revolt (in the 1790s, slaves in Santo Domingo slaughtered thousands of people, and Haiti became the first country ruled by blacks) as well as another Nat Turner, who led slave rebellions in Virginia in 1831. Nor did Southerners wish to fight against blacks; they felt it was a humiliation to be shot by one. Confederate war-department policy called for treating captured Federal black soldiers as rebellious slaves; their white officers were considered guilty of inciting slave revolt. For both, the penalty was death. Confederate Secretary of War James Seddon suggested that officers and men "be dealt with redhanded on the field of war or immediately after." The logical extension of this policy was to take no prisoners at all. The cries of "no quarter" were repeated many times over, wherever black troops fought.

According to a Confederate of the Ninth Texas Cavalry, in early 1864 he and his comrades routed a group of black Federal soldiers near the Yazoo River in Mississippi and rode among the kneeling, pleading captives telling them they would "blow their brains out and leave them to wilter in their own blood." To many Confederates, such behavior was the easiest way to deal

Gunners of Battery A, Second U.S. Colored Artillery, perform a drill (top, left) at their camp near Nashville, Tennessee. Like all black soldiers in Federal service, they faced the threat of execution if captured by the Confederates. The policy was never officially carried out, however, in part because President Lincoln threatened that Southern prisoners would meet "appropriate reprisals," as the cartoon at left shows.

with the situation. When he heard rumors that some of his troops had taken black prisoners, General E. Kirby Smith wrote to a subordinate, "I hope this may not be so, and that your subordinates . . . may have recognized the propriety of giving no quarter to armed negroes and their officers. In this way we may be relieved from a disagreeable dilemma."

The Confederates did put blacks to work as cooks, teamsters, stevedores, and laborers, though they were not regularly enlisted. But by late 1864, with Confederate manpower depleted, the South was desperate. Secretary of State Judah P. Benjamin argued, "We have 680,000 blacks capable of bearing arms who ought now to be in the field. Let us now say to every Negro who wishes to go into the ranks on condition of being free, go and fight—you are free." Robert E. Lee urged the arming of blacks because it was "almost certain that if we do not get these men, they will soon be in arms against us." Whether the Confederacy could have mustered in enough black troops to make a difference in the outcome on the battlefield remains doubtful.

For the Northerners who led the fight to get blacks into uniform, the decision to arm them was a victory that soon tasted bittersweet. For though it brought the North its first black regiment, the 54th Massachusetts, the regiment's first engagement—a heroic charge on Fort Wagner, South Carolina—was ill-fated. Robert Gould Shaw, the 54th's 25-year-old colonel, wrote in June 1863, "[If] the raising of coloured troops proves such a benefit to the country, and to the blacks . . . I shall thank God a thousand times that I was led to take my share in it." Forty-seven days later, while leading the 54th at Fort Wagner, Shaw was killed along with almost half his regiment.

Officers and civilian teachers stand behind a class of black troops (above), many of whom hold textbooks. Literacy rates were generally high among black troops recruited in the Northern states, but low in former Confederate territory, where volunteers were ex-slaves who had been denied an education by their owners.

A WARRIOR FOR FREEDOM
With the chevrons of a first sergeant on his sleeves, James Baldwin (above), of Company G, 56th U.S. Colored Infantry, poses before the flag. As the senior noncommissioned officer in his company, Baldwin played a gallant part in the July 26, 1864, battle of Wallace's Ferry, Arkansas. Despite the loss of their colonel and other officers, Baldwin and comrades held off a force of Confederate calvary. Wounded in the neck during the fight, Baldwin recovered and served to the end of the war.

ARMY TEAMSTERS
Outfitted in castoff uniforms, black teamsters gather for a photograph (opposite) at City Point, Virginia, the bustling supply depot for the Federal forces besieging Richmond and Petersburg in 1864. Paid a small salary for their work as laborers and wagon drivers, these former slaves, or "contrabands," were ubiquitous in Northern armies.

FROM SLAVE TO SOLDIER
Widely circulated in the North to encourage black enlistment in the Union army, the two photographs above contrast "Contraband Jackson," a runaway slave, with "Drummer Jackson," now proudly wearing the uniform of a musician in the United States Colored Troops.

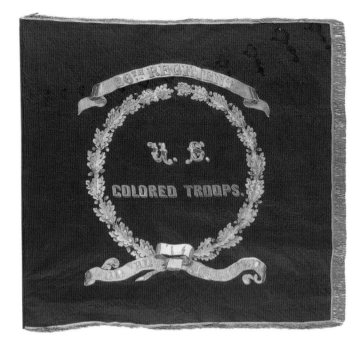

REGIMENTAL BANNER

In a ceremony held just before the unit's departure for the front, this flag (left) was one of a pair of embroidered regimental banners presented to the 26th U.S. Colored Troops, organized on Riker's Island, near New York City, in February 1864. The 26th left for its station in the Department of the South.

DETERMINED TO SERVE

Twenty-one-year-old Arnum (left), of Springfield and the 54th Massachusetts, exudes the earnest determination that was characteristic of black Federal soldiers who knew they might be executed if captured by the Confederates. A soldier of the 55th Massachusetts Colored Infantry wrote that if President Davis were to "enforce his threat of treating us as servile insurgents, there will be but little quarter shown to rebels who fall into our hands."

PROUD TO SERVE

Standing in formation, muskets at the position "in place rest," a detail of the 107th U.S. Colored Troops (left) prepares for guard duty at Fort Corcoran, an earthwork in the defenses around Washington, D.C. The regulation uniforms, white gloves, and military bearing of the sergeant (far left) and his men attest to the volunteers' rigid discipline and pride. The 107th was recruited in Kentucky in July 1864 and campaigned in Virginia and North Carolina. Like many U.S. Colored Troops units, the 107th was retained in service after the Confederate surrender to enforce political "reconstruction" in the South.

The 54th Massachusetts

MARCH TO GLORY
Sculptor Augustus Saint-Gaudens's memorial to Colonel Robert Gould Shaw and the 54th Massachusetts (left) depicts the regiment's farewell parade through Boston on May 28, 1863—"at last to help in breaking the chains," one black spectator exulted.

The first black regiment sponsored in the North, the 54th Massachusetts Infantry began recruiting in February 1863 and received widespread Northern support. Frederick Douglass, whose two sons joined the unit, exhorted the idealistic volunteers "to get at the throat of treason and slavery."

REGIMENTAL FLAG
This state color (inset) was carried by the 54th Massachusetts in its heroic but doomed charge on Fort Wagner, South Carolina. Confederate soldiers found the flag beneath a pile of dead.

RAISING A REGIMENT

Posters like the one below attracted volunteers to the 54th from far beyond Massachusetts. Recruiting agents, many of them prominent abolitionists, traveled to black communities throughout New England and the Midwest. The regiment ultimately included men from more than a dozen American states and Canada.

AN AWARD FOR VALOR

Sergeant William H. Carney, of Company C, 54th Massachusetts (left), was born in slavery, was freed upon the death of his master, and moved to the seafaring town of New Bedford, Massachusetts. During the attack on Fort Wagner, Carney seized the U.S. colors from a fallen bearer and planted the flag on the ramparts. Repeatedly wounded, he managed to crawl from the battlefield, the bloodstained banner in his arms. Carney's bravery earned him the Medal of Honor.

A GALLANT LEADER

Despite his initial misgivings, Robert Gould Shaw (above) accepted command of the 54th Massachusetts when his doting mother told him, "I feel as if God had called you up to a holy work." The 25-year-old colonel and his fellow white officers formed a powerful bond with their soldiers and sought the opportunity to lead them in battle. That opportunity came at Fort Wagner on July 18, 1863. Shaw died in the vanguard of the assault.

VETERANS AT LAST

Having endured the prejudice of their government and survived the hatred of their enemies, men of the 54th Massachusetts relax on James Island, South Carolina, near war's end. About 300 of the unit's men died in battle or from wounds or disease inflicted in battle; another 200 were wounded or captured. But the regiment's heroic ordeal, as Governor Andrew wrote, was "full of hope and glory."

NOW IN CAMP AT READVILLE!

54th REGIMENT!

MASS. VOLUNTEERS, composed of men of

AFRICAN DESCENT

Col. ROBERT G. SHAW.

☞ Colored Men, Rally 'Round the Flag of Freedom!

BOUNTY $100!

AT THE EXPIRATION OF THE TERM OF SERVICE.

Pay, $13 a Month!
Good Food & Clothing!
State Aid to Families!

RECRUITING OFFICE.

COR. CAMBRIDGE & NORTH RUSSELL STS.,
BOSTON.

Lieut. J. W. M. APPLETON, Recruiting Officer.

ZWELL & CO., Steam Job Printers, No. 37 Congress Street, Boston.

Turning Point

AFTER THE SOUTH'S VICTORY at Chancellorsville in early May 1863, Confederate fortunes in the eastern theater had never been better; Robert E. Lee and his army seemed unbeatable. In the West, however, Southern commanders were performing poorly. Federal gains along the strategically important Mississippi River threatened to counteract the

Lieutenant William O. Colt of the Fifth Corps of the Army of the Potomac purchased the Maltese cross–shaped badge below to commemorate his service with the 83rd Pennsylvania Infantry, which fought at Gettysburg in the defense of Little Round Top on July 2, 1863.

Confederate progress in Virginia. So the outcome of the war was still very much in doubt, and European governments again pondered the possibility of intervention on behalf of the Confederacy. "The truth is," wrote the U.S. ambassador to England, Charles Francis Adams, "all depends upon the progress of our armies."

Since October 1862 the Union army of Ulysses S. Grant, which had captured Forts Henry and Donelson earlier that year and then gone on to fight determinedly at Shiloh, had made little progress in its goal to capture Vicksburg, Mississippi, a fortified port on the great river and, along with Port Hudson, the Confederacy's last stronghold on the river. Vicksburg sat atop high bluffs, and its forts made an assault from the land impractical. The Federals controlled the river north and south of the city, but only by conquering Vicksburg could they gain the entire Mississippi. Only then would merchants in the West again be linked with the outside world, and only then would the Union succeed in splitting the Confederacy—in isolating Louisiana, Texas, and Arkansas from the other Southern states and Richmond. But taking Vicksburg would prove exceedingly difficult.

In his first attempt at the river stronghold, Grant combined the Union's land and water forces in a single offensive movement. An energetic Confederate defense, however, coupled with a spectacularly successful cavalry raid on the Federal supply depot, halted Grant far short of his goal in December 1862 and forced him to withdraw.

The Federals next attempted to dig their way to Vicksburg by scraping a canal deep enough through the bayous to permit gunboats and transports to bypass the city and operate against the defenses from the south. High water defeated this plan, known as the Bayou Expedition, in March 1863. Another excavation with the same goal—this one called the Duckport Canal—ended in failure when the water proved too low. While Duckport was in progress, Federals southwest of Vicksburg dug through the swamps trying to open a 400-mile route for the Union fleet to pass through a series of lakes and canals. This project too eventually failed.

Grant next turned his attention to the rivers and bayous just north of Vicksburg. In March 1863 he destroyed a levee at Yazoo Pass, allowing his fleet to enter the Tallahatchie River and steam southward to the Yazoo River, which led directly to Vicksburg. The Southerners responded by quickly building a fort on the Yazoo about 90 miles north of Vicksburg and beating back the gunboats, deftly foiling Grant's sixth attempt. Undaunted, the U.S. Navy tried to force its way up vine-choked Steele's Bayou, but this expedition ended when Confederate infantry halted and almost captured the gunboats struggling through the obstructed channels. The failure at Steele's Bayou marked nine months of frustration for the Federals in the Mississippi Valley.

But Grant would not give up. In early April he decided to march his troops past Vicksburg on the opposite shore and take his chances running the fleet of gunboats and transports past the city, directly under the noses of the Confederate gunners. The navy lost two ships and a few barges in the process, but Grant at last had his ground and water forces south of Vicksburg. By the first of May, most of his army had crossed the river and was less than 20 miles away.

The Northerners did not move directly on their goal, however. Instead, Grant marched boldly inland, toward Jackson, the state capital. After defeating several groups of small Confederate forces, Grant's men entered Jackson on May 14 and stood astride the Confederate supply line to Vicksburg. The South's commander at the river city was John C. Pemberton, a Pennsylvanian by birth. Though he had been ordered to evacuate and save his army of more than 30,000, he decided to stand firm and resist. On May 16 Grant's relentless advance reached Champion's

Watched by crowds of civilians, a column of Federal infantry marches through the streets of Gettysburg, Pennsylvania (top), during the dedication of the National Cemetery on November 19, 1863. It was there that President Abraham Lincoln (inset) delivered a "few appropriate remarks," which later became immortalized as the Gettysburg Address.

273

A key Union vessel in the war on the Mississippi, the ironclad *Essex* (top) docks at Baton Rouge, Louisiana, sometime in 1862. In January 1863 Drum Major Daniel B. Allen of the 77th Illinois sketched the powerful warship and the rest of the Mississippi Squadron (above) as they steamed out of the Yazoo River into the Mississippi.

Hill, just 10 miles from Vicksburg. Some 20,000 outnumbered Confederates made a determined effort to turn back the Northerners, but the swarming Federals now seemed indomitable. Pemberton's men slowly fell back to Vicksburg and prepared for the coming attacks. Grant assaulted the fortifications on May 19 and again on May 22, but he found them too strong. Unwilling to waste more lives, he settled down to a siege; he would starve the garrison out.

In Virginia, the end of May found Lee preparing for yet another bold stroke. After the victory at Chancellorsville, the general had presented President Davis with a plan for invading the North that Lee thought offered many advantages. Moving the war north would relieve battle-ravaged Virginia and bring the conflict's harsh realities to the Union—to Pennsylvania, where Lee and his men and animals could subsist on the fruits of Yankee farms. Davis approved the plan, and in the final days of May Lee reorganized his army under commanders James Longstreet, Richard S. Ewell, and A. P. Hill. A few days later, the army moved northward.

Federal commander Joseph Hooker had spent the weeks following his defeat at Chancellorsville resting his Army of the Potomac and skirmishing with his superiors in Washington. Though he had more than 80,000 men, Hooker claimed he needed reinforcements. To Lincoln, the request was all too familiar, and he came to the conclusion that Hooker was another George McClellan. When he did not get his way, Hooker, showing annoyance, asked to be relieved of his command, and on June 28 Lincoln replaced "Fighting Joe" with Pennsylvanian George G. Meade.

A crowd of newly freed slaves and Yankee soldiers gathers at the courthouse at Vicksburg on July 4, 1863 (left), to watch the raising of the Stars and Stripes proclaim the Federal occupation of the town. Ironclads and transports of the Mississippi Squadron under Rear Admiral David Dixon Porter (below) played an important role in the capture of the Confederate "Gibraltar of the West."

By the end of June Lee's army was well into Pennsylvania. It had fought and won a small battle at Winchester, Virginia, and streamed across the Potomac unchecked. One column appeared to threaten Philadelphia by moving on York on the Susquehanna River. Another column came within a few miles of the state capital, at Harrisburg. All along their marches, the Southerners collected food, forage, clothing, harness, shoes, and much else that had been in short supply for so long. As the invasion proceeded satisfactorily, with Confederate troops ranging unchecked through the rich summer countryside, the Federal army lagged far behind in Virginia. Not until June 29 did Lee have cause for concern. Through a Confederate spy, he learned that the Federals

THE ENEMY IS APPROACHING!

I MUST RELY UPON THE PEOPLE FOR THE

DEFENCE of the STATE!

AND HAVE Called THE MILITIA for that PURPOSE!

A. G. CURTIN, Governor of Pennsylvania.

THE TERM OF SERVICE WILL ONLY BE WHILE THE DANGER OF THE STATE IS IMMINENT.

Hagerstown Road west of Gettysburg (top) shows the effects of advancing Confederates carrying out Lee's plan to take the war to the North. A Pennsylvania poster (above) advises residents that the state militia has been mobilized.

had increased their rate of pursuit and would be upon him within days. The Virginian ordered his far-flung columns to cease their wanderings and gather at a crossroads called Gettysburg.

Meade also directed his army toward Gettysburg, thanks to an alert cavalry general named John Buford. On the hills west of Gettysburg, with just two small cavalry brigades, Buford found part of Lee's army and sent word to Meade that Federal infantry would soon be needed to resist the Southerners arriving from the west. On July 1, almost a third of the Army of the Potomac arrived at Gettysburg, but the Confederates, converging from three directions in great strength, steadily pushed the Northerners back. At sunset, what was left of the Federal First and 11th Corps took a strong position on high ground south of town. Lee's men had mauled the Federals, but, to the general's chagrin, had not destroyed them. Lee planned to attack again in the morning.

Meade hurried his troops forward, and by the morning of July 2 the Federals presented a strong line along the hills and ridges. As expected, Lee attacked. With the Confederates pressing hard on both ends of the Federal line, the fighting was fierce. But the Federals, with the advantages of good ground, excellent artillery, and the knowledge that for the first time in the war they were fighting on home soil, withstood every attack. Still, Lee was unwilling to give up, and he declared that if the enemy was still on the field in the morning he would attack again.

The Federal Third Corps suffered heavy casualties (top) during an assault at Gettysburg led by Confederate General James Longstreet (inset). The soldiers above fell in a trampled meadow near the Peach Orchard on July 2, 1863.

On the morning of July 3, about 12,000 Confederate infantrymen massed for an assault. The Southern artillery bombarded the center of the Federal line on Cemetery Ridge, trying to weaken it before the attack. By midafternoon, silenced Union guns led Lee to believe his men had succeeded and could assault the ridge. Moving forward across nearly a mile of open field, the Confederates presented one of the grandest spectacles of the war. But Pickett's Charge, as it became known—named for one of its commanders, General George Pickett—was a dismal failure. The Union battery had only been saving its ammunition. Row after row of Southerners fell, and the charge ended in a fury of fire and hand-to-hand combat. As his broken regiments limped to safety—Pickett lost more than half his men—Lee rode among them, lamenting, "It is all my fault." His bold gamble for a decisive victory on Northern soil had failed, and the attempt had cost him 28,000 men; the Federals lost 23,000. Gettysburg was the largest battle of the war, and it would come to be seen as high tide for the Confederacy.

Lee retreated from Pennsylvania, and a revived North rejoiced. There was more good news. On July 4 in the West, Pemberton surrendered to Grant. The two triumphs marked a turning point in the conflict. With Vicksburg captured and Lee out of the Keystone State, the North could presume that the war's darkest days had passed and that ultimate victory was possible.

BYPASSING THE REBELS

Yankees under General James B. McPherson excavate a canal (above) planned to connect the Mississippi River with Lake Providence north of Vicksburg. Grant hoped that the canal would provide access to bayous leading to the Red River, permitting his transports to bypass Vicksburg's formidable defenses. The Federals struggled for two months in mud and an atmosphere that one soldier described as "a saturated solution of gnats" before Grant determined that the route was impractical and the project was abandoned.

YANKEE GROUNDHOGS

Earthworks and individual bombproofs—shelters that protected soldiers from artillery fire—honeycomb the ground around Wexford Lodge (opposite), a house located amid the Federal siege lines north of Vicksburg. The home's owner, James Shirley, was a former New Englander and a strong Unionist; his family was relocated to a plantation behind Union lines. The earthworks surrounding the house were occupied by men of the 45th Illinois Infantry who took part in a bloody assault on the Confederate lines on June 25, 1863.

COMING TO TERMS

Ulysses S. Grant (below, at left) and Confederate General John C. Pemberton meet in the shadow of the Third Louisiana Redan to discuss surrender terms for Vicksburg and its defenders. Theodore Davis, a young artist working for *Harper's Weekly*, was present to sketch the July 3 meeting.

THE FIRST ASSAULT

General Grant's army advances on Vicksburg in a naive watercolor (above) by an unknown artist. Although the painter added many fanciful elements, such as the wagon-borne brass band (foreground), he accurately conveys the rugged nature of the ravines and ridges surrounding the city. Grant launched his first direct attack on Vicksburg on May 19, 1863.

SILENCED GUNS

Captured cannon, among the 172 pieces of artillery surrendered at Vicksburg, stand in an improvised ordnance park (opposite) in the seized town. Nearly 20,000 Confederate soldiers were paroled after the surrender. One Rebel fighter recalled that some soldiers "broke their trusty rifles against trees," rather than turn them over.

A YANKEE FORAY

Artillerymen of the Federal Sixth Corps pause near their pontoon bridges (above) after crossing the Rappahannock River near Fredericksburg in early June 1863. Hooker had dispatched General John Sedgwick's corps on a reconnaissance across the river to determine the location of the Confederate forces. When Sedgwick collided with some of A. P. Hill's men, who had remained behind to screen the westward movement of the rest of Lee's army, Sedgwick concluded that the entire enemy force was still in place, and withdrew.

PATH OF THE STAMPEDING CORPS

Neat houses line Carlisle Street where it passes through the center of Gettysburg (above). After heavy fighting west of the town on July 1, 1863, the shattered Federal llth Corps retreated south along this route to take up positions on Cemetery Ridge. Confederates under General Richard S. Ewell occupied the town and held it during the remaining two days of fighting at Gettysburg.

A BATTERED HEADQUARTERS

The Leister farmhouse stands surrounded by dead horses and shattered stone walls in this photograph (left) taken a few days after the Battle of Gettysburg. Located behind the Federal lines on Cemetery Ridge, the building was used as a headquarters by the commander of the Army of the Potomac, George G. Meade. The modest dwelling was splintered by Southern artillery fire during the bombardment that preceded the final Confederate assault on July 3.

HIGH-WATER MARK

On July 3, troops of General Alexander Webb's Philadelphia Brigade (above) rush forward to reinforce the wavering Union line, blunting the onslaught of Virginia Confederates under General Lewis Armistead. A Federal soldier who faced the Rebel charge on Cemetery Ridge wrote that the fighting was "foot to foot, body to body and man to man as they struggled, pushed and strived and killed." The scene was sketched by *Harper's Weekly* artist Alfred Waud.

VENERATED RELIC

The 24th Michigan Infantry's bullet-riddled regimental flag (right) attests to the ferocity of combat that the unit endured in McPherson's Woods on July 1. Battling desperately to stem the Confederate offensive, the 24th and the rest of General Solomon Meredith's Iron Brigade stood resolute in the face of repeated attacks. In the course of the action, nine of the 24th's color-bearers were killed, and 23 bullets pierced the regiment's silk banner. The photograph, a *carte-de-visite*, was taken shortly after the battle.

Flag - 24th Mich. Vols. After Gettysburg.

A NEW COMMANDER

A grizzled veteran of the Mexican War, Major General George Gordon Meade (opposite) took command of the Army of the Potomac on June 28, 1863, just three days before the Battle of Gettysburg. An able if uninspired leader, Meade was known for his irascible temper. A staff officer wrote, "I don't know any thin old gentleman with a hooked nose and cold blue eyes who, when he is wrathy, exercises less of Christian charity than my well beloved Chief."

HOMETOWN COMPANY

In the photograph above, taken at Fairfax Station, Virginia, in June 1863, Captain Henry M. Minnigh (left foreground) stands in front of Company K of the First Pennsylvania Reserves. The company was organized in Adams County, Pennsylvania, in and around the town of Gettysburg, and many of the men shown here fought virtually within sight of their homes. On July 2, the First Reserves, part of Colonel William McCandless's Brigade of the Federal 5th Corps, participated in the defense of Little Round Top.

CAPTURED BUT DEFIANT

Three Confederate soldiers, probably stragglers captured after Gettysburg, pose by a rail breastwork on Seminary Ridge (left) for one of Mathew Brady's photographers. The men were among the more than 5,400 prisoners who fell into Federal hands; another 6,800 were left behind wounded. Confederate prisoners were sent to camps such as Point Lookout, Maryland, and Johnson's Island, in Lake Erie. Many of the Confederates captured at Gettysburg were not released until the winter of 1865.

THE LAST POST

A young Confederate soldier lies dead behind a stone breastwork in Devil's Den (opposite), a jumble of massive boulders overlooking Plum Run at the foot of Little Round Top. Evidence suggests that photographer Timothy O'Sullivan moved the body about 40 yards and positioned the rifle to improve the composition of his image. The soldier may have been a member of the Georgia Brigade killed during the assault on Devil's Den on the afternoon of July 2.

Soldier Life

When not in battle, the typical Civil War soldier—
Union and Confederate—spent much of his time
performing the monotonous drudgery of military
life: endless rounds of fatigue duty, drills, guard duty.
To combat boredom, soldiers turned to activities
like letter writing, music, sports, and gambling.

BREAD AND AMUSEMENTS
The basic component of the Civil War soldier's field ration was the flour-and-water biscuit (left) dubbed "hardtack" for its rock-hard consistency.
Federal officers on the staff of General George McClellan (above) kill time with a game of dominoes in their camp near Yorktown, Virginia.

HOMESPUN DIVERSIONS

Seated in church pews, Yankee troops (right) pass the time in their Virginia camp mending clothes, writing letters, and reading newspapers. Most soldiers carried pocket-sized sewing kits called "housewives," and many became adept at patching their tattered uniforms. No diversion, however, occupied as much time as letter writing. Postage was relatively inexpensive—about three cents—and surprisingly efficient postal systems allowed soldiers to maintain contact with loved ones at home. A Confederate soldier from Virginia remarked, "Everybody is writing who can raise a pencil or a sheet of paper."

A RARE WASH

Federal soldiers (left) take advantage of a lull in the fighting of June 1864 to bathe near the wrecked railroad bridge over the North Anna River south of Fredericksburg, Virginia—probably their first chance to wash in weeks. One soldier concluded that some of his comrades were "not over clean and if not pretty sharply looked after would not wash themselves from weeks end to weeks end."

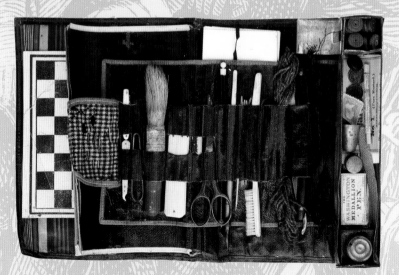

COMFORTS AND NECESSITIES

Private G. W. Green of the First Massachusetts Cavalry purchased this Brooks' Patent toilet and writing kit. The kit's oilcloth cover fit around a tinned box for storage and contained a wide variety of items—a writing set, shaving kit, and checker board, for example.

A Leader, at Last

WHEN ABRAHAM LINCOLN learned of the fall of Vicksburg, he lost all sense of the decorum befitting his position as chief executive of the United States. Throwing his arm around the bearer of the glad tidings, Secretary of the Navy Gideon Welles, he exclaimed, "I cannot, in words, tell you my joy over this result! It is great, Mr. Welles, it is great!"

At the headquarters of one of America's most powerful men, Grant's liquor cabinet stood as a potent symbol of human weakness. Though Grant had joined the Sons of Temperance in 1851, he was unable to keep his pledge and gained a reputation—too often exaggerated—as a heavy drinker.

Undoubtedly, the president's exuberance in July 1864 was largely due to the Union's sudden reversal of fortunes—the decisive victory at Vicksburg came one day after the Federals won at Gettysburg. But his reaction probably had something to do with General Grant's performance in Mississippi too. Competent generals had been hard to come by, especially in the East, so when Grant proved that he would not only fight, but also could win, Lincoln prized him. Neither Secretary of War Edwin Stanton nor General in Chief Henry Halleck had admired Grant in the first two years of the war, but Lincoln had sensed the man's mettle after the Union's disheartening performance at Shiloh in April 1862 and stood by him. "I can't spare this man," he said then. "He fights."

Hiram Ulysses Grant was born in 1822 in Point Pleasant, Ohio, and 17 years later entered the U.S. Military Academy, where a clerical error listed him as Ulysses S. Grant. An indifferent student, he excelled only in horsemanship and making friends. After graduating, he served in the infantry and fought courageously in the Mexican War, receiving recognition for his bravery. He then fell into the languid life of a junior officer in the peacetime army. Long tours of duty at remote posts kept him away from his wife, to whom he was intensely devoted. "You can have but little idea of the influence you have over me, Julia," he wrote. "If I feel tempted to do anything that I think is not right I am sure to think, 'Well now if Julia saw me would I do so?'" While on duty on the Pacific coast, he acquired a reputation for drinking. By 1854 he had had enough of the loneliness and left military service to join his wife and two sons in St. Louis.

The next six years were marked by hardship. Grant hoped to become a farmer, but had little success. He had neither money nor property. On land near St. Louis that his father-in-law let him use, Grant built an unattractive log house and called it "Hardscrabble." The crops didn't grow, and he and his family didn't have much to live

A devoted husband and father, Grant maintained exceptionally close bonds with his family. His wife, Julia, and youngest son, Jesse (both at left), brought a domestic warmth to army headquarters in 1864. Grant's chief of staff, John Rawlins (below), served as his conscience, encouraging Grant in his dedication to duty and vigorously opposing any drinking.

on. In the winter he hauled cordwood into St. Louis and tried to sell it himself on the streets. He pawned his gold watch for $22. He tried working as a rent collector, but because his partner, whom he grew to hate, was unscrupulous and cruel, Grant could not stand the job and quit. Finally, at what must have been his lowest point, Grant sought the help of his father, who consented to give him a job as a clerk in the family leather store in Galena, Illinois. During the years that Grant struggled, other men who would become generals in the Civil War prospered: John C. Frémont made a fortune in gold in California and ran for president, acquiring powerful friends; Halleck practiced law in California; and George McClellan drew $10,000 a year as a railroad president in Cincinnati.

At Grant's headquarters, Charles A. Dana (left) served as the war department's eyes and ears. He admired Grant as "a simplehearted, unaffected, unpretending hero ... Not a great man, except morally." Grant's subordinate, William S. Rosecrans, who was as popular as Grant in some quarters, as evidenced by the song-sheet cover below, could not agree with Dana. To his dying day, Rosecrans insisted that a jealous Grant had treated him unjustly and with pettiness.

ROSECRANS' VICTORY MARCH

The Civil War saved Grant by giving him a job; it also changed him. After the fall of Fort Sumter, he helped organize Galena's first company of Union volunteers, became colonel of the 21st Illinois Infantry in June 1861, and, after transforming the inexperienced soldiers into effective troops, was appointed a brigadier general and sent to Kentucky. He forced himself to be active and aggressive, despite a nagging fear of failure. He found—or developed—a sense of purpose and began to look at himself in a new light. In 1861, as he led his regiment toward a Confederate camp in Missouri, he had an epiphany. He wrote in his memoirs: "As we approached the brow of the hill from which it was expected we could see [the] camp and possibly find the men ready formed to meet us, my heart kept getting higher and higher until it felt to me as though it was in my throat. I would have given anything then to have been back in Illinois, but I had not the moral courage to halt and consider what to do; I kept right on. The Confederates were gone. My heart resumed its place. It occurred to me at once that [the Confederate commander] had been as much afraid of me as I had been of him. This was a view of the question I had never taken before; but was one I never forgot afterwards. From that event to the close of the war, I never experienced trepidation upon confronting an enemy, though I always felt more or less anxiety. I never forgot that he had as much reason to fear my forces as I had his. The lesson was valuable."

In February 1862 Grant became a hero after leading 17,000 men and a flotilla of gunboats under Commodore Andrew Hull Foote in the capture of Tennessee's Forts Henry and Donelson. At Fort Donelson, Grant's terse demand for unconditional surrender angered Southerners and delighted the North. Despite disagreements with more sluggish superiors, Grant continued to rise until he became one of the North's principal commanders; he was well liked, as a man and a leader, and respected. Wrote Assistant Secretary of War Charles Dana, "Grant was an uncommon fellow, the most modest, the most disinterested, and most honest man I ever knew, with a temper that nothing could disturb." Though his friend and chief lieutenant, General William T. Sherman, thought him "a mystery, and I believe he is a mystery to himself," he also saw him as "the greatest soldier of our time if not of all time. He dismisses all possibility of defeat. If his plan goes wrong he is never disconcerted but promptly devises a new one and is sure to win in the end." One British observer frankly stated that he thought Grant was "ordinary-looking, dull and silent." But after penetrating Grant's reserve, he found

Under Grant, members of the Eighth Kansas Infantry (top) strike a warlike pose in 1862. Grant was popular with his troops, as were most successful generals. His demeanor—"as cool as patience on a monument," said one soldier—inspired confidence, despite the fact that he spent his troops' lives freely, as one soldier's marked cartridge-box plate (inset) suggests.

A BAD EGG FOR JEFF DAVIS—CHATTANOOGA.

the general to be "a man of sterling good-sense as well as of the firmest resolution . . . humane, simple, modest; from all restless self consciousness and desire for display perfectly free."

After winning at Vicksburg, and bringing the Mississippi River back into the Union, Grant was called to manage Federal military operations throughout the western theater. In the autumn of 1863, after responding swiftly to a crisis in southwestern Tennessee, Grant won yet another triumph. That September, General William S. Rosecrans, the Union hero of the Battle of Stones River, had positioned his army of 60,000 men to capture and occupy the vital railroad town of Chattanooga, Tennessee. "Rosy" forced the Confederate defenders—50,000 men under General Braxton Bragg—to abandon the town, but Bragg did not withdraw far. On September 18, near Chickamauga Creek in northern Georgia, Bragg began maneuvering his army—now swollen to about 65,000—to

strike at Rosecrans. For three days the two armies mauled each other in what was to be the last great battle west of the Alleghenies. Together the armies' casualties totaled almost 35,000, and though the Confederates drove the Federals from the battlefield and claimed victory, they had gained little. The Federals still held Chattanooga.

Thrown by the defeat, Rosecrans told Lincoln, "We have met with a serious disaster," and warned, "We have no certainty of holding our position." Fortunately for Rosecrans, Bragg did not follow up his victory in Georgia with an immediate attack in Tennessee. Instead, he lay siege to Chattanooga and the Federals suffered severely from hunger. Washington rushed supplies and 40,000 reinforcements to resist the siege, but Lincoln had lost confidence in Rosecrans, who, he said, was "confused and stunned like a duck hit on the head." In October command of the theater went to Grant, who immediately replaced Rosecrans with George H. Thomas and then proceeded to Chattanooga. In less than a month, under Grant's influence, the Federals solved their

The Federal victory at Chattanooga in late November 1863 was a crushing blow for Jefferson Davis and the South (opposite, bottom) and a boon to the war-weary North. For months after the battle, exultant Union soldiers posed on the craggy summit of Lookout Mountain above Chattanooga. Members of the Eighth Kentucky Infantry (opposite) were credited with being the first to raise the Stars and Stripes on the embattled crest on November 25. General Joseph Hooker (above, third from right, with his staff around the time of the battle) achieved his greatest victory at Lookout Mountain.

supply problems and developed a plan to break the siege. On November 24 and 25, Grant launched a three-pronged attack with 70,000 men that drove Bragg's army from its strong position atop Missionary Ridge, sending the Confederates reeling into Georgia.

The victory held enormous importance for the Federals: The Confederate army had been soundly defeated and badly hurt. Chattanooga was secure, as was Tennessee, and the Northerners could now begin planning a campaign into the heart of Georgia and on to the Atlantic coast. Chattanooga also brought Grant more recognition. All the Confederate forces in the West— save the remnants of Bragg's force, now in Georgia (Bragg would soon be replaced by General Joseph Johnston)—had been defeated and dispersed, and Lincoln saw that Grant was responsible for the victories. The president was sure he had found the general who would end the war.

On March 9, Lincoln received Grant in Washington at a meeting of the cabinet. The president handed the general a commission as lieutenant general of the U.S. Army, making him the highest-ranking officer in the service and commander of all U.S. forces. Grant accepted the honor modestly; navy secretary Welles thought Grant looked embarrassed. The new commander quickly made a decision: He would make his headquarters in Virginia with the Army of the Potomac; his target would be Robert E. Lee's army.

HASTY RETREAT

An uncompleted contemporary sketch (left) portrays the hasty withdrawal of Colonel Robert Minty's cavalry brigade from Reed's Bridge on Chickamauga Creek on the afternoon of September 18, 1863. Minty's men were tearing down the span— "a narrow, frail structure, which was planked with loose boards and fence-rails"—when Confederates surprised them. After putting up severe resistance, the Federals abandoned their work and retreated. Another Federal brigade burned the bridge the next day.

BLOODY CHICKAMAUGA

On September 19 and 20, 1863, in what would be the bloodiest battle of the war in the western theater, Generals William S. Rosecrans and Braxton Bragg slugged it out along Chickamauga Creek in northwest Georgia. Fighting swirled around Lee & Gordon's Mills on the banks of the creek, ensuring that the structure (opposite) would become a popular post-battle subject for photographers.

DRUMMER BOY

At the age of 10, Ohioan Johnny Clem (right) enlisted as a drummer boy. He was, according to his sister, "an expert drummer, and being a bright and cheery child, soon made his way into the affections of officers and soldiers." He served with the 22nd Michigan Infantry in its major battles and earned fame throughout the North as the "Drummer Boy of Chickamauga" through a song of that name. He rose to sergeant before the end of the war and remained in the army, retiring as a major general.

SUPPLY LINE

By law, every soldier in the Union army was to have three pounds of food per day, and every horse and mule about 24 pounds. No army could be effective if undersupplied, so commanders worked long hours at solving logistical problems. Federals at Chattanooga endured hard times until they established the "Cracker Line"—a tenuous supply line that used ferries like the ones above and makeshift bridges to cross the Tennessee River.

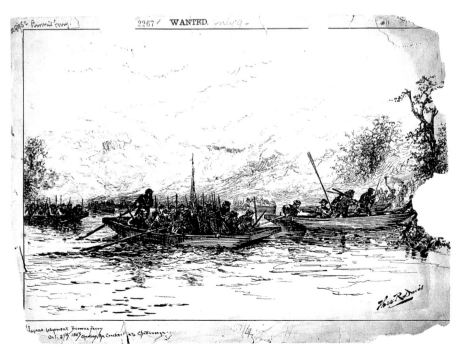

NIGHT MISSION

A sketch (right) by artist Theodore R. Davis portrays some of the 1,500 handpicked men of General William B. Hazen's command who daringly floated down the Tennessee River past Confederate sentinels in the predawn darkness of October 27, 1863. At Brown's Ferry, Hazen's men used their boats to build a pontoon bridge and open part of the famous Cracker Line.

MOUNTAIN PERCH

From their aeries atop Lookout Mountain, Confederates commanded a panoramic view (above) that included Moccasin Point in the Tennessee River and Chattanooga (upper right, on the right bank of the river). In October 1863 the Southerners controlled access to the city, but the Cracker Line—formed by bridges and ferries in the two river bends and the narrow neck of land in the center of the image—saved the Federal garrison. Joseph Hooker's troops took this vantage point when they drove the defending Confederates off the mountain on November 24, 1863.

HARPER'S HISTORY OF THE GREAT REBELLION.

566

[November, 1863.

THE STORMING OF MISSIONARY RIDGE.

UNSCHEDULED DASH

Grant's attempts to break out of Chattanooga on November 25, 1863, faltered in the face of the strong Confederate positions on Missionary Ridge. Braxton Bragg's Southerners had built three lines of earthworks on the slopes and crest. Late in the day, while taking enormous losses in the stalled offensive, Federal troops ignored orders and dashed up the slopes of the ridge on their own initiative. Confederate artillerymen tried desperately to bring the muzzles of their guns to bear on the attackers (left), but the Federals took the crest, along with 37 guns and 2,000 prisoners.

ROMANTICIZED BATTLE

Noting that "the side of Lookout Mountain was rugged, heavily timbered, and full of chasms," Grant believed that, had Bragg deployed his men wisely, "a hundred men could have held the summit against the assault of any number of men." But Hooker's men fought their way to, and eventually over, the mountaintop. An artist's imaginative lithograph (right) romanticized the fighting in heavy fog on the crest, which became known, equally romantically, as the "Battle Above the Clouds."

STORMING AND CAPTURE OF LOOKOUT MOUNTAIN,
November 24, 1863,
By Major General JOSEPH HOOKER, Commanding,
SUPPORTED BY OSTERHAUS' DIVISION OF THE 10TH, CRAFTS OF THE 4TH, AND GEARY'S OF THE 12TH CORPS.

COMMON MAN

With members of his staff, Grant, in his undistinguished uniform and smoking his usual cigar, views the battlefield on Lookout Mountain (above). To many, the commanding general's unmilitary bearing came across unfavorably. "General Grant," wrote one soldier, "is a short thick set man and rode his horse like a bag of meal. I was a little disappointed in the appearance. He was more plainly dressed than any other general on the field."

WINTER OF DISCOMFORT

Federals in winter camp in Chattanooga (opposite) naturally tried to make their existence as comfortable as possible, but a shortage of materials defied their efforts. The boards on a fence—erected, perhaps, as a windbreak—still bear the wallpaper from dismantled houses. Building materials and firewood were in chronically short supply, and soldiers and civilians alike suffered from the cold. The winter-long occupation by an army reduced to scavenging left Chattanooga in a state of squalor and its residents in poverty.

MELANCHOLY JOURNEY

Grant claimed 6,000 prisoners at Chattanooga. Since both North and South had begun keeping, rather than exchanging, their captives, the armies had to provide for the transportation and care of large numbers of unwanted guests. At left, Confederate prisoners wait in a Chattanooga train yard for the long, cold ride to a Northern prison.

HALLOWED GROUND

Federal soldiers wander over the battlefield of Lookout Mountain near the ruins of a house on the Cravens farm (left). Scavenging for souvenirs or firewood, the troops picked the area clean through the winter. The fighting on the slope had been intense, and Confederate defenders had made good, but ultimately futile, use of the rocks. The palisades of the mountain's summit, which Grant had considered almost impregnable as a defensive position, loom in the background.

The signal telegraph train as used at the battle of Fredericksburg

A. R. Ward

The Telegraph

The widespread use of the telegraph during the Civil War revolutionized warfare. For the first time in history, field commanders could maintain almost hourly communication with distant subordinates and superiors—including, for better or worse, their presidents.

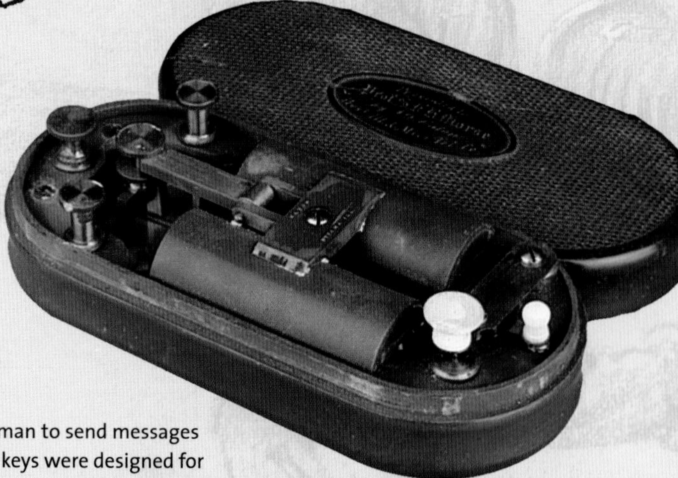

HIGH-LEVEL COMMUNICATIONS

Pocket telegraph keys (right) made it possible for a field commander with a trained signalman to send messages from any point along a telegraph line. Not much bigger than a bar of soap, these portable keys were designed for repairmen who traveled along the wires and reported trouble; one such "line walker" is shown at left. Telegraph lines required a high level of upkeep, since wind, weather, and enemy raiders routinely knocked the wires down. Skillful eavesdroppers with pocket telegraph keys could intercept enemy dispatches from atop a pole, and even sow chaos with bogus messages.

VISIBLE MEANS OF SUPPORT

The U.S. Signal Corps (above) was responsible for establishing new telegraph lines. The poles they used varied in height but were to be no less than five inches in diameter at the top—more if they were to support several wires—and set into the ground at least five feet. The heavy galvanized-iron wires that carried the signals required that the poles be stout, especially in high winds.

REAL TIME

Because they moved with the armies and were able to set up shop anywhere a wire could be strung, signalmen often worked in primitive conditions. The Federal field station above, near City Point, Virginia, helped Grant communicate with subordinates in operations against Petersburg. A good key operator working in good conditions could send about 42 words per minute—about 2,000 words an hour—in Morse code, though the transmission rate in the field was probably lower.

CAREER TRAINING

Alfred Waud sketched this signalman (left) using a Beardslee telegraph. Learning to send and receive signals via key was exacting work and required skill. "To become an expert operator requires much time and patience, and the most unwearied application," read a training manual of the time, which also proclaimed that such hard work would be rewarded. "The time will seldom or never be found when a thoroughly competent operator cannot obtain immediate and remunerative Employment."

TO LONG ENDURE

Rivers of Blood

WHEN ULYSSES S. GRANT, the new general in chief of the Union army, went to Virginia in March 1864, those who had known him in the West wondered if the reticent, strong-willed soldier from Illinois would be able to tolerate Washington's involvement in the operations of the eastern army. Since the war began, congressmen, members of the cabinet,

These twisted ramrods (left) were recovered from the Wilderness battlefield, where Grant fought Lee early in the new general in chief's overland campaign. The rods became twisted when overheated muskets ignited cartridges before the soldiers could withdraw the rammer.

and the president had all sought some measure of control over the army, and more often than not the result was detrimental. In early April 1864, Grant's friend William T. Sherman tried to forestall Washington's meddling by writing to his brother, Senator John Sherman: "Let him alone . . . Grant is as good a leader as we can find. He has honesty, simplicity of character, singleness of purpose, and no hope or claim to usurp civil power. Let him alone. He wants no help." Lincoln agreed. The president gave Grant carte blanche, declared that he did not even wish to know his plans, and promised every assistance in his power. It was a good thing that the new general had so much presidential support, because Grant's operations in the spring and summer of 1864 would spill rivers of blood, causing even unflinching Northerners to quail at the extent of the slaughter.

Grant went east convinced that there could be no peace until "the military power of the rebellion was entirely broken." Previous commanders had made Richmond their objective, but Grant aimed to destroy the Confederate armies, which he saw as acting independently and without concert, "like a balky team, no two ever pulling together." In the spring of 1864, Grant determined—as McClellan had in 1862—that the best plan was a simultaneous advance of all Federal armies on Confederate armies and Southern cities from Virginia to Louisiana. With the Confederates stretched to their limits, the Federals, in Grant's words, would "hammer continuously against the armed force of the enemy and his resources, until by mere attrition, if in no other way, there should be nothing left to him but . . . submission."

The two main Federal thrusts would be in Georgia and Virginia. Grant ordered Sherman to smash Joseph Johnston's army north of Atlanta and drive into the interior of Georgia as far as possible, inflicting along the way all the damage he could upon the South's war resources. Meade's Army of the Potomac, meanwhile, would attempt to crush Lee's army. The plan's key element was determination, something Grant possessed in abundance. When some officers cautioned that Lee was cunning and aggressive, Grant's temper flared: "Some of you always

Wounded Federals rest beneath a tree in the yard of a house at Fredericksburg (left). The severity of the fighting at nearby Spotsylvania and the Wilderness turned the town into a vast hospital. A soldier of the 11th Mississippi, wounded on May 10, used the last of his strength to write a poignant, blood-stained farewell (below) to his father.

seem to think Lee is suddenly going to turn a double somersault, and land in our rear and on both of our flanks at the same time," he said. "Go and try to think what we are going to do ourselves, instead of what Lee is going to do."

Lee understood well the dilemma before him. The Federal armies continued to grow: Grant, who accompanied Meade's army, could bring almost 120,000 men against Lee's less than 70,000. The Southern general concluded that he must strike a delicate balance between concentrating his troops against Grant's immense force and detaching men to defend or threaten other points. The Virginian also knew that, with the 1864 presidential election looming, Lincoln would be desperate for victories. "The importance of this campaign to the administration of Mr. Lincoln and General Grant," he wrote to Jefferson Davis, "leaves no doubt that every effort and every sacrifice will be made to secure its success." The Confederacy could spare no less.

The sacrifices began on May 4, 1864, when Grant, moving south into central Virginia, sought to get his army around Lee's flank in an area of scrub timber and tangled undergrowth called the Wilderness. Lee, in position just a few miles west of where he had fought the battle of Chancellorsville a year earlier, blocked Grant's advance and the battle began. The thick woods obstructed the armies and restricted the movement of wheeled vehicles, mitigating the Federal advantages in men and artillery. It became an infantry fight in which foot soldiers

Officers on the staff of Union commander John Sedgwick's Sixth Corps (left) relax beside their comfortable log hut in the winter campground near Brandy Station, Virginia. Major Thomas Hyde, seated with outstretched legs (far left), noted that the arrival of General Grant (below) was greeted with guarded optimism, as "the record and Lincoln's opinion were in his favor."

charged and countercharged and fought at close range. On the battle's second day, May 6, the Federals nearly gained Lee's flank and rear, but timely reinforcements under General James Longstreet prevented a Confederate rout, though Longstreet himself fell badly wounded. That night, Grant decided not to attack again. He had made no headway and lost more than 15,000 men, many of whom burned to death in the forest fires kindled by the shooting in the tindery undergrowth. Lee had earned a tactical victory but at a cost of more than 12 percent of his army.

Previous Federal commanders in Virginia who had sustained enormous casualties against Lee had withdrawn afterward to let their armies recuperate. Not Grant. If his troops did not yet know that they had a different kind of general, they knew now. The men of the Army of the Potomac learned on May 7 that their general was not pulling back, but moving forward, southward, in an attempt to get between Lee and Richmond.

Lee reacted quickly and again blocked the Federals, this time at Spotsylvania. For more than a week, the armies maneuvered and fought, with the climax coming on May 12. In a driving rain, Grant launched an assault on the Confederate earthworks known as the "Mule Shoe," for its rounded shape. The Federals made it into the trenches, where the hand-to-hand fighting was fierce. So heavy was the firing that an oak tree nearly two feet in diameter standing

just behind the Confederate line was completely cut down by bullets. A desperate Confederate counterattack stemmed the Federal advance. Grant lost more than 17,000 men, bringing his losses to about 33,000 in just over two weeks. He remained determined, however, and told Washington that he would continue to move on Richmond. "I will take no backward steps," he told the war department. "I propose to fight it out on this line if it takes all summer."

In Georgia and on schedule, Sherman, intent on destroying Joseph Johnston's army, had moved southward in the first days of May with nearly 100,000 men. The two generals would thrust and parry for weeks in a series of brilliant offensive and defensive movements. Johnston was badly outnumbered—he had only about 65,000 men—so he determined to fight a defensive campaign to conserve his precious manpower. The armies fell into a pattern: The Confederates would dig in and discourage or perhaps repel a frontal assault, then Sherman would send a flanking column toward the Confederate rear, forcing Johnston to withdraw to a new position, where the pattern would repeat.

Sherman's men forced the Southerners to retreat from Dalton, Georgia, but a counterattack at Resaca almost unhinged the Federal advance. The armies sparred at Adairsville and Cassville, but more energetic marches by the Federals forced Johnston to withdraw first to Dallas and then,

In the late afternoon of May 4, 1864, photographer Timothy O'Sullivan recorded the opening of Grant's offensive as the rearmost units of the Sixth Corps marched across a pontoon bridge spanning the Rapidan River at Germanna Ford (above). The army's supply wagons crossed that evening, and the Ninth Corps the following morning. While O'Sullivan was taking his photographs, the Fifth Corps was already pushing south toward the Wilderness, where the Federals would battle Lee's army on May 5.

In May 1864, while Grant was facing Lee in Virginia, General William Sherman (inset) advanced on the Rebel army in Georgia. Before joining Sherman's march in the South, soldiers of the 78th Pennsylvania—battle-tested veterans of Stones River, Chickamauga, and Chattanooga—doffed their hats for a group photo (right) atop Lookout Mountain. At Pickett's Mill on May 27, the Pennsylvanians fought with what their brigade commander called "heroism worthy of all praise."

after heavy fighting at New Hope Church and Pickett's Mill at the end of May, to Kennesaw Mountain. "The whole country is one vast fort," Sherman informed Washington, "and Johnston must have at least 50 miles of connected trenches with abatis and finished batteries." Sherman saw Kennesaw as "the key to the whole country," and departed from his flanking strategy long enough to launch a futile assault on June 27 that cost him 3,000 men, three times the Confederate loss. By early July, however, Sherman had managed to outflank the Confederates and force them to withdraw. The Federals had battled through nearly 100 miles of mountainous country and stood just 15 miles from Atlanta. The cost had been high, however: 17,000 casualties (the Confederates lost 14,000) in just over two months.

In Joseph M. Brown's drawing of Kennesaw Mountain (above), on June 27, 1864, Confederate soldiers pour volleys of musketry into their Yankee assailants from behind the field fortifications of an area that projected so far out it was called the "Dead Angle." Tennessean Sam Watkins, awed by the bravery of his foes, noted, "They seemed to walk up and take death as coolly as if they were automatic or wooden men."

Johnston continued to withdraw, forced back by Sherman. When he got his army across the Chattahoochee River, outside of Atlanta, the Confederate government decided Johnston was too passive. Jefferson Davis replaced him with General John Bell Hood, who was as aggressive as Johnston was conservative. Hood attacked, and the armies clashed in a series of encounters—at Peachtree Creek, Ezra Church, Jonesboro, and Atlanta itself—but Sherman continued to tighten his ring around the city, and Hood's diminished army grew increasingly powerless.

In Virginia too the Confederates searched in vain for ways to stand up to the Federals. Lee's army had fought well, badly bloodying Grant at the North Anna River and at Cold Harbor in late May and early June, but the North continued to sidestep the Southern lines and push southward. Grant decided that the key to Richmond was Petersburg, a railroad hub 23 miles south of the capital. On June 15 and 18, he launched assaults with most of his troops—first with units of the Army of the James and then with elements of the Army of the Potomac—but, due to poor coordination, could not crack the Confederate defenses. He again maneuvered around a Confederate flank, and by late June had begun siege operations.

By August 1864 Grant was firmly established in siege lines at Richmond and Petersburg, but his overland campaign had cost the Union 50,000 casualties in three months. Lee had lost fewer men, but a higher percentage of his total force. Sherman had closed in around Atlanta, and though the Confederates in both Georgia and Virginia were still dangerous, they were weak and on the defensive. Lee admitted that, with the Federals knocking at the heart of the Confederacy and the South's armies badly reduced through incessant fighting, Southern prospects were dim. It was, he confessed, "only a matter of time."

Regl Band

Sergt. C.R. Todd right Genl Guide.

17th Maine Inf. Vols.
(taken May 3, 1864)

Surgeon N. A. Hersom   Chaplain J. F. Lovering   Capt. J. C. Perry Co D. acting field officer   Capt. G. W. Verrill Co E. acting Adjutant   Asst. surgeon N. B. Coleman

Colonel George Warren West.

POISED FOR BATTLE

On May 3, 1864, the 507-strong 17th Maine Infantry (above) poses for a regimental photo during the unit's daily dress parade at Brandy Station. By the end of the week, 192 of the men would be casualties, victims of the two days of fighting in the Wilderness. Another 69 were lost at Spotsylvania.

DIGGING IN

Shallow rifle pits and a robust breastwork of logs (opposite) mark the line defended by General Richard Ewell's Confederates in the Battle of the Wilderness on May 5 and 6. Posted astride the Orange Turnpike, Ewell's men used their cover to advantage, repulsing a series of Yankee attacks. As the campaign progressed, soldiers in both armies dug in whenever a battle seemed likely.

THE HUMAN COST

Stark evidence of the futility of Grant's assaults at Cold Harbor were the Union soldiers who remained unburied where they fell in early June 1864 until the war's end, when this photograph (left) was taken. Soldiers assigned to bury the dead were able to identify some individuals, but many were interred as unknowns in the nearby National Cemetery.

THE MULE SHOE

Log and earth breastworks constructed by Southerners defending the salient, an outward projecting area, called the Mule Shoe (above) for a time prevented Yankees at Spotsylvania from breaking through in the battles of May 10 and 12. "Give a man protection for his body and the temptation is very strong to put his head under cover too," noted Confederate McHenry Howard. "Behind works not a few men will crouch down doing nothing."

OUT OF THE WAR

Herded together in a field at White House Landing on the Pamunkey River, near Richmond, captured Confederate soldiers (above) await transport to the Northern prison at Point Lookout, Maryland. Photographed by one of Mathew Brady's cameramen on June 9 or 10, the men were most likely captured during the fighting near Cold Harbor a week earlier. They joined thousands of other captives from the battles at Spotsylvania.

AWAITING BURIAL

Confederate dead (left) are laid out prior to their burial in a mass grave at Alsop's Farm, near Spotsylvania. Photographer Timothy O'Sullivan recorded the grisly scene on May 20, the day after Ewell's division was driven back by counterattacking Federal troops. The unpleasant task of interring the fallen from both sides was assigned to men of the First Massachusetts Heavy Artillery.

OVERLAND CAMPAIGN

STANDOFF AT NORTH ANNA

War-weary Federal soldiers (above) rest on the banks of the North Anna River at Jericho Mills, a bridgehead established by George Meade's Army of the Potomac on May 23. For three days, combat flared along the river bluffs, as Lee successfully stymied the Union offensive. But when Grant began shifting his forces east, threatening the Confederate right flank and rear, the Southern troops were compelled to pull back in order to safeguard the capital at Richmond.

COUNCIL OF WAR

In the wake of the bloody battle at Spotsylvania, Generals Grant and Meade summoned their staffs for a conference in the yard of Massaponox Church (opposite) on May 21, 1864. Timothy O'Sullivan photographed the commanders' council of war from his vantage point in a second-story window, producing a series of images that stand as a remarkable example of early photojournalism. In the view shown here, the generals and their subordinates sit in pews carried into the churchyard; wagons of the Fifth Corps rumble past in the background. Among the officers consulting maps is General Meade, seated at the far end of the left-most pew. Grant, apparently absorbed in thought, sits with legs crossed, in front of the trees at center.

THE GENERAL'S SERENADE

Perched in a bandstand resembling a huge bird's nest, regimental musicians of the 38th Illinois Infantry prepare to serenade Brigadier General William P. Carlin and his staff at their headquarters near Ringgold, Georgia. Formerly colonel of the 38th, Carlin (third from left, with a double row of buttons on his coat) had won promotion for his bravery at Perryville and Stones River and would soon lead his brigade in the campaign for Atlanta.

GUARDING THE RAILROAD

Assigned to guard a strategic bridge on the Nashville & Chattanooga Railroad near Whiteside, Tennessee, Federal infantrymen (left) break beside their tents and the log blockhouse that would become their refuge if they were attacked by Rebel raiders. Recognizing the importance of safeguarding his lines of supply for the impending advance into Georgia, General Sherman emphasized, "Every foot of the way had to be strongly guarded against the acts of a local hostile population and of the enemy's cavalry."

GENERAL SHERMAN'S CAMPAIGN—GENERAL WILLIAMS'S DIVISION OF HOOKER'S CORPS DRIVING THE REBELS THROUGH T

CONFEDERATE BREASTWORKS

Relentless in his drive for Atlanta, Sherman committed the 20th Corps to an assault on a strong Rebel position near New Hope Church on May 25. Sheltered behind earthworks like the one at left, photographed by George N. Barnard, Confederates in Alexander Stewart's division repelled their blue-clad assailants. One Yankee survivor described the attack as "simply slaughter," noting that "scores and hundreds of men surged right up to the breastworks and died there."

OS.—Sketched by Theodore R. Davis.—[See First Page.]

FIGHT AGAINST KOLB'S FARM

On June 22, 1864, Union troops in Brigadier General Alpheus Williams's First Division, 20th Corps, forced Rebel skirmishers under Hood to fall back on their main line of battle near Kolb's Farm. Hood soon mounted a counterattack, which was repulsed with heavy losses. Based on a sketch by artist-correspondent Theodore Davis, the scene was published as an engraving (left) in the July 2 issue of *Harper's Weekly*.

RELIEVED OF COMMAND

General Joseph E. Johnston (right) was greatly admired by his troops, but his inability to resist Sherman's forces strained Johnston's already testy relationship with President Davis. On July 17 Johnston was ordered to relinquish command of the Army of Tennessee to General John Bell Hood. A Texan who likened the news of Johnston's removal to "a clap of thunder from a clear sky" noted that the "men were astonished beyond expression and for the first time appeared disheartened."

BLOODY KENNESAW

The commanding heights of Kennesaw Mountain and Little Kennesaw appear in the background of this rare composite photograph (above), taken soon after Sherman's costly offensive on June 27. Despite the almost suicidal gallantry of the Yankee attackers, Johnston's position at Kennesaw proved impossible to capture by direct assault. "How so many of us escaped wounds or death, God only knows," Captain John Gillespie of the 78th Ohio wrote after the fight. "Yet hundreds of mothers will weep tears of sorrow when the details of yesterday's great battle reaches them." Five days later the Rebels abandoned their stronghold, and Sherman resumed his advance on Atlanta.

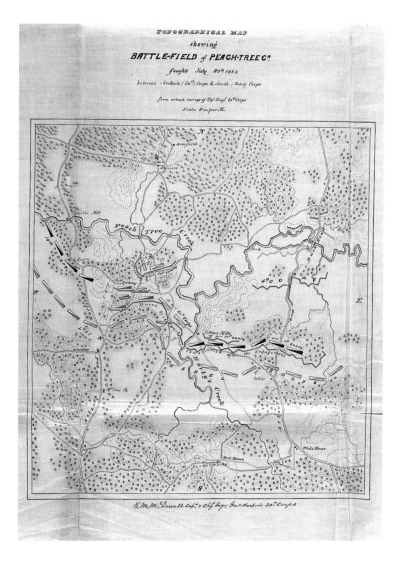

BATTLE AT PEACHTREE CREEK

Captain Robert M. McDowell, chief topographical engineer for the left wing of Sherman's Army of Georgia, prepared the map above of the July 20, 1864, Battle of Peachtree Creek. Determined to drive the Yankees from the northern outskirts of Atlanta, the newly appointed Confederate commander, John Bell Hood, launched a counterattack on the Federal 14th and 15th Corps. Portions of the Union line gave way, but the Rebel charge was ultimately checked, and Sherman tightened his grip on Atlanta's beleaguered defenders.

As his armies closed in on Atlanta, General Sherman assured his Washington superiors that "whether we get inside Atlanta or not, it will be a used up community by the time we are done with it." Complex and astute, driven and at times ruthless, William Sherman saw no glory in war—only a grim reality.

HARD AS STEEL

The photograph at left shows Sherman's characteristic intensity—what poet Walt Whitman called his "stern open air." One subordinate thought Sherman's "sharp blue eyes" were "kindly as a rule, but cold and hard as steel sometimes." Soldiers who liked their commander's unostentatious style called him "Uncle Billy." All Sherman's men wore corps badges—the one above belongs to the 20th—which he ordered so he could identify them.

William T. Sherman

COMMANDER FATHER

Seated in front of a map of the Deep South, Sherman clasps nine-year-old Thomas Ewing Sherman (left). The general was a loving but demanding parent, and his relationship with "Tommy" was often strained.

AMBITIOUS STEPFATHER

One of 11 siblings, Sherman was nine years old when his father died. He was taken in—though never officially adopted—by Thomas Ewing (below). A U.S. senator from Ohio, Ewing appointed his ward to West Point. Three of Ewings own sons served as Union generals.

AMATEUR ARTIST

Drawing was a required course at West Point, and though Sherman never became an accomplished artist, he enjoyed sketching scenes on his letters home. His drawings at right are of an officers' mess tent in Mississippi and a fortified Federal battery at Vicksburg.

A DIFFICULT MARRIAGE

In May of 1850 Sherman married Ellen Ewing (above), the daughter of his foster father, Senator Thomas Ewing. A devout Catholic, she waged a lifelong and unsuccessful battle to convert her husband, whose temperament was in many ways far different from hers.

Cavalry Charge

I N THE EARLY 1860S, before the conflict robbed Americans of their romantic notions about war, the cavalryman was their ideal soldier. Resolute and spirited, he swept down on the enemy like the wind, his raised saber and thundering horse making him both alluring and terrifying. Foes cringed or fled before the onslaught. The victorious

cavalier not only triumphed; he did so with verve and panache. In jangling spurs, heavy gauntlets, and perhaps a plumed hat or scarlet neckerchief, he strode boldly through life. Glamour surrounded the cavalryman, and the hard-working infantryman hated him for it. Foot soldiers, who bore the heaviest burdens in war, believed the horseman was all style and no substance. "Whoever saw a dead cavalryman?" infantrymen sneered.

Most leaders North and South accepted the foot soldier's view in the early days of the war and attached little value to large bodies of horsemen. Of the 70,000-odd soldiers present at the Battle of Bull Run in July 1861, only about 1,000 were cavalrymen. Few of the men who built the armies of the Civil War saw the wisdom in Napoleon's declaration that "an army weak in cavalry rarely achieves great success." Fewer still could have expected that in the last two years of the war horsemen would sweep by the thousands across Virginia, Pennsylvania, Georgia, and Alabama. What began in both armies as the most ignored branch of the service slowly grew to be perhaps the most important.

The Confederacy had the advantage in mounted arm early in the war. The leaders who proved themselves most adept as cavalry chieftains were Southerners, and Southern troopers seemed to have an affinity for horses that their Northern counterparts lacked. Federal cavalrymen marveled at the superb Southern horseflesh that flew over fences like deer and easily outran the less fleet animals that came from pastures north of the Mason-Dixon Line. The problem for Northerners, and, to a lesser degree, Southerners, as well, was inexperience. Few soldiers of the Civil War received much training, and cavalrymen felt the effects of this policy more than men in the infantry or artillery. Raw cavalry recruits had to learn how to ride as well as fight, and a man did not become accustomed to the saddle overnight. An officer from New York wrote, "Some of the boys had never ridden anything since they galloped on a hobby horse, and they clasped their legs close together, thus unconsciously sticking the spurs into their horses' sides. Blankets slipped from under saddles and hung from one corner; saddles slipped back until they were on

the rumps of horses; others turned and were on the under side of the animals; horses running and kicking; tin pans, mess-kettles flying through the air"—hardly useful on the battlefield.

Cavalrymen also had to learn to care for their mounts. Because neither army established any sort of veterinary service, and cavalrymen, especially in the North, tended to ride their horses to death, a trooper who could neither ride well nor maintain his animal's health was a significant liability. Wrote one Federal officer about the many small precautions a man had to take to keep his horse fit: "Sore backs became common with the hard-ships of campaigning, and one of the first lessons taught the inexperienced trooper was to take better care of his horse than he did of himself. The remedy against recurrence of sore backs on horses was invariably to order the trooper to walk and lead the disabled animal. With a few such lessons, cavalry

In a column of fours, Confederate troopers (above) canter down a country road with the dashing spirit that made them the envy of their Yankee counterparts. Much of the success of the Southern horsemen in the eastern theater was due to their intrepid and flamboyant commander, General James Ewell Brown (Jeb) Stuart (inset).

By 1864 the Northern cavalry had gained the upper hand under hard-hitting commanders like Philip Sheridan (third from left). Here he stands with his subordinates, Generals Davies, Gregg, Merritt, Torbert, and Wilson.

Daring leadership was an important factor in the Confederate cavalry's ability to outmaneuver the Federal mounted arm in the early years of the war. The dashing John Hunt Morgan (inset, left) and the iron-willed "Wizard of the Saddle" Nathan Bedford Forrest (right) proved formidable foes to hapless Yankees in the West.

soldiers of but short service became most scrupulous in smoothing out wrinkles in saddle blankets, in dismounting to walk steep hills, in giving frequent rests to their jaded animals, and when opportunity offered, in unsaddling and cooling the backs of their mounts after hours in the saddle. Poor forage, sudden changes of forage, and overfeeding produced almost as much sickness and physical disability as no forage at all."

It took at least a year to make a reasonably competent cavalryman, and just as long to train a cavalry horse. European armies, by contrast, took two years to train a mount, because only excellent horsemen and carefully trained mounts, so the thinking went in Europe, could charge with any effectiveness over broken ground, and a furious gallop on the battlefield was likely to do more damage to untrained men and horses than the enemy could.

American cavalrymen of the late 1850s were greatly influenced by the classical—as opposed to the dragoon—European cavalry tradition, which held that horsemen served first and foremost

as the "eyes" of the army commander. The troopers were to reconnoiter, to follow the enemy columns and bring information to army headquarters. Cavalry regiments were also to operate defensively by keeping opposing cavalry at a distance, thereby screening the movements of their own army. Finally, European cavalrymen were used as shock troops. When a commander needed to apply a swift, sharp blow to the enemy, he called on his cavalry. In battle, the cavalry typically guarded the army's flanks, and if the enemy were beaten, the horsemen would surge into the mass of withdrawing troops, terrifying the foot soldiers with a charge of pounding hooves and slashing sabers. A well-timed cavalry charge could easily turn a defeated foe into a routed mob.

Unfortunately, it was the mythic idea of the bold and dashing horse soldier, based in large part on the European classical tradition, that motivated many of the young men who enlisted in cavalry regiments in 1861 and 1862. Not only did these men misunderstand the real nature of a cavalryman's work; they were unaware that the dragoon European cavalry tradition—less

In a hard-fought engagement near Aldie, Virginia, on June 17, 1863, Union staff Captain George Armstrong Custer leads the charge of the First Maine Cavalry (above) as Colonel Calvin Douty falls dead from his horse (left) and General Judson Kilpatrick lies pinned beneath his wounded mount. Twelve days later, the audacious young Custer was promoted to brigadier general and given command of the Michigan Brigade. The summer of 1863 was a significant period in the history of the Union cavalry, with the Yankee troopers playing an important role in the successful Gettysburg campaign.

Empty Federal stables in the shadow of Tennessee's Lookout Mountain (top) await the arrival of fresh animals. Thousands of horses died from exhaustion and starvation—a grim counterpoint to the cavalry's romantic image, exemplified by the plumed officer's hat above.

established than the classical and more varied in form—had taken root in America in the 1850s when Congress authorized two regiments of this hybrid branch of service, which combined elements of the infantry and the cavalry. Dragoons could serve in traditional cavalry roles, but could also fight on foot. Commanders used dragoons as mounted infantry; dragoons used their horses mainly to get into and out of action, where they fought on foot.

The Confederates were more willing than the Federals to experiment with their cavalry, giving the South another advantage early in the war. They organized their mounted troops into large, independent bodies, for example, so that talented and daring leaders like James Ewell Brown (Jeb) Stuart, Nathan Bedford Forrest, and John Hunt Morgan could successfully lead long raids on the enemy. The less imaginative Federals used their horsemen more traditionally—as scouts, couriers, and "screens." While the Southerners banded whole regiments of horsemen into brigades and brigades into divisions, Federal commanders broke their regiments up into smaller pieces and dispersed the companies and battalions throughout their armies. The result was a completely dominant Southern cavalry that seriously hampered Federal operations. Not until 1863, after the North had reorganized its cavalry into brigades and divisions and corps, did the Federal cavalry become ascendant.

YANKEE SWASHBUCKLER

Cocky, flamboyant, and brave, the golden-haired George Armstrong Custer (above), a general at 23, was one of the Union's most celebrated cavalrymen. By 1865, the time of this photo, he had seen action in most engagements in the eastern theater. A subordinate described Custer as "the idol, as well as the ideal of his men ... the foremost cavalry officer of his time."

REBEL SCOUTS

Members of the Eighth Texas Cavalry, the rough-and-ready Confederate troopers above were part of a 30-man detail assigned to serve as scouts under Captain Alexander Shannon. As General Sherman's forces cut a swath of destruction through Georgia and the Carolinas, Shannon's scouts hung on the flanks of the Federal columns, waylaying isolated Yankee patrols, supply wagons, and foragers. The scouts showed no mercy to pillagers. "In the morning we found 3 Yanks driving off a lady's cows," Texan Enoch D. John wrote of one encounter. "We soon scattered their brains and moved on."

FINE HORSEFLESH

Superbly mounted, with the saddlecloth and accouterments befitting his rank, and accompanied by a cavalry escort, Brigadier General Rufus Ingalls (opposite) prepares to ride the lines of the winter encampment near Brandy Station. As chief quartermaster of the Army of the Potomac—a position he filled with credit from 1862 to the war's end—Ingalls had his pick of the best horses in the Federal remount depots. By 1864 the Union Cavalry Bureau had largely overcome its earlier problems with corruption and mismanagement, and was efficiently seeing to the purchase, care, and supply of animals to units at the front.

Jeb Stuart

Perhaps the most famous horseman of the Civil War, James Ewell Brown (Jeb) Stuart waged war with rollicking flair. "He was always cheerful," General Lee wrote of his cavalry commander, "always ready for work, and always reliable."

ALLURING— AND TERRIFYING

Broad-shouldered and powerfully built, with an outgoing personality and hearty laugh, Jeb Stuart habitually sported high boots, jangling spurs, and a plumed hat (right)—attire that epitomized the dashing cavalryman. The flashy general was prepared to fight as well as to lead, and his personal armament reflected his intentions. In addition to a saber, Stuart carried a formidable Le Mat revolver (top), a veritable arsenal, holding nine .42-caliber rounds with a second, lower barrel capable of firing a charge of buckshot. Stuart's zeal for combat ultimately cost him his life when he rode forward to fire upon retreating Yankee troopers in the May 1864 Battle of Yellow Tavern and was mortally wounded by a pistol shot from a dismounted foe.

RAIL PRIZE

Dismounted Confederate troopers under Stuart fire on a Yankee supply train (above) at Tunstall's Station on the Virginia peninsula during the June 1862 ride around McClellan's army. The locomotive managed to break through the ambush, keeping $125,000 in Union soldier's monthly pay from the clutches of the Southern raiders. Stuart's audacious foray wreaked havoc on Federal depots and convinced McClellan that even behind the lines his forces were vulnerable to Confederate attack.

RIDING A RAID

A jaunty song composed in the wake of Stuart's June 1862 ride around McClellan's army on the peninsula, "Riding a Raid" became even more popular following a second circumvention of McClellan's forces, in October 1862. The sheet-music cover above depicts Stuart in all his glory, and the image reinforced his stature as a Southern hero.

THE CLASS OF '54

Jeb Stuart stands at center (above) with two comrades from West Point: Robert E. Lee's son Custis (left), who ranked first in the 1854 class, and an unidentified cadet. In 1855 Stuart married Flora Cooke (right), daughter of Lieutenant Colonel Philip St. George Cooke, who as a Union cavalry general battled his son-in-law's men in the peninsular campaign.

Black Flag

AFTER THREE YEARS of increasingly brutal fighting, soldiers on both sides of the conflict were ready to ignore what politicians and editors had been calling "the rules of civilized warfare." In 1861 Northerners and Southerners alike had hoped that everyone would respect these rules, which involved treating prisoners decently and leaving civilians

A Confederate prisoner confined in a Yankee compound at Rock Island, Illinois, crafted this wooden bracelet with a metal cross (below). Many Civil War captives took to carving trinkets from wood, bone, and other materials at hand.

alone. But by 1864 participants in the war began to value conquest over human decency, and they grew ever more ruthless in their conduct, descending, at times, into barbarism. In 1864 women and children were burned out of their homes and livestock were slaughtered in the fields. Captured soldiers were hanged or shot. Captors starved and neglected their prisoners. "You might as well appeal against the thunder storm as against these terrible hardships of war," wrote General William T. Sherman in September 1864. "They are inevitable. War is cruelty, and you cannot refine it."

General Sherman only articulated what many commanders, North and South, now believed: Neither side would surrender until the pain became unbearable. The only way Southerners could gain peace, Sherman wrote, was by admitting that the war "began in error and is perpetuated in pride." In the meantime, the Federals would wage war with increasing earnestness.

In the summer of 1864, in Virginia, Federals under General David Hunter burned portions of the Shenandoah Valley, including the Virginia Military Institute and the home of the governor of the commonwealth, in Lexington. In response, Confederates under General John McCausland entered Chambersburg, Pennsylvania, and demanded $100,000 in gold as reparations. When the residents failed to raise the ransom, McCausland burned the town. That autumn, General Grant, while attempting to surround Lee at Petersburg, sent orders to General Philip Sheridan, also in the Shenandoah, telling him to make the region "a barren waste . . . so that crows flying over it for the balance of this season will have to carry their provender with them." Sheridan reported that his cavalrymen had "destroyed over 2,000 barns filled with wheat, hay, and farming implements; over seventy mills filled with flour and wheat; have driven in front of the army over 4,000 head of stock, and have killed and issued to the troops not less than 3,000 sheep." Sheridan assured Grant that "the Valley, from Winchester up to Staunton, ninety-two miles, will have little in it for man or beast."

Everywhere, Federal commanders stepped up their war against Confederate guerrillas who harassed the invading Northerners and had become ubiquitous since 1861. The most troublesome was Colonel John S. Mosby, leader of the 43rd Battalion, Virginia Cavalry. Since early 1863, Mosby had led mounted rangers in operations behind enemy lines. The raiders so dominated a portion of northern Virginia that the region became known as "Mosby's Confederacy," where no Federal rider, scout, sentry, or picket post was safe. Mosby's men disrupted communications, waylaid wagon trains, and captured unwary Federals by the score and sent them southward to prison. In 1864 the Federals came down hard on Mosby and his men. Because the Rebel rangers lived among civilians until called together for a specific operation, Grant ordered Sheridan to take the war to the people by burning crops, mills, and barns, and confiscating livestock. The policy enraged the Southerners, and the fighting was desperate whenever the cavalries of Mosby and Sheridan clashed, for no man on either side wished to become a prisoner. Wrote one Federal, "To be caught by Mosby's men then was almost certain death." Soldiers reported finding bullet-riddled bodies by the roadside and corpses dangling from trees. To the shirt of one dead guerrilla, Northerners pinned a note: "This will be the fate of Mosby and all his men." It was, wrote one New York cavalryman, "not a good time to be taken prisoner."

Indeed, in the new war of stern measures and harsh retaliation, the prisoners of war suffered perhaps more than anyone. In 1861 both armies paroled prisoners quickly and were generally

The Union locomotive at top was derailed by Confederates in Virginia. Bands of Southern guerrillas, including John Mosby's Partisan Rangers, preyed upon Yankee supply lines. General Jubal Early (above) used Mosby's men in an effort to counter the destruction wrought by Federal armies in the Shenandoah Valley.

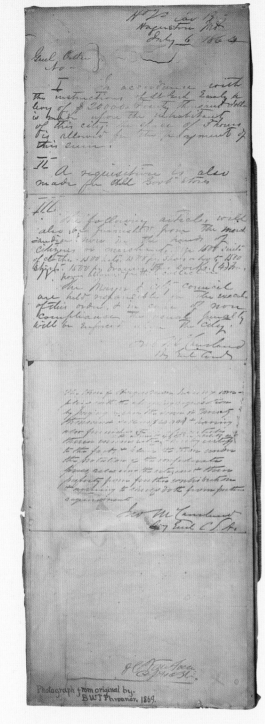

On July 6, 1864, Confederate General John McCausland made demands (listed above) on the residents of Hagerstown, Maryland. They were able to save their town from the torch by coming up with the $20,000 ransom.

humane in their treatment of captives. In July 1862 Richmond and Washington had established a cartel that allowed prisoners to return home upon parole, having promised not to fight again until they were exchanged—that is, until the bureaucrats and administrators agreed to swap the names of paroled prisoners. Once officially exchanged, and if they were healthy, they returned to their regiment and the war. The cartel worked well until mid-1863, when the Confederates, reacting to the increasing presence of black soldiers in the Union army, adopted a policy calling for the enslavement of captured black U.S. soldiers and the execution of their white officers. The Federals suspended the cartel and held Confederate prisoners hostage against the South's threat to enslave and execute captured Union soldiers.

Both sides hoped for a humane agreement, but both took liberties in the meantime. After the surrender of Vicksburg in July 1863, Grant paroled some 30,000 Confederate captives. Confederate authorities later deemed many of these paroles invalid, declared the men "exchanged," and returned them to duty. This happened again with wounded Confederate prisoners left at Gettysburg. But when Grant recaptured some of his Vicksburg prisoners months later at

Chambersburg, Pennsylvania (opposite), unlike Hagerstown, failed to escape McCausland's torch when residents could not pay $100,000 in gold. The shell of the Virginia Military Institute (left) shows the destruction wrought by Federals under General David Hunter (below). Captain Henry Dupont, who accompanied Hunter, described him as "dominated by prejudices." One Yankee cavalryman recalled that Hunter "chuckled with delight" as he watched the inferno.

Chattanooga and called attention to what he considered Southern duplicity, the Confederates denied any wrongdoing. Grant had felt all along that the cartel favored the Confederacy, and when he became general in chief in the spring of 1864 he insisted that "no distinction whatever will be made in the exchange between white and colored prisoners." But the South refused to budge on the issue of black troops until President Jefferson Davis partially relented and agreed to exchange only black soldiers who had enlisted as freemen, but not those who were escaped slaves. On this the South stood firm, so the Federal war department declared that the Union army would not exchange any prisoners unless they all could be exchanged equally. At this point, the only option was for both sides to keep large numbers of prisoners.

Stockades and prison pens sprang up all across the country. Warehouses, barns, and abandoned factories—often overrun with vermin—housed prisoners, as did stock yards, railroad depots, fairgrounds, empty city lots, even rural clearings. Overcrowding and exposure to the elements exacerbated the spread of disease, and inmates died by the thousands. At least 56,000 prisoners died in captivity during the war, and many thousands who survived the ordeal died later of diseases they contracted while in prison.

At Johnson's Island, Point Lookout, Fort Delaware, and other Northern prisons, Confederates shivered through the winter and died of disease in the summer. Those who survived the prison at Elmira, New York, forever afterward called it "Hellmira." The Federals freely admitted that they

The Union's Major General Philip H. Sheridan—shown above in a rare moment of relaxation in the summer of 1864—was hot-tempered, hyperactive, and ruthlessly determined to achieve victory, at any cost. A charismatic leader despite his diminutive stature, Sheridan displayed an uncanny ability to galvanize his troops in battle. "His influence on his men was like an electric shock," a subordinate recalled. "They simply believed he was going to win, and every man was determined to be on hand to see him do it." Sheridan's scourging of the Shenandoah Valley fostered a bitter campaign of retaliation and counterreprisals.

underfed their captives and deprived them of blankets and other necessary items, but claimed they did so only in retaliation for the poor treatment Union soldiers received in Southern prisons. Indeed, the Southern stockades at Florence, Salisbury, and elsewhere were at least as bad as the Northern prisons. The worst was Andersonville, in Georgia. With a planned capacity of 10,000 men, Andersonville held three and a half times that in the summer of 1864. The captors provided neither sufficient food nor shelter, and in just 14 months 13,000 men died of disease, starvation, and exposure. A Confederate surgeon who inspected the camp thought that "the haggard, distressed countenance of these miserable, complaining, dejected, living skeletons, formed a picture of helpless, hopeless misery, which it would be impossible to portray by [words or brush]." Indicative of the spirit of the times is a remark published by the *Atlanta Intelligencer* in August 1864: "During one of the intensely hot days of last week more than 300 sick and wounded Yankees died at Andersonville. We thank heaven for such blessings."

Davis declared that at a time when Confederate soldiers in the field suffered from hunger and supply shortages the South simply could not care for its prisoners. He accused Grant of knowing

this and cold-heartedly wishing to burden the South with caring for tens of thousands of prisoners in the hope that it would hasten the Confederacy's demise, regardless of how many prisoners died. Grant tacitly admitted as much. "It is hard on our men held in Southern prisons not to exchange them," he wrote, "but it is humanity to those left in the ranks to fight our battles."

Humanity was in short supply in America in 1864, as Richmond hospital administrator Pheobe Pember recognized. A special exchange had brought a group of prisoners, Union and Confederate, to Richmond in 1864, and Pember, who saw them, was deeply affected. "Can any pen or pencil do justice to those squalid pictures of famine and desolation?" she wrote. "Those gaunt, lank skeletons with the dried yellow flesh clinging to bones enlarged by dampness and exposure? Those pale, bluish lips and feverish eyes, glittering and weird when contrasted with the famine-stricken faces—that flitting, piteous, scared smile which greeted their fellow creatures, all will live forever before the mental vision that then witnessed it. When we review the past, it would seem that Christianity was but a name—that the Atonement had failed, and Christ had lived and died in vain."

In August 1864 hundreds of ragged captives (above, left) gather near a gate at the infamous Andersonville stockade to receive their meager rations. "Inside the camp death stalked on every hand," wrote a survivor, "the poor fellows rotted by inches." At war's end, Federal authorities arrested Andersonville's Swiss-born commandant, Captain Henry Wirz (above), and convicted him of war crimes. Wirz was hanged on November 10, 1865.

MOSBY'S CONFEDERACY

John S. Mosby's Partisan Rangers swoop down on a Yankee wagon train in the imaginative period engraving above that, despite its errors (most of Mosby's men carried pistols, not sabers), captures the essence of Mosby's tactics. "If you are going to fight," the famed Rebel raider, known as the "Gray Ghost," asserted, "then be the attacker." Though his 43rd Virginia Battalion rarely fielded more than 300 horsemen at a time, the band thwarted many times that number of Federals in fruitless pursuits and escort duties. The raider's zone of operations in northern Virginia's Loudoun and Fauquier counties was dubbed "Mosby's Confederacy."

THE GRAY GHOST

For a studio portrait taken in 1865, Colonel John Singleton Mosby (right) carried a sword—a weapon he had no use for in action. "My men were as little impressed by a body of cavalry charging them with sabres," he once stated, "as though they were armed with cornstalks." The former lawyer's fierce reputation belied his slight build—he weighed a mere 125 pounds. "There was nothing ferocious in his appearance," a Federal officer recalled, "but when in the saddle he was not a man one would care to meet singlehanded." One of Mosby's men thought the secret of his power was in his piercing blue eyes, noting that "when he spoke they flashed the punctuation of his sentences."

PURSUING A PHANTOM

Standing with fellow officers of the 13th New York Cavalry, Colonel Henry S. Gansevoort (above, center) launched frequent expeditions into "Mosby's Confederacy" from the Federal base of operations near Falls Church, Virginia. Educated at Princeton and Harvard Law School, Gansevoort was a first cousin of novelist Herman Melville and the grandson of a Revolutionary War general. The genteel New Yorker found Mosby's Rangers to be a formidable but elusive foe. "They fight with desperation when attacked," Gansevoort wrote, "but principally confine themselves to dashes here and there, and long pursuits of small bodies of our forces. The night does not know what the morning may disclose."

TAGGED AND INCARCERATED

A motley group of Confederate prisoners of war (above), wearing ill-fitting Federal overcoats issued by their captors and identification tags pinned to their shirts, stand in front of a barracks at Camp Douglas, Illinois. The third-largest military prison in the North, Camp Douglas, near Chicago, was initially so poorly guarded that Mayor Julian S. Rumey feared "the prisoners will break through and burn the city." In fact, the captives were more concerned with survival than escape. When this photograph was taken, in February 1862, there was only one surgeon on duty for about 7,000 prisoners, many of whom were in poor health.

BLEAK FUTURE

Late in the war, Union cavalrymen escort thousands of captured Confederate soldiers (right) to prison. After the collapse of the cartel in 1863, prisoners faced a bleak and uncertain future, since there was no longer a policy for paroling and exchanging captives. The numbers of prisons and prisoners escalated. At the Federals' Camp Douglas, for example, captives were quartered in 33 barracks that were built to house 6,000 men, but by December 1864 the prison population was double that. Overcrowding and the frigid Northern climate fostered the spread of disease. A Federal inspector admitted, "The mortality of the prisoners is quite large, attributed to their wretchedly broken-down condition."

THE RAGGED SURVIVORS

Recently freed from a Rebel prison, a weary contingent of Iowa volunteers (above) awaits transportation from New Orleans to the North. Made feeble by malnutrition and clad in tattered, lice-infested garments, most were too exhausted to celebrate. One survivor of Andersonville recalled that Union medical attendants "wept as children at the condition of their comrades, who had been into the mouth of Hell and returned."

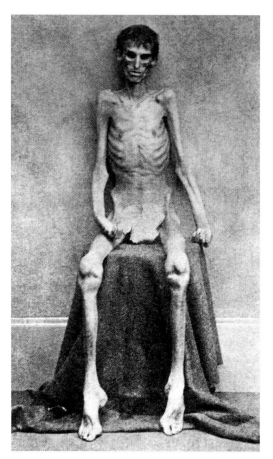

MAN'S INHUMANITY TO MAN

One of a series of horrifying images of former prisoners, the photograph at right, of a skeletal Federal soldier, fueled the cry for vengeance against Southern officers deemed responsible for such inhumanity. Eventually, Andersonville's commandant, Henry Wirz, became the symbolic focus of Northern outrage. But the shocking accounts of conditions in the Confederacy's prison pens left a legacy of bitterness that failed to dissipate with the passage of time.

MAKESHIFT PRISON

Confederate guards relax outside the ruins of a covered bridge (right) made into a prison for captured Yankees. Spanning the Pearl River at Jackson, Mississippi, the rickety structure was sketched by Colonel Thomas Clement Fletcher of the 31st Missouri, one of 400 captives who endured deplorable conditions on the bridge during the winter of 1862–63.

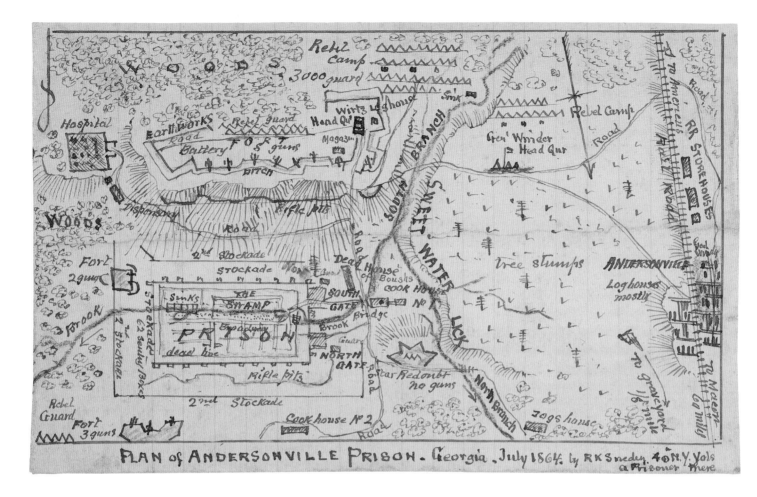

PLAN OF ANDERSONVILLE PRISON. Georgia. July 1864. by R K Sneedy 40 N.Y. Vols a Prisoner there

MAP OF HELL

This plan of Andersonville prison (left) shows the stockade as it appeared in July 1864. Robert K. Sneden, a soldier of the 40th New York who had been captured in Virginia on November 27, 1863, while serving as a topographical draughtsman, drew the map after his release. Among the first captives to be sent to the compound, Sneden survived the harsh conditions and was paroled in December 1864.

WHERE DISEASE FLOURISHED

In August 1864 a Macon, Georgia, photographer named Andrew Jackson Riddle made several images of the Andersonville stockade, including the view at right, which shows the camp's open latrine—located close to the prisoners' crude shelters and alongside the stream in which the inmates bathed and drew their water supply. "You could see numbers of men wading from knee to waist deep in the liquid, fetid filth," recalled prisoner Charles Hopkins of the First New Jersey. "Woe to him that had the slightest sore or abrasion of the skin which might come into contact with that polluted mass."

A GRIM TASK
Granted extra rations so they might be strong enough to carry out their grim task, Federal prisoners at Andersonville (left) inter the victims of hunger, disease, and exposure in a burial trench north of the stockade. In August 1864 the death rate exceeded 100 captives per day. "The wet weather for the past few days has been very hard on the sick men, and they are dying off rapidly," prisoner Eugene Forbes noted in his diary. "A dead man in rear of our tent this morning, and any number throughout the camp . . . The men are dying inside like rotten sheep."

Mourning

During the Civil War, thousands of families mourned the death of a loved one. People showed their bereavement with attire that symbolized their loss and by observing a ritualized period of mourning that might last months or even years.

THE RELICS OF LOSS

The death of a national hero sometimes prompted entire communities to express their grief. When Stonewall Jackson died, the ladies of Williamsburg, Virginia, showed their respect by wearing a mourning badge (inset, left). In late 1862 the famed Confederate cavalry leader Jeb Stuart lost his five-year-old daughter to disease, and a few months later his trusted comrade and friend, Major John Pelham, was killed in action. The cased ferrotype photograph (top left) shows Stuart and his wife in mourning clothes; the lock of hair might be their daughter's or Pelham's.

A TABLEAU OF GRIEF

The photograph at left shows symbolic mementos of General W. H. L. Wallace, a Federal division commander killed at the battle of Shiloh. Arranged in front of his home, in Ottawa, Illinois, are Wallace's portrait, his riderless horse, and the flag for which he died.

TOKEN OF REMEMBRANCE

A brooch containing two entwined locks of hair (above) was worn in remembrance of a fallen Confederate cavalryman. A woman in mourning would typically wear black clothing and a piece of jewelry that evoked her lost loved one. Some women dressed this way for more than two years.

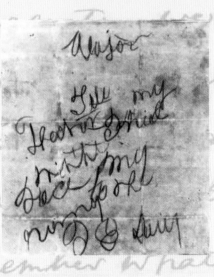

LAST MESSAGE

On July 2, 1863, Colonel Isaac E. Avery of the Sixth North Carolina was struck down by artillery fire as he led a Confederate brigade in the final charge on Gettysburg's Cemetery Ridge. With his life ebbing away, Avery scrawled a last message (left) to his subordinate, Major Samuel M. Tate: "Tell my father I died with my face to the enemy." Such relics of devotion and sacrifice were treasured and often displayed in the homes of families whose loved ones would never return.

MOURNING A HERO

Mourners (right) remember Stonewall Jackson beside his grave in Lexington, Virginia. The parklike landscaping and elaborate memorials typical of nineteenth-century cemeteries reminded the living of the deeds and ideals of those interred.

Referendum on Resolve

TWO DAYS AFTER independence day 1864, 15,000 Confederate soldiers crossed the Potomac River to invade Maryland. Led by General Jubal Early, the raiding force had been spurred northward by Robert E. Lee. Under siege by Ulysses S. Grant's troops at Petersburg, Lee saw that the only way he could hope to damage Union prospects was by dividing Grant's

A campaign lapel decoration (below), with a portrait of General George McClellan, strongly resembles a military medal. Relieved of command by President Lincoln in November 1862, McClellan was the Democratic Party's nominee to run against his former commander in chief in 1864.

attention. If Early could threaten Washington, Grant might be forced to weaken his lines in Virginia. On July 9, Early defeated a body of Federals at Monocacy, near Frederick, Maryland, and marched eastward on the capital of the United States. Grant did indeed detach and hurry troops to the defense of Washington, but Early, deciding not to test the strong fortifications around the city, withdrew, content with having given the Lincoln administration a good scare.

Early's raid sharply underscored the vast problems bedeviling Abraham Lincoln less than four months before he was to stand for reelection. Though the war campaigns of 1864 had been the bloodiest of the conflict, and the death toll continued to rise, the battles had not stopped Lee and other Confederates from doggedly resisting the Federal armies and denying the Union both Richmond and Atlanta. A war-weary North cried for progress, for some sign that victory was near and the immense sacrifice of life was not in vain. Instead, they received the appalling news that a Confederate army was threatening their national capital and that their president was calling for a half-million more troops. "I see no bright spot anywhere," wrote one New Yorker, "only humiliation and disaster." Abolitionist Wendell Phillips wrote, "Lincoln is doing twice as much today to break this Union as [Confederate President] Davis is," and he told Senator Charles Sumner, "We are paying thousands of lives and millions of dollars as penalty for having a timid, ignorant President." "Mr. Lincoln is already beaten," wrote Republican editor Horace Greeley of the *New York Tribune*. "He cannot be elected."

Lincoln himself expected defeat in the fall elections. "This morning, as for some days past," he wrote in late August, "it seems exceedingly probable that this Administration will not be re-elected. Then it will be my duty to so co-operate with the President elect, as to save the Union between the election and the inauguration; as he will have secured his election on such ground that he can not possibly save it afterwards." Most observers expected the new president to be Lincoln's old nemesis, General George B. McClellan. The Democrats had made the Young Napoleon their candidate and peace their platform. Clement Vallandigham, the antiwar "Peace

A month after Lincoln and his running mate, Andrew Johnson of Tennessee (above), were officially nominated in June 1864, Confederates threatened Washington but thought better of attacking the bristling ring of earthworks, including Fort Slemmer (top), that defended the capital city.

Democrat" convicted of crimes against the government and exiled a year earlier, was back and exerting great influence on Democratic Party policy. Vallandigham wrote the critical plank in the party's platform: "After four years of failure to restore the Union by the experiment of war . . . [we] demand that immediate efforts be made for a cessation of hostilities, with a view to an ultimate convention of the states, or other peaceable means, to the end that, at the earliest practicable moment, peace may be restored on the basis of the Federal Union." McClellan apparently endorsed the plank; he was quoted as saying, "If I am elected, I will recommend an immediate armistice and a call for a convention of all the states and insist upon exhausting all and every means to secure peace without further bloodshed."

Southerners, of course, were delighted. Confederate Vice President Alexander Stephens said it presented "the first ray of real light I have seen since the war began." What staunch Unionists objected to, meanwhile, was the Democrats' saying that peace was more important

Just five miles from the White House, Fort Stevens (above) was the northernmost of nearly 70 earthen fortifications protecting Washington. Salvos from Fort Stevens's 17 cannon and mortars stopped Jubal Early's Rebel offensive in July 1864. Abraham Lincoln and his wife visited the fort during the battle, and the president attracted Confederate fire when he climbed atop a parapet for a better view of the action. Lincoln was not hit, but Surgeon C. C .V. Crawford, of the 102nd Pennsylvania, was wounded at the president's side.

than union. After hundreds of thousands of Northern men had died, a settlement with the South that did not include union would mean that all those men had died in vain, a prospect that many Northerners could not accept. Still, Lincoln seemed unelectable. His own party, the Republicans, openly sought another candidate.

Once again, abolition emerged as a key issue. Lincoln had but two conditions for peace: restoration of the Union and the abolition of slavery. His enemies in the Democratic Party emphasized the latter in their campaign against him, declaring, "Tens of thousands of white men must yet bite the dust to allay the negro mania of the President." The Republicans urged him to abandon the abolitionist cause, but Lincoln, after wavering momentarily, realized he could not. The war, he wrote, "is & will be carried on, so long as I am President for the sole purpose of restoring the Union. But no human power can subdue this rebellion without using the Emancipation lever as I have done." What of the 130,000 black men already in Federal uniforms? he asked. They had been given freedom, and it had been promised to their brothers and sisters. To break that promise, Lincoln argued, would be the ruination of the Union cause. "All recruiting of colored men would instantly cease, and all colored men now in our service would instantly desert us. And rightfully too. Why should they give their lives for us, with full notice of our purpose to betray them? Abandon all the posts now possessed by black men, surrender all these advantages to the enemy, & we would be compelled to abandon the war in 3 weeks. I should be damned in fire & in eternity for so doing. The world shall know that I will keep my faith to friends & enemies, come what will." Privately, Lincoln believed his stand would cost him the election. "I am going to be beaten," he said, "and unless some great change takes place *badly* beaten."

That great change did come—and suddenly. On September 2, after months of maneuvering and thousands of casualties, Sherman took Atlanta. "Atlanta is ours, and fairly won," the general wired to Washington. The people of the North finally had their sign of progress. Militarily, the fall of the Southern railroad hub further isolated Virginia and the Carolinas from the rest of the Confederacy. Politically, Sherman's victory had an immediate effect on Lincoln's chances in the election. With ultimate victory now a distinct possibility, the Democrats' negotiated-peace platform looked far weaker than it had before Atlanta fell. McClellan realized this, and in accepting the Democratic nomination, to the chagrin of party leaders

The sketch at top, of Pennsylvania troops using paper ballots to cast their vote for president, is by war correspondent William Waud. Members of other regiments voted by choosing a white ball or black cube from the front of a box (above) and then slipping the token into the rear compartment. An officer periodically opened the box to count the results.

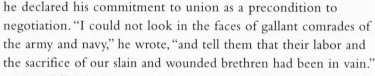

The six-foot-four Lincoln once commented that, while his rival for the presidency, George McClellan, was more handsome, "I am the longest." The successes of Farragut at Mobile Bay and Sherman in Atlanta, and the decisive actions and victories of Sheridan and his men in Virginia's Shenandoah Valley (above), led voters to reelect Lincoln. A newspaper cartoonist drew the portrait titled "Long Abraham Lincoln a Little Longer" (left) to commemorate the event.

he declared his commitment to union as a precondition to negotiation. "I could not look in the faces of gallant comrades of the army and navy," he wrote, "and tell them that their labor and the sacrifice of our slain and wounded brethren had been in vain."

McClellan had narrowed the gap between Lincoln and himself. Voters now had two Union candidates to choose from. One was committed to union and abolition, while the other cared little for the black man. Both had significant weaknesses. Lincoln was viewed as a poor administrator whose efforts to direct the war had cost the country much blood and money; McClellan's party included antiwar, pro-Southern Northern agitators known as "Copperheads." McClellan had endorsed a Copperhead in the Pennsylvania gubernatorial contest in 1863, and the Democratic candidate for vice president was Ohio congressman George Pendleton, a collaborator of Vallandigham's who had consistently opposed war measures in Congress. McClellan's association with these men turned many voters against him. The race looked as if it would be close, but as the campaign progressed, Little Mac received the worst possible news for his candidacy: Federal armies were winning the war.

In September and October, General Philip Sheridan fought Jubal Early in the Shenandoah Valley and beat him soundly. In battles at Winchester, Fisher's Hill, and Cedar Creek, Sheridan dealt Early's army—and the Confederacy—crippling blows. After Cedar Creek, just three weeks before the election, Early's army was so damaged and worn down that it could no longer

YOU TRIED TO RIDE THEM TWO HOSSES ON THE PENINSULA FOR TWO YEARS MAC BUT IT WOULDN'T WORK

LITTLE MAC (confidentially)—Curse them baulky Horses—I can't manage the Act no how. One threw me in Virginia, and the other is bound the wrong way.

PEACE.

WAR

LITTLE MAC, IN HIS GREAT TWO HORSE ACT, IN THE PRESIDENTIAL CANVASS OF 1864.

Union troops begin to camp in Atlanta's main square (above) in September 1864, two months before the presidential elections. The Federal victory over the key Southern city convinced many Northerners that Lincoln was handling the war successfully. As the political cartoon at top right suggests, some began to believe that McClellan and the so-called Peace Democrats were incapable of handling either war or peace.

defend the Shenandoah Valley, leaving Lee's position at Richmond and Petersburg vulnerable to attack.

So as November 8, Election Day, arrived, Lincoln appeared less inept as a war leader. He would also be helped by the voting laws in many states that permitted soldiers in the field to vote. For despite the Army of the Potomac's lingering affection for McClellan, and the western armies' indifference toward, even antipathy for, emancipation—and despite the fact that the troops had more to gain by an armistice than anyone—the voters in the ranks were in favor of seeing the job through to victory. The election became a referendum on resolve. "Seldom in history," wrote Ralph Waldo Emerson, "was so much staked on a popular vote, I suppose never in history."

The troops voted against McClellan. "Not that the soldiers dislike the man so much as the company he keeps," explained one man in uniform. "There are a good many soldiers who would vote for McClellan but they cannot go Vallandigham." So Lincoln was the favorite all around. He won slightly more than half the popular vote (about 55 percent of the roughly four million votes cast) and most—about 90 percent—of the 233 electoral votes. The numbers shocked observers. An American correspondent for a London newspaper declared himself "astonished" at the extent and depth of the Northerners' determination. They were, he thought, "earnest in a way the like of which the world never saw before, silently, calmly, but desperately in earnest."

With the charged election behind them, Northerners turned with equal earnestness to the grim business before them. The path ahead was now clear. As one Federal soldier wrote to his father, "This election has relieved us of the fire in the rear and now we can devote an undivided attention to the remnants of the Confederacy."

DEATH KNELL OF THE CONFEDERACY

The color sergeant of the Second Massachusetts Infantry stands on the steps of Atlanta's municipal courthouse (above). When Federals raised the Stars and Stripes over the building after occupying the city, one observer noted that "such a cheer went up as only a conquering army, flushed with victory, can give." Federal General William Sherman saw the victory as the start of a campaign that would sound the "death knell of the Southern Confederacy."

YANKEE CONVENIENCES

As Union comrades lounge about the ramparts of a captured Confederate fort (right), a soldier quietly reads in the mouth of a bombproof dugout. Contemplating the formidable cordon of defenses that ringed Atlanta 12 miles around, one Union soldier wrote, "It is astonishing to see what fortifications they had every side of the city. All in vain for them, but quite convenient now for us."

SHERMAN'S HAIRPINS

Before beginning his March to the Sea, Sherman ordered the destruction of Atlanta's transportation infrastructure. Carrying out the general's order that "the destruction be so thorough that not a rail or tie can be used again," a demolition squad (above) tears up a section of track in Atlanta's rail yard. The rails, after being heated red hot on a fire of burning ties and twisted out of shape, became known as "Sherman's Hairpins."

"HEAPS OF DESOLATION"

Amid the rubble of Atlanta's roundhouse (right), train crews pose on captured locomotives and freight cars. The devastation of Atlanta by Sherman and his troops was so complete that one Union officer claimed that "the crash of falling buildings and the change of strong walls and proud structures into heaps of desolation make a dreadful picture of the havoc of war." Wrote one Union private in a letter home: "I don't think any people will want to try and live there now."

POE'S PROJECT

Leaning against the breech of a 20-pounder Parrott gun at a Union fort in Atlanta, General Sherman (above, in the foreground at right) stands with members of his staff during the Federal occupation of the city. The Confederates left behind a ring of defensive points that stretched 12 miles around Atlanta, but this fort—a new one—was part of Sherman's attempt to contract the city's lines of defense. His chief engineer, Captain Orlando Poe (behind the cannon, fourth from left), directed the project.

PREEMPTIVE DEVASTATION

Not all of the devastation in and around Atlanta was the work of Sherman's wrecking crews. As General John Bell Hood's Confederates abandoned the city on the night of September 1, 1864, they torched an ordnance train loaded with explosives to prevent it from falling into Yankee hands. Scattered axles and wheels of obliterated boxcars, warped steel rails, and the leveled walls of a rolling mill (right) attest to the force of the resulting explosion.

FREE AT LAST
Recently freed by Lee's surrender to Grant at Appomattox, blacks await the mules that will tow their canal boat (left), loaded with all their worldly possessions, out of occupied Richmond. Even when the fighting was over, the torrent of refugees continued. This image is one of a series of Richmond images taken by photographer Alexander Gardner in April 1865.

Refugees

The Civil War uprooted hundreds of thousands of Southerners, black and white. Leaving their homes, they might escape the uncertainty of enemy occupation only to face another equally difficult ordeal: a tortuous journey full of hardship and danger.

"HARD ON ALL"
With their wagon loaded, a family (right) abandons its home as the war engulfs them. Said one Confederate, "It is hard on all; but to see the poor women with their children on one arm ... is enough to move the hardest heart."

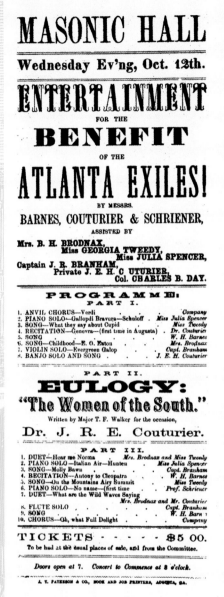

MASONIC HALL

Wednesday Ev'ng, Oct. 12th.

ENTERTAINMENT

FOR THE

BENEFIT

OF THE

ATLANTA EXILES!

BY MESSRS.

BARNES, COUTURIER & SCHRIENER,

ASSISTED BY

Mrs. B. H. BRODNAX,
Miss GEORGIA TWEEDY,
Miss JULIA SPENCER,
Captain J. R. BRANHAM,
Private J. E. H. COUTURIER,
Col. CHARLES B. DAY.

PROGRAMME:

PART I.

1. ANVIL CHORUS—Verdi . . . . . Company
2. PIANO SOLO—Gallopdi Bravura—Schuloff . Miss Julia Spencer
3. SONG—What they say about Cupid . . Miss Tweedy
4. RECITATION—Geneva—(first time in Augusta) . Dr. Couturier
5. SONG . . . . W. H. Barnes
6. SONG—Childhood—E. O. Eaton . . . Mrs. Brodnax
7. VIOLIN SOLO—Evergreen Galop . . . Capt. Branham
8. BANJO SOLO AND SONG . . . J. E. H. Couturier

PART II.

EULOGY:

"The Women of the South."

Written by Major T. F. Walker for the occasion,

Dr. J. R. E. Couturier.

PART III.

1. DUET—Hear me Norma . . Mrs. Brodnax and Miss Tweedy
2. PIANO SOLO—Italian Air—Hunten . Miss Julia Spencer
3. SONG—Molly Bawn . . . . . Capt. Branham
4. RECITATION—Antony to Cleopatra . . W. H. Barnes
5. SONG—On the Mountains Airy Summit . Miss Tweedy
6. PIANO SOLO—No name—(first time . Prof. Schrener
7. DUET—What are the Wild Waves Saying .
Mrs. Brodnax and Mr. Couturier
8. FLUTE SOLO . . . . . . Capt. Branham
9. SONG . . . . W. H. Barn..
10. CHORUS—Oh, what Full Delight . . . Company

TICKETS - - - - $5 00.

To be had at the usual places of sale, and from the Committee.

Doors open at 7. Concert to Commence at 8 o'clock.

A. T. PATERSON & CO., BOOK AND JOB PRINTERS, AUGUSTA, GA.

FEW OPTIONS

Southern blacks had little say in where they went. Many were forced to remain on their plantation, some fled with masters deeper into Southern territory, others were simply abandoned. Many, like the family at left, escaped to freedom but were disillusioned by the reception they received. Federal soldiers could rarely supply them with sufficient food, and frequently handled them roughly.

"A TERRIBLE THING"

As fires rage, fulfilling Sherman's promise to "make Georgia howl," panicked Southerners (left), clutching a few possessions and driving some livestock before them, attempt to flee the destruction. Strikes against civilians were intended to crush the spirit of the people who supported the Confederate war effort. One of Sherman's aides commented, "It is a terrible thing to see the terror and grief of these women and children."

RARE WELCOME SIGN

The handbill above, which circulated in Augusta, Georgia, shows that refugees were occasionally welcomed. Proceeds from the night of lively music and dramatic readings went to benefit exiles from recently fallen Atlanta. Refugees often put more strain on already depleted resources and were usually not so heartily supported.

PERMITTED TO TRAVEL

Permits were frequently needed to travel in the South. The one at right gave its bearer permission to journey from Jackson, Mississippi, to Charleston, South Carolina. The traveler promised not "to communicate . . . for publication any fact ascertained, which, if known to the enemy, might be injurious to the Confederate States of America."

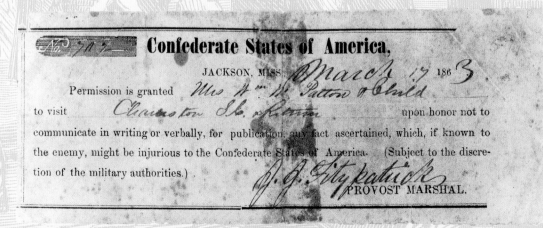

Confederate States of America,

JACKSON, MISS. *March 17* 186*3*

Permission is granted *Mrs. Wm. W. Patton & Child*

to visit *Charleston S.C. Home* upon honor not to communicate in writing or verbally, for publication any fact ascertained, which, if known to the enemy, might be injurious to the Confederate States of America. (Subject to the discretion of the military authorities.)

J. B. Fitzpatrick
PROVOST MARSHAL.

The South at Bay

"WITHOUT SOME INCREASE of our strength," Robert E. Lee had written to the Confederate war department in the summer of 1864, "I cannot see how we are to escape the natural military consequences of the enemy's numerical superiority." By the end of autumn, with Grant still bearing down at Petersburg, Lincoln reelected to office, Atlanta fallen, and

A Federal soldier fashioned the torch below from wood splints and hemp during the burning of Columbia, South Carolina, on February 17, 1865. His commander, General William T. Sherman, asserted, "I have never shed any tears over the event, because I believe that it hastened what we all fought for, the end of the war."

Confederate resources dwindling, the chances of the South escaping those consequences looked even more remote. "Where is this to end?" wrote one Confederate general. "No money in the treasury—no food to feed General Lee's army—no troops to oppose General Sherman. . . . Is the cause really hopeless?" The answer coming from Tennessee and Virginia—and Georgia, the Carolinas, Petersburg, and practically everywhere else the war was being waged—was yes.

After losing Atlanta, General John B. Hood regrouped his army and devised a plan to defeat William T. Sherman and reclaim Confederate fortunes in the West. He would ignore the Union armies in Georgia and march northward, deep into Sherman's rear army, and sever the Federal supply line there. He would then defeat the Union armies in Tennessee and Kentucky, and move on to Virginia to help Lee defeat Grant. All this Hood intended to do with what remained— just 40,000 men—of the once-proud Army of Tennessee and the tens of thousands of volunteers he hoped to enlist en route. President Jefferson Davis encouraged him.

The Confederate general entered Tennessee in the last week of November and advanced on the entrenched Federals on the Harpeth River near Franklin. Hood, known as a hard, rather than smart, fighter, ordered a frontal assault on the Federal position. His corps commanders protested, Hood overruled them, and 22,000 men went forward on November 30. The fighting was desperate and continued long after the sun went down. During the night, the Federals withdrew to Nashville. But Hood's victory was a Pyrrhic one: He had lost 7,000 men—three times the Federal loss; 12 Confederate generals had been wounded, six mortally; and more than 50 regimental commanders were casualties. Hood had nearly destroyed his own army. Yet he was not finished. Though outnumbered (the hoped-for recruits were nowhere to be found), Hood followed the Federals to Nashville, tempting fate. The Union commander there, General George Thomas, had twice as many men as Hood, and on December 15 and 16 Thomas attacked. Hood's army fought gamely until the second day, when it could resist no more and promptly fell apart. For two weeks the Southerners, now a fragmented, disorganized mass, streamed southward into Mississippi, where Hood could collect only about half of the men he had a month earlier. In mid-January Hood resigned.

In his annual message to Congress the previous December, Lincoln had tried to show Southerners, especially those who were not yet convinced of the hopelessness of their cause, what they were up against. He noted that the U.S. Navy, with 671 ships, was the largest in the world, that the North's industrial capacity continued to grow, and that crop harvests and exports were at record highs. Undoubtedly addressing Southern readers, Lincoln declared that "material resources are now more complete and abundant than ever. . . . we have *more* men *now* than we had when the war *began*. . . . We are *gaining* strength, and may, if need be, maintain the contest indefinitely."

Federal commanders, meanwhile, were seeing to it that there would be no such need. Just before Hood moved north to cut Sherman's supply line, the Ohio general had abandoned his ties to the rear and embarked on one of the more spectacular and controversial movements of the war. Sherman's "March to the Sea" involved 62,000 Federals tearing a swath of destruction across the state of Georgia. After leaving Atlanta in flames, they headed for Savannah, plundering and burning as they went. "We are not only fighting hostile armies," Sherman wrote, "but a hostile people, and must make old and young, rich and poor, feel the hard hand of war." The

To watch the fighting of December 15, 1864, Federal soldiers at Nashville (top) cluster around the casement—a covered position for artillery—of a fort overlooking the Nashville & Decatur Railroad. In two days of fighting, the army of General George Thomas (inset, right) routed the forces of Confederate commander John Bell Hood (left).

371

THE PEACE COMMISSION.
Flying to ABRAHAM'S BOSOM.

Federals encountered little resistance; even the 10,000 defenders of Savannah fled without a fight. On December 22, 1864, Sherman telegraphed Lincoln, "I beg to present you, as a Christmas gift, the City of Savannah, with 150 heavy guns . . . & about 25,000 bales of cotton."

Roughly 230 miles north, Federals under General Ben Butler sought to close the last remaining port open to blockade runners: Wilmington, North Carolina. Fort Fisher, an enormous coastal fortification at the mouth of the Cape Fear River, had long kept Wilmington in business, and Butler schemed to knock out the fort. He floated a hulk ship packed with 215 tons of gunpowder up to the fort and detonated the charges. The spectacular explosion, on Christmas Day, caused almost no damage, so three weeks later more than 6,500 Federal troops—soldiers, sailors, and marines—stormed the fort and were successful. The fall of Fort Fisher closed Wilmington and marked a triumph for the U.S. Navy. The Confederacy was now isolated.

Faced with this fact, Confederate authorities approached the Lincoln administration about the possibility of a negotiated peace. Confederate Vice President Alexander Stephens and two other commissioners met with Lincoln on February 3 aboard the steamer River Queen in Hampton Roads, Virginia. In the four-hour meeting, Lincoln insisted that any settlement include three conditions: union, emancipation, and no armistice until the agreement was executed. If the Confederates would simply cease fighting immediately, however, they would be offered lenient surrender terms and possibly even be compensated for slaves lost to emancipation. The Confederates balked, and the war went on.

On February 1, 1865, Sherman and 60,000 men left Savannah for the heart of secession, Columbia. "The truth is," he wrote General Henry Halleck, "the whole army is burning with an insatiable desire to wreak vengeance upon South Carolina. I almost tremble at her fate, but feel that she deserves all that seems to be in store for her." And suffer the Palmetto State did. "In Georgia few houses were burned," recalled a Federal officer, "[in South Carolina] few escaped." Bypassing Charleston, the invaders reached Columbia on February 17. Sherman did not order the state capital burned, but it burned anyway. Fires were set by citizens fleeing the "Yankee hordes" and by drunken Federal soldiers; high winds fanned the flames until Columbia was ashes. It was a heavy blow to Southern morale. Wrote one Carolinian: "All is gloom. . . . The power to do has left us. To fight longer seems madness."

Many in Lee's army felt the same way. Since the previous summer they had been defending the Richmond-Petersburg line from Grant's siege. The men existed in a world of muddy trenches, dugouts, sharpshooters' bullets, steady bombardment, and unrelenting discomfort. The army was very nearly destitute; some were literally starving. "If some change is not made and

The end of 1864 and the beginning of 1865 brought a series of disasters to the Confederacy. A photograph taken from Winstead Hill (opposite, above), south of Franklin, Tennessee, shows the open ground traversed by attacking Confederates during their calamitous assault on November 30. On January 15, a Union fleet, shown above in a painting by Xanthus Smith, bombarded the Rebel defenses at the mouth of the Cape Fear River in North Carolina, part of a combined army-navy operation to close the Confederacy's last usable seaport at Wilmington. Confederate efforts to negotiate peace in February 1865 were ridiculed in a Northern political cartoon (opposite).

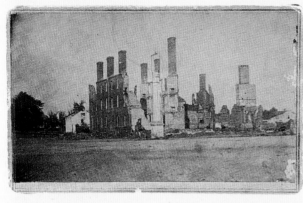

The three photographs above show the destruction wrought in Columbia, South Carolina, by Federals under General Sherman. They were taken by a local photographer who lost everything but his camera. Official military photographer George N. Barnard accompanied Sherman on his campaigns and took the fourth image (above right), also of Columbia.

the commissary department reorganized," Lee wrote to the war department, "I apprehend dire results. The physical strength of the men, if their courage survives, must fail under this treatment." "There are a good many of us," a Marylander wrote, "who believe this shooting match has been carried on long enough. A government that has run out of rations can't expect to do much more fighting, and to keep on in a reckless and wanton expenditure of human life." Inevitably, the pervading sense of futility began to chip away at the soldiers' resolve. "Hundreds of men are deserting nightly," Lee declared, predicting that the mass exodus would "bring us calamity." In a five-week period in February and March 1865 nearly 3,000 of Lee's men—about a tenth of his force—walked off. Most were from North Carolina, men who were desperate to get home and protect their families from the advancing Northern armies.

It was during this crisis that Lee was elevated to supreme commander of all the Confederate forces. The move was a gesture more than a practical step, for with the Confederacy collapsing all around him, the general could do little. Still, he welcomed the opportunity to try. "If I can relieve you from a portion of the constant labor and anxiety which presses upon you, and maintain a harmonious action between the great armies," he wrote to President Davis, "I shall be more than compensated for the addition to my present burdens."

Privately, however, Lee had no illusions about what lay ahead, and he knew the end would come soon; the bright hopes of 1862 and 1863 were extinguished. Lee knew he had done everything he could, and that his men had succeeded in trying whatever he asked of them, but he knew as well that many in Richmond lacked the selfless patriotism that their experiment in self-government demanded. He fumed at the selfishness and irresponsibility in Richmond. "I have been up to see Congress," he told a friend, "and they do not seem to be able to do anything except eat peanuts and chew tobacco, while my army is starving." When a legislator told him to "cheer up, General," because he and his colleagues had passed a bill to raise more troops, Lee responded grimly, "Yes, passing resolutions is kindly meant, but getting the men is another matter." Perhaps the result was inevitable. "When this war began," he told his son, "I was opposed to it, bitterly opposed to it, and I told these people that unless every man should do his whole duty, they would repent it; and now they will repent it."

Embrasures and rows of sharpened stakes (top) guard the massive walls of Fort Harrison, a key Confederate redoubt in the outer lines of Richmond's eastern defenses. Federal troops under General Edward O. C. Ord captured the fort on September 28, 1864. In February 1865, when Sherman began his march through the Carolinas, General P .G. T. Beauregard (inset) was placed in command of all Confederate forces in South Carolina.

NASHVILLE

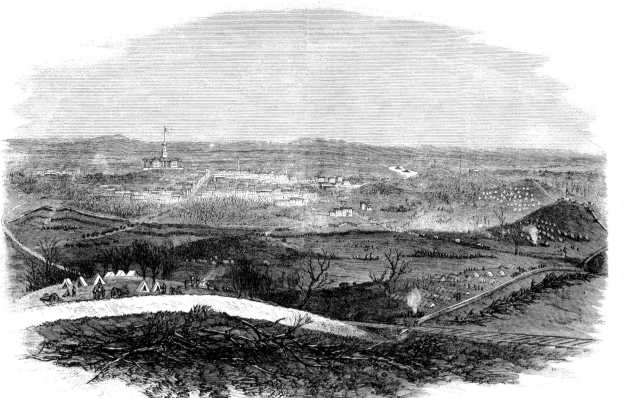

WELL-GUARDED BASTION

Camps of Federal troops dot the hilltops surrounding Nashville (left) in this 1865 newspaper engraving. The view, looking north, shows Federal gunboats anchored in the distant Cumberland River and the double line of earthworks that circled the city. Nashville's formidable defenses were never challenged. When the Army of Tennessee approached the city in December 1864, commander John Bell Hood chose not to attack with his weakened force of 25,000 men. The Federal counteroffensive on December 15 crushed Hood's forces and ended Confederate attempts to recapture the city.

ARTILLERY POST

Protected by sheet iron and layers of massive wooden timbers, a Federal casement (right) guards Nashville's eastern approaches near the Nolensville and Franklin & Columbia Turnpikes. During their two-and-a-half-year occupation of the city, Federal engineers constructed a 10-mile-long network of fortifications to protect the city from a possible Rebel attack. Brigadier General Z. B. Tower, the Federal Inspector of Fortifications, complained that many of Nashville's defenses were incomplete due to the "uncommon mortality" of the black laborers hired to perform the work.

AWAITING NEWS OF THE BATTLE

Huddled against the cold, Federal infantrymen man the trenches in the outer line of Nashville's defenses in this photograph taken on December 16, 1864. A ditch lined with sharpened stakes, called a fraise, and an abatis—felled trees arranged to form a barrier against attacking infantry— are visible in front of the earthworks. Rough, temporary board shelters, dubbed "shebangs" by the soldiers, clutter the area immediately behind the earthworks. A wagon train, parked in the field in front of the works, indicates preparations to join in the pursuit of Hood's beaten Confederates.

OCCUPIED REBEL STATEHOUSE

In the earthworks surrounding the Tennessee statehouse at Nashville, Federal gunners (above) man two formidable 30-pounder Parrott rifles. Engineers under Brigadier General James S. Morton fortified the capitol hill because of its excellent command of the city. The defenses consisted of earth parapets and stockades around the capitol grounds large enough to mount 15 guns and allow room for a regiment of infantry. The heavy guns never fired a shot in anger, and in 1865 the unsightly stockade was removed at the request of the Unionist state legislature.

IMPROVISED DIVISION

Soldiers of the Nashville garrison (right), possibly men of the quarter-master's division, sit in their camps in this December 1864 photograph taken during the Battle of Nashville. Under Federal occupation, the city became a major supply depot for the Union armies fighting in Tennessee and Georgia. When Hood's army threatened the city, Colonel James L. Donaldson's quartermaster's division, a force composed of quarter-master corps clerks and employees, was armed and sent to man part of the city's defenses. The unit was not engaged and remained behind when Major General George Thomas's forces departed to pursue the retreating Rebels.

A UNIFIED COMMAND

William Tecumseh Sherman (center) sits flanked by six of his senior subordinates: (from left) Major Generals Oliver O. Howard, John A. Logan, William B. Hazen, Jefferson C. Davis, Henry W. Slocum, and Joseph A. Mower. Of the efficiency and unity of his command, Sherman wrote, "It is impossible to conceive a march involving more labor and exposure, yet I cannot recall an instance of bad temper by the way, or hearing an expression of doubt as to our perfect success in the end. I believe that this cheerfulness and harmony of action reflects upon all concerned quite as much real honor and fame as 'battles gained' or 'cities won.' "

MAKING GEORGIA HOWL

A Federal infantryman, assisted by a sword-wielding cavalry trooper, attempts to subdue a pig as foragers run amok on a Georgia plantation in this engraving (left) by war correspondent James E. Taylor. In the background, other Yankees drive away livestock and burn buildings and a massive cotton-bale press. A clergyman's daughter described the looting of her family plantation and the "forty or fifty men in the pantry, flying hither and thither, ripping open the safe with their swords and breaking open the crockery cupboards. . . . [The Federals then] flew around the house tearing open boxes, everything that was closed." Worse than the foraging parties were the dreaded "bummers," gangs of renegade soldiers who hung around the flanks of Sherman's army and preyed on the defenseless civilian population along the line of march.

WRECKING THE RAILS

Soldiers of Sherman's army systematically wreck a section of a Southern railroad (above) while an officer watches through his telescope as a distant cavalry party burns a wagon bridge. A hardworking division could destroy more than 10 miles of track in a day. The wooden ties, recalled a Federal soldier, "would be gathered and piled up crosswise to a height of four feet with the rails placed on top. When the ties were fired the rails would become red hot and could be twisted and destroyed."

DEATH OF A REBEL RAM

In the woodprint at right, the Confederate ironclad CSS *Savannah* explodes shortly before dawn on December 21, 1865. When Federal troops under Brigadier General John W. Geary entered Savannah, the Rebel ram, anchored in the Savannah River, fired several shots before being set afire by her own crew to keep her from falling into enemy hands. Confederate authorities also burned several smaller gunboats and laid waste to the nearby navy yard.

SHERMAN'S MARCHERS

This late-war photograph (opposite) depicts veteran soldiers of the 17th Ohio Infantry Regiment, part of General Jefferson C. Davis's corps. Organized in 1861, the 17th served in both the Army of the Ohio and the Army of the Cumberland, and fought in nearly every major engagement in Tennessee, Georgia, and North Carolina. Two hundred thirty-two of the regiment's officers and men died in battle or from battle wounds or disease by the time the 17th was mustered out of the service, in July 1865.

UNCLE SAM'S CHRISTMAS SURPRISE

A jubilant General Sherman, relieved that the Confederates had surrendered Savannah without a fight, dispatched news of the port's capture to President Lincoln in a brief telegram sent on December 22: "I beg to present to you as a Christmas gift the City of Savannah with 150 heavy guns & plenty of ammunition & also about 25,000 bales of cotton." A cartoonist sketched the incident—with Sherman stuffing the port of Savannah into a sleeping Uncle Sam's Christmas stocking (above)—for the January 14, 1865, issue of *Frank Leslie's Illustrated Newspaper*. With Savannah captured, Sherman ended his "March to the Sea" and turned his army toward the Carolinas.

PAPER-COLLAR SOLDIERS

Resplendent in their chasseur-style uniforms, a company of the 33rd New Jersey Infantry (right) stands at "rest." Formed in Newark, the 33rd, along with the rest of the 20th Corps, was transferred from the Army of the Potomac to Sherman's army in October 1863. When western troops derided the easterners—a more formal and disciplined group than the rest of Sherman's men—as "paper collar and white glove fellows," a 20th Corps veteran responded that his unit had "surpassed the Western Army as much in its fighting quality as it does in appearance, drill and discipline. It seems that the men can make a neat appearance on dress parade and fight well too."

AN ENGINEERING TRIUMPH

Photographed from the top of a Federal supply wagon, a party of horsemen (above) approaches the pontoon bridge at Wilcox's Landing on the James River. At 4:00 p.m. on June 15, 1864, the engineer battalion under Captain George H. Mendell began the task of bridging the half-mile wide river. Working against a strong tidal current, Mendell's 450 bridge builders floated 101 heavy wooden pontoons into place. To help withstand the current, the structure was lashed to transport schooners moored above and below the bridge. By 11:00 p.m., the flooring was laid and the bridge complete. Mendell proudly reported that "the greater part of the infantry and artillery, all the wagon trains, and droves of beef-cattle of the army passed this bridge safely and without interruption."

THE RAILROAD ARTERY

Locomotives of the U.S. Military Railroads pass the conical Sibley tents of a Federal camp (left) flanking the rail line at City Point, Virginia. Located at the confluence of the Appomattox and James Rivers, City Point became the principal supply base for Grant's operations around Petersburg. Workers of the 2,000-man U.S. Military Railroads Construction Corps repaired the City Point Railroad and laid nearly 21 miles of new track to connect it with depots near the front lines. At the landing, the corps built an extensive complex of repair shops, water tanks, and locomotive sheds. To satisfy the army's demand for rail transport, a fleet of steamers, tugboats, and barges delivered two dozen engines and more than 275 rail cars to City Point. Barges were fitted with rails to ship fully loaded boxcars. At City Point, a specially designed loading dock allowed the cars to be rolled from the ship directly onto rail lines on the pier.

MASTERS OF SIEGE CRAFT
The army assigned engineer officers to oversee the construction of field fortifications, roads, and bridges. In the trench fighting at Petersburg, staff engineers of the Army of the Potomac (above) coordinated their efforts to ring the Rebel city with a massive system of trenches, siege batteries, protected roads, and bombproof shelters. During the brutal battles of Grant's overland campaign, the rapid construction of field works became crucial, and staff engineers played an important role in the planning of rifle pits and defensive lines.

INGENIOUS DEFENSES
Gabion revetments—wattle cylinders filled with stone and earth (left)—line the traverses and parapets of Fort Sedgwick, a Federal fortification on the Jerusalem Plank Road southeast of Petersburg. The traverses were earthwork barriers constructed at right angles to a trench line to protect soldiers from enfilading fire. A fraise and brushwood abatis, obstacles to attacking infantry, are visible beyond the ditch that surrounds the outer walls. Earthworks like Fort Sedgwick could withstand artillery bombardments that would shatter walls of brick or stone.

HARDTACK MOUNTAIN

Men of the U.S. Army Quartermaster's Corps stand atop two giant stacks of hardtack boxes (left) at a depot near City Point. Hard tack—flour-and-water crackers—was one of the main field rations of the Federal army. The large, wood-hooped barrels piled in the foreground contain either salt pork or beef, the other primary field ration. City Point's vast storage warehouses maintained a 30-days' supply of food at all times. Each day, tons of supplies—from shoes to artillery projectiles—were transported to the army in the field by hand, wagon, or rail. The ability of the Federal authorities to deliver such masses of matériel proved to be a vital factor in the Union's ultimate victory.

FORT HELL

A warren of bombproofs, traverses, and trenches clutter the interior of Federal Fort Sedgwick in this 1865 photograph (left). One of 41 such earthwork strongholds located in the inner and outer rings of the Federal siege works at Petersburg, the fort formed the pivot point where the Union lines shifted from north-south to east-west. As a result, Fort Sedgwick came under constant artillery bombardment and rifle fire. So severe was the shelling that soldiers quickly dubbed the post "Fort Hell" and assigned the name "Fort Damnation" to nearby Rebel Fort Mahone. Duty in the trenches in the hot Virginia summer was arduous in the extreme. A soldier from New Hampshire recalled how the men suffered "tortures from the fierce heat and the swarms of flies that seemed to be determined to devour them."

A MONSTER GUN

Colonel Henry L. Abbott (in high boots, right), commander of the First Connecticut Heavy Artillery, stands in front of the "Dictator," the largest of the Federal guns operated against Petersburg. Work crews laid a special narrow-gauge rail line to move the 17,000-pound weapon into its firing position northeast of the beleaguered city. The Dictator went into action on July 9, 1864, lobbing its 200-pound shells a distance of more than two and a half miles.

NAPOLEON IN BRONZE

On the docks at City Point (below), a soldier of the U.S. Colored Troops stands guard over a line of light 12-pounder "Napoleon" howitzers, limbers, and caissons. The Napoleons, named for their prototype, developed in France under Emperor Napoleon III, were massive smoothbores that fired a four-and-a-half-inch round projectile. Introduced in 1861, the bronze 12-pounders soon became the workhorses for both the Federal and Confederate artillery.

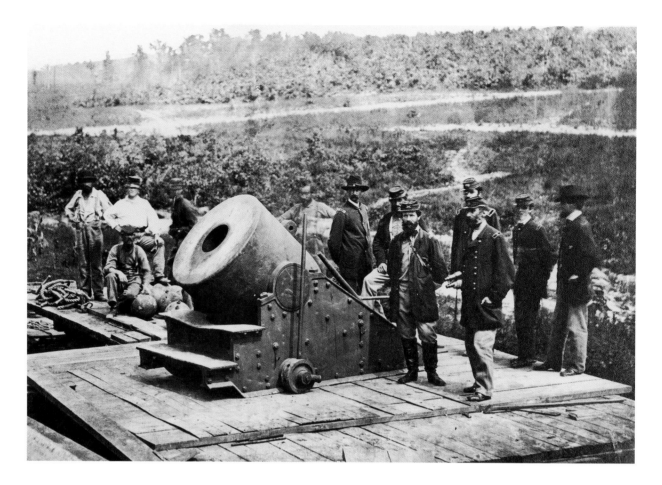

A DEADLY STOCKPILE

Gunners (opposite) of the First Connecticut Heavy Artillery stand around the entrance to the magazine at Fort Brady, a fortification on the north bank of the James River near Dutch Gap. Used to house powder and projectiles for the fort's heavy siege guns, the magazine was protected from enemy fire by layers of timbers and cut logs covered by more than 10 feet of packed earth. Soldiers entered the double-chambered magazine, in the center of Fort Brady, by a central corridor.

UNDERGROUND COMMAND POST

Federal soldiers (above) lounge at the entrance to the bombproof that was dug under
the Pulpit Battery, a stronghold at the northern end of Fort Fisher, formerly a Confederate
post. The Confederates removed the battery's guns and sealed the embrasures to provide
sheltered headquarters for the fort's commanding officer, Colonel William Lamb. Fort Fisher
was stormed by men of the Federal 10th Corps in fierce hand-to-hand fighting that left
Colonel Lamb, after leading a desperate counterattack by men drawn from the fort's improvised hospital, severely wounded. A Yankee sailor who viewed the scene after the battle wrote
that "if hell is what it is said to be, then the interior of Fort Fisher is a fair comparison."

YALE GENERAL

Major General Alfred Howe Terry (right, center) sits amid his staff beneath the headquarters flag of the Federal 10th Corps. In February 1865, Terry led the corps in the joint army-navy operation that captured Fort Fisher and closed the port of Wilmington. A Yale-educated lawyer, Terry rose from the rank of colonel in 1861 to command an army corps by spring of 1864. Widely viewed as one of the army's finest volunteer officers, Terry was awarded two brevets and received the official thanks of Congress for his capture of Fort Fisher.

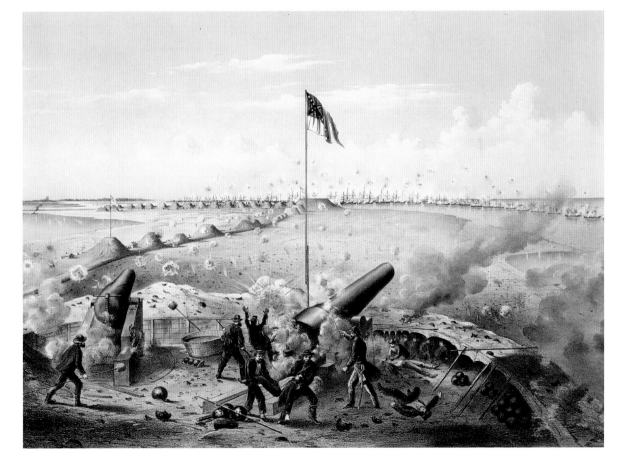

AN IRON HAIL

Exploding Federal shells decimate Rebel gun crews (left) inside the Mound Battery, a stronghold at the southern end of Fort Fisher, the Rebel bastion guarding Wilmington, North Carolina. A fleet of 150 ships under Rear Admiral David Porter bombarded the Confederate works in preparation for a landing by more than 6,500 Federal troops. Fort Fisher's commanding officer, Colonel William Lamb, wrote that "all day and night on the 13th and 14th of January the navy continued its ceaseless torment . . . along the parapet, scattering shrapnel in the darkness. We could scarcely gather up and bury our dead without fresh casualties."

CRATER CHARGE

A column of soldiers of the 23rd U.S. Colored Troops (left) rushes toward the huge crater that was the result of a mine explosion on July 30. General Edward Ferrero's Division of black troops attacked in support of General James Ledlie's Division when the white soldiers stalled in the gaping hole and surrounding debris-filled trenches. Widespread confusion gave the Confederates time to surround the crater and block the Federals inside it.

The Crater

In July 1864, men of the 48th Pennsylvania Infantry dug a 500-foot tunnel under a Confederate redan near Petersburg. On July 30 they exploded a mine that obliterated a Rebel battery. Federal troops charged into the hole left by the explosion, becoming easy targets for Confederate counterattackers.

A FIGHTING GENERAL

Confederate Brigadier General William Mahone (left), dubbed "Little Billy," graduated from the Virginia Military Institute and by 1861 was president of the Norfolk & Petersburg Railroad. Mahone's competence and dash at the Crater earned him a battlefield commission to Major General.

MORTAR PROTECTION

Empty platforms for light mortars line the bottom of a lunette—a crescent-shaped earthwork for artillery (left)—in this post-war photograph. The battery provided covering fire for troops attacking toward the Crater. Moments after the mine was exploded, Federal batteries poured heavy fire into the Confederate lines. The mortars were manned by gunners of the First Connecticut Heavy Artillery.

OUT OF THE CRATER

The shovel below was recovered from the Crater in the years following the battle. The large number of bullet holes, each the size of a .58-caliber rifle bullet, suggest the shovel was used for target practice or to draw the fire of Federal sharpshooters.

A BROTHER'S TRIBUTE

The grave marker above, improvised from a supply crate, identified the grave of Lieutenant George L. Vaughn of the 48th Georgia Infantry, who fell in the fighting at the Crater on July 30, 1864. The lieutenant's brother carved the headboard shortly after the battle.

THE YANKEE MINERS

A miner of the 48th Pennsylvania digs toward Rebel lines in this wartime newspaper engraving (left). Behind him, soldiers fill cracker boxes with some of the 18,000 cubic feet of earth that had to be removed from the 500-foot tunnel. The spoil had to be disposed of out of view of Rebel sentries.

Full Cycle

SATURDAY, MARCH 4, 1865, brought rain and high winds to Washington, D.C., where the reelected president of the United States was to take the oath of office. Four years earlier, Abraham Lincoln had stood on the same spot and alluded to the storm ahead. Now, after four years of bloodshed, he rose to speak just as the sun, which according to one observer

An illuminated broadside (below), published soon after Lincoln's second inaugural address, delivered on March 4, 1865, reproduced the president's magnanimous words. The vignettes include depictions of his Illinois home, his delivery of the speech, and the White House.

From
Abraham Lincoln's Second Inaugural Address
March 4, 1865

...With malice toward none; with charity for all; with firmness in the right, as God gives us to see the right, let us strive on to finish the work we are in; ...to do all which may achieve and cherish a just and lasting peace among ourselves, and with all nations.

had been obscured all day, "burst forth . . . and flooded the spectacle with glory and with light." "Did you notice that sunburst?" Lincoln later asked a friend. "It made my heart jump."

The reelected president spoke just 701 words. He mentioned how both political parties "deprecated war; but one of them would make war rather than let the nation survive; and the other would accept war rather than let it perish." He observed that Northerners and Southerners "pray to the same God; and each invokes His aid against the other. It may seem strange that any men should dare to ask a just God's assistance in wringing their bread from the sweat of other men's faces; but let us judge not that we be not judged. The prayers of both could not be answered; that of neither has been answered fully." He revealed his vision of what lay ahead. "Fondly do we hope—fervently do we pray—that this mighty scourge of war may speedily pass away. . . . With malice toward none; with charity for all; with firmness in the right, as God gives us to see the right, let us strive on to finish the work we are in; to bind up the nation's wounds; to care for him who shall have borne the battle, and for his widow, and his orphan—to do all which may achieve and cherish a just and lasting peace, among ourselves, and with all nations."

Lincoln's peace would be gentle, as free as possible from recriminations. But first that peace must be won, and it was to this that Ulysses S. Grant was applying himself in Virginia. The Federal commander balanced his thrusts at the Confederate line, striking at Petersburg and then toward Richmond, forcing Lee to spread his dwindling manpower across a 37-mile front. Grant took great advantage of his numerical superiority (he had 110,000 men, almost twice as many as Lee), relentlessly extending his lines westward, south of Petersburg, cutting the railroads and forcing Lee to stretch himself ever thinner.

In late March, seeing that time was running out, Lee authorized a desperate, preemptive surprise attack on Grant's line at Fort Stedman. Early success in the predawn hours of March 25 brought the Confederates little, however, and Federal reinforcements prevented a victory. Grant kept the pressure on, sending General Philip Sheridan to break the last rail line into

When Lincoln posed for photographer Alexander Gardner on February 5, 1865 (inset), a month before his second inaugural address, the hint of a smile came through a face made haggard by war. Knowing that Union victory was near, Lincoln stressed in his speech the need for reconciliation between North and South. In Gardner's photograph of the ceremony (left), Lincoln sits to the left of the small lectern. The actor John Wilkes Booth, soon to be Lincoln's assassin, is believed to be among the spectators behind the railing (upper right).

In March 1865, buglers and troopers (top) who were part of Grant's escort assemble at City Point, Virginia, the principal supply base during the Petersburg siege. A series of clashes in February and March made it clear that the Federal noose was tightening around Petersburg's defenders. The map above shows some of the Union lines as they appeared on April 1; the next day an all-out Federal assault broke through the Rebel entrenchments.

Petersburg on April 1. In a stunning victory at Five Forks, Sheridan gained access to the railroad, and on the next day Grant pressed the advantage again by launching a general assault. Lee's beleaguered right flank at last gave way, and Federal troops poured through the breach. That night, Lee evacuated Petersburg and headed west in the hope of joining General Joseph Johnston's army, struggling through the Carolinas. On April 2, Richmond fell.

For six days, Lee's hungry army stumbled westward. Lee expected to lead his men to supply trains at Farmville, where he could burn the bridges behind him and the army could rest. But the Federals pressed too vigorously in pursuit, and Lee could not safely halt his weary brigades. The loss of General Richard Ewell's corps at Sailor's Creek on April 6, where nearly a third of the retreating Confederates became casualties or were captured, caused Lee to exclaim, "My God, has the army dissolved?"

When fast-moving Federal troops worked their way in front of Lee's advance and forced the Confederates under General John B. Gordon to fight at the village of Appomattox Court House, Lee found his army trapped. Opposed by cavalry and infantry, Gordon reported that he could not hold on unless strongly reinforced. Lee had no men to send, for the rest of his troops were holding off the pursuing Federals in the rear. Lee knew the end had come. "There is nothing left me but to go and see General Grant," he said, "and I would rather die a thousand deaths."

Lee wrote to Grant requesting a meeting. Grant later said that he had been suffering an intense migraine headache that morning, but as soon as he received Lee's note the pain vanished. He at once wrote to Lee that he would meet him as soon as possible and was on the way.

A Federal wagon train (left) rumbles westward out of Petersburg on April 10, 1865—a week after Yankee troops occupied the former Confederate stronghold. The caravan carried supplies to the hard-marching Union column that pursued Lee's army toward Appomattox.

"Unless he offers us honorable terms," General James Longstreet said to Lee, "come back and let us fight it out." This Lee would not have to do.

Lee directed two officers to find a suitable meeting place. One of them spoke with Wilmer McLean, in the village of Appomattox Court House, about the use of his house. McLean, who had lived next to the Manassas battlefield in July 1861, when Confederate officers used his home as a headquarters, agreed. This time he would host one of the great events in American history.

Lee, resplendent in his best uniform, entered the McLean parlor around 1 P.M. Grant, having ridden hard to find Lee, arrived a half-hour later, his boots and field uniform (he wore a private's shirt) spattered with mud. He explained that he had come directly to the meeting rather than delay matters by seeking out a better uniform. The two men spoke cordially. Grant reminded Lee that they had met years ago while fighting in the Mexican War. "I have always remembered your appearance," said Grant, "and I think I should have recognized you anywhere." "Yes," Lee replied, "I know I met you on that occasion, and I have often thought of it and tried to recollect how you looked, but I have never been able to recall a single feature."

Lee finally brought up the matter at hand and asked what terms of surrender Grant would offer. Knowing Lincoln's wish to heal the wounds of war as quickly as possible, Grant offered generous terms. As he committed them to paper, he explained that Lee's men must simply stack

A telegram (above) from President Lincoln to General Grant emphasized that the decisive moment of the war was at hand: "General Sheridan says 'If the thing is pressed I think that Lee will surrender.' Let the thing be pressed."

Mathew Brady's photograph of Robert E. Lee (above), taken in Richmond a week after the general surrendered at Appomattox, captures the Confederate commander's dignity and strength of character—traits that impressed the soldiers of both armies. "All appreciated the sadness that overwhelmed him," recalled Grant's aide, Horace Porter, "and he had the personal sympathy of everyone who beheld him." Troops of the 188th Pennsylvania (opposite) pose in front of Appomattox Court House during occupation duty, part of the war's aftermath, in the summer of 1865.

their arms, turn over all Confederate property, and promise not to take up arms against the United States. Grant added that officers could keep their sidearms and their private horses and baggage. "This done," he wrote, "each officer and man will be allowed to return to their homes, not to be disturbed by United States authority as long as they observe their parole and the laws in force where they may reside." When Lee informed him that enlisted men as well as officers in the Confederate army used their own horses rather than government-owned animals, Grant promised to allow any Confederate who claimed a horse or mule to take it home with him. The Union commander went even further. When Lee stated that his men had eaten little for some days, Grant immediately offered to send rations across the lines to feed them.

On April 10, Lee issued his final official words to his army. He told them they could go home and that they had fought well. With "admiration of your constancy and devotion to your country," he wrote, "and a grateful remembrance of your kind and generous consideration of myself, I bid you all an affectionate farewell." Lee went to join his family in Richmond.

Although the last Confederate army would not lay down its arms for several weeks, the war all but officially ended at Appomattox. Joseph Johnston surrendered to Sherman in North Carolina before the end of April, and the Confederate government disbanded. Though much

hardship lay ahead, especially for the impoverished South, Grant's magnanimous treatment of Lee allowed Americans on both sides to hope that a true reconciliation would come, one without bitterness and acrimony. Lincoln had, after all, spoken of "malice toward none and charity for all," and he had repeatedly declared that he was for a hard war and a soft peace.

Just days after the surrender at Appomattox, however, the future suddenly grew less bright. On the evening of April 14, 1865, actor and rabid Confederate sympathizer John Wilkes Booth entered a section of boxed seats at Ford's Theater in Washington and fired a bullet into Abraham Lincoln's brain. The president died the next morning. After a daring escape, Booth was pursued and killed 12 days later by a cavalry unit. His co-conspirators—one of whom had attacked and stabbed Secretary of State William Seward that same evening—were tried and hanged. Swift justice would not help the South, however. The reconstruction of the broken nation would now be overseen by a U.S. Congress controlled by vengeful men harboring years of anger. They sought not charity for all, but retribution, and the South would be made to pay for its waywardness. Ironically, with the death of Abraham Lincoln, perhaps the most hated man in the Confederacy, whose election in 1860 had triggered secession, the South had lost a friend and its greatest hope for a "just and lasting peace."

A week after the assassination, the war department issued a wanted poster (above) offering large rewards for the capture of John Wilkes Booth and fellow conspirators John Surratt and David Herold. Photographic images of all three men adorned the poster, though both Surratt's and Herold's names were misspelled. Six days later, Booth was killed and Herold surrendered; John Surratt managed to elude authorities and flee the country, though his mother, Mary, was among four conspirators tried, convicted, and sentenced to death.

RICHMOND IN FLAMES

Riding across a bridge spanning the James River, a Rebel cavalry detachment (above) escorts the carriages of Confederate officials evacuating Richmond late on the night of April 2. "It was a sad, a terrible & a solemn sight," General E. Porter Alexander recalled. "The whole river front seemed to be in flames, amid which occasional heavy explosions were heard & the black smoke spreading & hanging over the city seemed to be full of dreadful portents." As he rode away, Alexander sensed "a peculiar . . . feeling of orphanage."

A CAPITAL IN RUINS

Undamaged except for a few broken windows, the classic facade of the Virginia statehouse, which served as the Confederacy's capitol, stands above the ruins of Richmond's business district. Visible at far left, next to the steeple of the Broad Street Methodist Church, an equestrian statue of George Washington overlooks the parklike capitol grounds. The devastating conflagration began when Southern soldiers preparing to evacuate the city set fire to military warehouses along the James River. By dawn on April 3, entire blocks were engulfed in flames.

A GUTTED SHELL

Most of Richmond's business district was heavily damaged by the fires that ravaged the abandoned Confederate capital. Many structures, like the building above, were completely gutted. Colonel Charles Francis Adams, Jr., of the Fifth Massachusetts Colored Cavalry, found the city "quiet and silent as a graveyard," and the surrounding countryside "a curious region of desolation . . . swept with the besom of destruction."

PICKETING THE DEBRIS

Federal cavalry horses wait along a rail fence (right) amid the ruins of Richmond, across the street from the Confederate treasury building (far right). "As the sun rose on Richmond, such a spectacle was presented as can never be forgotten," recalled resident Sallie Putnam. "Above all this scene of terror, hung a black shroud of smoke through which the sun shone with a lurid angry glare . . . as if loath to shine over a scene so appalling."

TROPHIES OF WAR

Delegated to oversee the transfer of 71 Confederate flags from Appomattox to Washington, Major General John Gibbon (left, center, with left hand on belt) poses with his staff and a group of Federal soldiers, each awarded the Medal of Honor for capturing a Rebel banner in battle. More than a colorful piece of cloth, a flag embodied the very heart and soul of the unit it represented, and to capture one in combat was deemed an act of daring that merited recognition. It wasn't until 1905 that these revered symbols were returned to Confederate veterans associations.

SOLDIERS NO MORE

Recently paroled Southern soldiers (opposite), disarmed but still clad in Confederate gray, mingle with Federal troops and local civilians beneath the equestrian statue of George Washington in Richmond's Capitol Square. The image, made by photographer James Reekie on April 14, captures the odd tranquillity that had settled over the war-torn capital as Yanks and Rebs took the first tentative steps toward national reconciliation. Their good will would soon be put to the test, for that very evening Lincoln was assassinated in Washington.

A CELEBRATION OF VICTORY

Within 24 hours of Lee's surrender, word of the Federal victory had been telegraphed across the North, prompting joyous patriotic celebrations like the one announced in a Detroit broadside (right). It was also a time for reflection, as countless families scarred by war could at last return to their everyday lives. "I felt a strange and tender exaltation," poet James Russell Lowell wrote on hearing the news. "I wanted to laugh and I wanted to cry, and ended by holding my peace and feeling devoutly thankful."

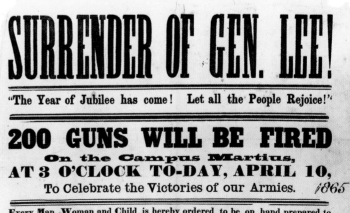

SURRENDER OF GEN. LEE!

"The Year of Jubilee has come! Let all the People Rejoice!"

200 GUNS WILL BE FIRED

On the Campus Martius,

AT 3 O'CLOCK TO-DAY, APRIL 10, 1865

To Celebrate the Victories of our Armies.

Every Man, Woman and Child is hereby ordered to be on hand prepared to Sing and Rejoice. The crowd are expected to join in singing Patriotic Songs.

ALL PLACES OF BUSINESS MUST BE CLOSED AT 2 O'CLOCK.

Hurrah for Grant and his noble Army.

By Order of the People.

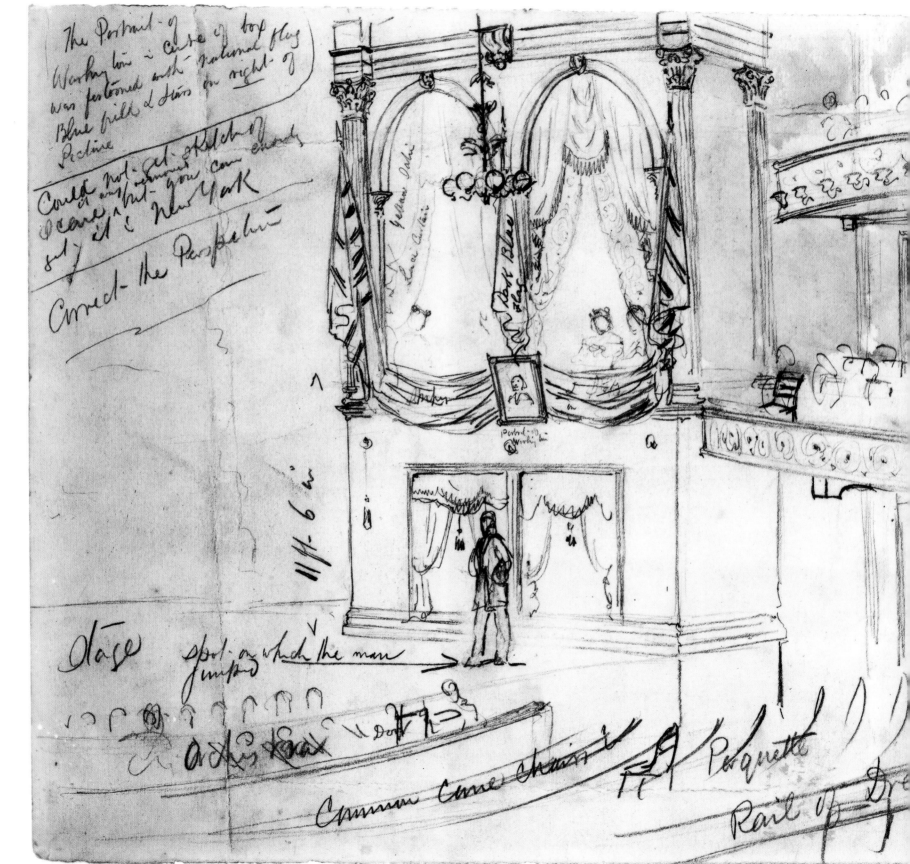

The Portrait of Washington in centre of box was festooned with national flag Blue field & Stars on right of Picture

Could not get Mitchell & care mysterious but you can Scene & did get it in New York

Correct the Perspective

11′- 6″

Stage   spot on which the man jumped

Actor's Box   Door

Common Cane chairs   Perquette

Rail of Dr

CELEBRITY TURNED MURDERER

Dapper, handsome, and renowned for his fiery performances in Shakespearean roles, the actor John Wilkes Booth (below) came from a family of talented thespians. As a celebrity of the stage, Booth was often photographed, and he enjoyed presenting images of himself—like the one below—to his admirers. Few suspected his bitter hatred for the Union government and its chief executive, and when the fatal shot was fired at Ford's Theater, public adulation turned to unmitigated rage. "Do recognize him some where," one former devotee scrawled on a photograph of Booth, "& kill him."

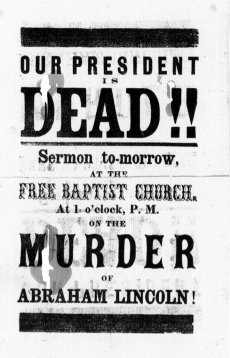

A SOMBER EASTER

Bordered in black, a church broadside (above) announces a sermon on the death of President Lincoln, the subject of every minister's text on Easter Sunday 1865. The assassination on Good Friday prompted widespread comparisons between the martyred president and Jesus Christ. But a desire for vengeance, rather than forgiveness, was the overwhelming feeling among Americans who believed the former leaders of the Confederacy were responsible for the murder.

TRAGEDY ON STAGE

Alfred Waud's sketch of Ford's Theater (left) shows the flag-draped box where the president and first lady were seated with their guests, Major Henry Rathbone and Clara Harris, on the evening of April 14. After firing the fatal shot into Lincoln's head, Booth stabbed Major Rathbone and leapt to the stage, shouting, "Sic semper tyrannis!" (Thus always to tyrants). The figure in Waud's drawing stands where Booth landed, beside a startled actor performing in the comedy *Our American Cousin*.

A SORROWFUL PARADE

After having lain in state in the East Room of the White House, Lincoln's body was transferred on April 9 to the recently completed rotunda of the U.S. Capitol for a public viewing by thousands of grief-stricken citizens. The photograph above depicts a portion of the immense funeral cortege that paraded down Pennsylvania Avenue toward Capitol Hill. The lines of dark-clad figures that at first glance appear to be soldiers are actually representatives of Washington's black community holding hands and marching 40 abreast in 100 ranks—a striking and appropriate tribute to the "Great Emancipator."

FUNERAL TRAIN
Curious onlookers observing President Lincoln's funeral train (above) as it waits on a trestle after arriving in Chicago on May 1, 1865, gather on the shore of Lake Michigan. Heavily draped in black crepe, the engine and its nine cars departed Washington on April 21 and stopped in nine cities—the president lying in state in each one—before Lincoln's casket reached its final destination: Springfield, Illinois.

HOME AT LAST
A large delegation of mourners gathers in front of the Lincoln house (left) at Eighth and Jackson Streets in Springfield. While the president's coffin rested in the Illinois statehouse, hundreds of people— dignitaries, old neighbors, the bereaved, and the curious—posed for images taken by an enterprising photographer who set up his camera across the street from the president's former home. On May 4, 20 days after Lincoln died, his body was finally laid to rest in Springfield's Oak Ridge Cemetery.

AWAITING THE PARADE

On May 23 and 24, 1865, the victorious Union armies paraded up Pennsylvania Avenue in an awe-inspiring "Grand Review." Eager to get a look at famous generals and fighting regiments, at bullet-torn banners and sun-browned veterans of great battles, spectators (left) packed the sidewalks and bleachers. "Any man in uniform was . . . the rage today," one officer wrote. "It certainly is pleasant to be made much of by pretty women, especially after four years of absence from female society."

EXECUTIVE HONORS

A contingent from the Veteran Reserve Corps stands at attention in front of the elaborate presidential reviewing stand (left), reserved for high-ranking government and military officials. Among those visible on the platform are President Andrew Johnson, Secretary of the Navy Gideon Welles, and Generals Grant, Sherman, and Meade. "The wild enthusiasm, the inspiring cheers, seemed sufficient recompense for all those years of blood," a Massachusetts veteran recalled, "beyond the power of tongue or pen to ever faithfully portray."

CROWNED WITH GLORY

Photographed from the grounds of the Treasury Building, a Federal regiment (above) prepares to right-wheel up Pennsylvania Avenue at 15th Street as crowds line the sidewalk in front of Willard's Hotel, at left. Riding with the soldiers of the Fifth Corps, General Joshua Lawrence Chamberlain exulted over the pageantry: "At the rise of ground near the Treasury a backward glance takes in the mighty spectacle: the broad Avenue for more than a mile solid full, and more, from wall to wall, from door to roof, with straining forms and outwelling hearts. In the midst, onpressing that darker stream, with arms and colors resplendent in the noon-day sun, an army of tested manhood, clothed with power, crowned with glory, marching to its dissolution!"

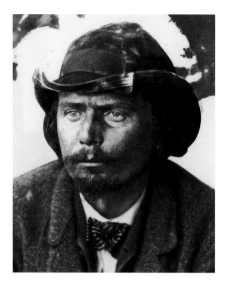

CONSPIRATOR OR VICTIM?

Mary Surratt (above), an affable 42-year-old widow, managed a boardinghouse in Washington where Booth and his accomplices—including Mary's son John—met to plot the attack on President Lincoln and other Federal officials. She was sentenced to death despite pleas for mercy by five of the nine military officers who tried the conspirators.

A RELUCTANT PARTNER

German-born George Atzerodt (above), of Port Tobacco, Maryland, smuggled supplies, escaped prisoners, and Confederate sympathizers into Virginia. Atzerodt failed to follow through on his part in the conspiracy—the murder of Vice President Johnson—but his clear knowledge of the assassination plot led to his conviction.

FAITHFUL ACCOMPLICE

An associate of John Wilkes Booth in a failed plot to kidnap Lincoln, David Herold (above) served as a liaison between the actor and the other conspirators, and accompanied Booth during the 12 days that the assassin eluded the authorities. Raised in a prosperous family and educated at Georgetown, Herold turned 23 years old during the trial that resulted in his hanging.

POWERFUL CONFEDERATE

A former Confederate soldier, and at 21 the youngest of the conspirators sentenced to die, Lewis Powell (above) was also the most imposing. Over six feet and powerfully built, he was good-looking and had an inscrutable attitude that mesmerized observers during the trial. Powell wounded Secretary of State Seward and four others in a brutal rampage through Seward's home.

FINAL JUSTICE
On the sweltering afternoon of July 7, 1865, minutes after the trap was sprung, the bodies of the four condemned conspirators—Mary Surratt, Lewis Powell, David Herold, and George Atzerodt—hang motionless from a gallows in the courtyard of Washington's Old Arsenal Prison (left). The grim image is from a series taken by photographer Alexander Gardner. His execution pictures mark a milestone in the history of photojournalism.

Davis Imprisoned

There was little doubt in the minds of many Federal officials that the Confederacy's chief executive, Jefferson Davis, had authorized Lincoln's assassination. It was an incorrect assumption, but when Davis was apprehended by Union troops, he had every reason to fear that a desire for vengeance would triumph over reason and justice.

A LOYAL SPOUSE

The former Confederate president had no stauncher ally than his wife, Varina Howell Davis (below). She was only 18 when she married the austere and ambitious widower, who at 36 was twice her age. But in their 20 years together, Varina displayed an independent spirit, strength of character, and steadfast loyalty—qualities that would be severely put to the test during Davis's imprisonment.

SUFFERING IN SILENCE

Jefferson Davis sits in his spartan quarters (above) in Fortress Monroe. During his two years of confinement, he was guarded round the clock by soldiers who were forbidden to converse with him. Worldwide sympathy for Davis's plight ultimately brought about his release. On Christmas Day 1866 Pope Pius IX sent Davis a crown of thorns (top) that the pontiff made with his own hands.

ROUGH CAPTURE

Early on May 10, 1865, Davis, his family, and a small escort were surrounded and captured by Federal cavalry near Irwinsville, Georgia. Davis emerged from his tent and advanced to meet them. It was a chilly morning and he was wearing an overcoat and a shawl (left) that his wife had impulsively thrown over his shoulders. The haphazard attire would make Davis an object of ridicule. Rumors spread that he had attempted to flee disguised in his wife's clothing—bonnet, hoop skirt, and petticoats. The story was featured in cartoons and popular songs (below).

ULTIMATE REDEMPTION

A proud man, Jefferson Davis (left) was deeply aggrieved by the absurd accounts of his attempting to escape in female attire and the very real possibility that he would be tried for treason and hanged. Though indicted, Davis was never brought to trial. Released on bail in May 1867, he was granted amnesty by presidential proclamation on Christmas Day 1868.

A Long, Dark Road

W HEN PRESIDENT ABRAHAM LINCOLN reviewed the Army of the Potomac at Falmouth, Virginia, in April 1863, he sat exceptionally quietly among a cluster of generals as the thousands of volunteers marched by, flags fluttering and bands playing bright military airs. The president, one general noticed, seemed lost in thought as he took in the panorama.

"Carpetbaggers," opportunistic Yankees seeking to make a fortune in the postwar South, got their name from the inexpensive suitcases they carried, which were made from carpeting (below). Few of them achieved financial success. One Ohioan recalled his venture as "a fool's errand."

Suddenly Lincoln turned to General Darius Couch and asked, "What do you suppose will become of all these men when the war is over?" Couch, caught off guard, could not reply, but the incident impressed him deeply, and he later wrote, "It struck me as very pleasant that somebody had an idea that the war would sometime end."

When the war at last did end, not a few soldiers on both sides were asking themselves Lincoln's question. They would go home, of course, but to what? America had changed drastically in four years. Emancipation had turned Southern society inside out, and invading armies had left the South impoverished and a veritable wasteland. The North was feeling the effects of having been bitterly divided over the war along political as well as class lines. Copperheads, War Democrats, moderate Republicans, "Radical" Republicans, had all vied for control of the Union, and working men had rioted in New York City and elsewhere, protesting what they believed was a "rich man's war and a poor man's fight." In the North and the South, emancipation meant that white men would now have to compete with large numbers of free black men for jobs. And what would those jobs be? Would former employers in shops and factories welcome the veterans back to the fold? And what about the enormous gaps that the war left in communities and family circles? Some 258,000 Southern men and about 365,000 Northern men lay in soldiers' graves.

Of course, the men themselves—those who were fortunate enough to return home healthy and as they had left, with two arms and two legs—had changed. No longer were they the innocents who had marched off to find glory. What they had seen and suffered could not have failed to affect them inwardly; they could never again look at the world as they had. What's more, they had bonded as brothers with those who had endured the same experiences. As one veteran put it, "We have shared the incommunicable experience of war; we have felt, we still feel, the passion of life to its top." Breaking such strong bonds, especially for those who had been victorious, was difficult. "I wish it was possible to

Not all troops went home after the war. In an attempt to locate the bodies of thousands of men who were missing in action, soldiers helped scour battlefields. Many fatalities had been buried in shallow graves; others, like the skeletal remains at Cold Harbor (left), had been exposed to the elements for months. In the former Confederate states, large numbers of Federal troops were stationed to ensure the safety and political enfranchisement of the newly freed slaves, who might be harmed by vindictive ex-Confederates, a situation caricatured in the cartoon below.

express my feelings," wrote one Northerner, "and make plain our experiences when we started homeward. Sunshine and shadows seemed to play with us. We had hoped and prayed for the end of strife; we were overjoyed that we had won victory and that the end had come; but as comrades we were attached by devoted ties, we loved one another." They also suspected that their return to civilian life would not be easy. "It seemed to me," wrote one soldier, "that to be without a musket and with no more camps or campaigns to look forward to, we would be out of an occupation and without a commission. Settling down to routine daily employment in a slow shop [or] store was not favorable to our habits of life; we felt kind of lost."

In the South, with no victory to lessen their feelings of alienation, men in tattered uniforms ambled through the countryside, some walking a thousand miles or more to return home. They looked sick and exhausted, one Northerner thought, "they have a care-worn and anxious look, a played out manner." An Alabama woman watched them and remembered them into her old age. "Often as I sit in the twilight and drift back into the past," she wrote, "it is not easy to restrain tears, as memory views those soldiers in their worn gray, marching home sad and depressed, with the cause they had so warmly espoused, lost."

Though the ex-Confederates had been vanquished on the battlefield, few found that defeat had altered their views on what the South stood for. They still believed in the justness of their cause, and the idea of submitting to Federal authority was repugnant to them. Hatred of the Yankees had never been stronger than it was at the end of the war, and the antipathy

421

only worsened with Washington's heavy-handed efforts from 1865 to 1877 to "reconstruct" the South by creating new state governments run by coalitions of blacks, carpetbaggers, and Southerners who sided with the first two. Reconstruction alienated most Southerners, and many sustained a spirit of resistance toward everything Northern, as the popular 1866 song "O, I'm a Good Old Rebel" made clear:

> Three hundred thousand Yankees is stiff in Southern dust.
> We got three hundred thousand before they conquered us.
> They died of Southern fever and Southern steel and shot,
> I wish they was three million instead of what we got.
>
> I can't take up my musket and fight them now no more,
> But I ain't gonna love them, now that is certain sure.
>   And I don't want no pardon for what I was and am.
>   I won't be reconstructed, and I don't care a damn.

Again, Robert E. Lee emerged as a leader. He was the most respected man in the South and would come to symbolize all that was good and powerful and admirable about the Confederacy. In 1865 he made no secret of the course he would follow: The fact was, the war was over and the South had been defeated. "The duty of its citizens appears to me too plain to admit of doubt," he wrote. "All should unite in honest efforts to obliterate the effects of war, and to restore the blessings of peace. They should remain . . . in the country; promote harmony and good feeling; qualify themselves to vote; and elect to the State and general Legislatures wise and patriotic men, who will devote their abilities to the interests of the country, and the healing of all dissensions."

But it would not be easy; the Southern psyche was wounded too deeply. "We were engaged in a just and holy war," wrote one Virginian, echoing the opinion of millions of Southerners who could not accept that their sacrifice had been in vain. As they suffered through Reconstruction—as they had suffered through the war—they came to cherish their hardships and see them as honors. Their trials defined them as Southerners, and the Confederate experience—equal parts battlefield valor and stoic defiance in defeat—played a significant part in determining the meaning of Southern heritage.

With the passing of the decades, Americans gained a perspective on what they had endured in those four years of war, and they came to see the conflict as a watershed event. Northerner

Whether they had been privates or generals, Civil War veterans in 1865 had to resume life among civilians. Despite the loss of both forearms at the Battle of Perryville, Union artilleryman Samuel H. Decker (above), equipped with artificial limbs of his own design, became a doorman for the U.S. House of Representatives. When Robert E. Lee (inset, at right) and Joseph Johnston (left) met for a reunion in 1870, Lee was president of Washington College and Johnston had embarked on a business career.

Cooper Shop SOLDIERS HOME
Race & Crown Sts. Philadelphia April 20th 1866
received of Soldiers Aid Society of Grason &
Vicinity Thirty one & Two Dollars.

Treasurer

George Ticknor thought the war had created a "great gulf between what happened before in our country and what has happened since, or what is likely to happen hereafter. It does not seem to me as if I were living in a country in which I was born." In his dysphoria, Ticknor could not have been alone. In much less than the span of a lifetime, America underwent a series of shock waves—the enormous influx of immigrants, the rise of industrialization, westward expansion, secession, emancipation, Shiloh, Antietam, Stones River, Gettysburg, the March to the Sea, assassination. As the graves of hundreds of thousands testified, the war could not be erased, ignored, or forgotten.

Ironically, the peace that did eventually come—and it was by no means an encompassing one—was achieved by the same men who had fought each other in deadly earnest. In the 1880s and '90s, and into the twentieth century, aging veterans rediscovered and attempted to relive the exciting days of their youth. Books, memoirs, essays, and addresses appeared by the

After the war, Philadelphia's Cooper Shop—the site of a notable wartime "Refreshment Saloon," where civilian staff workers provided food, coffee, and comfortable barracks for Union soldiers en route to the front—continued to serve the veterans as a privately funded caregiving facility. The elaborate testimonial above was issued as a receipt for charitable donations to the project. With the National Soldiers Home in Washington unable to meet the demand of needy veterans, in 1865 the government established additional asylums in Maine, Ohio, and Wisconsin.

In the decades following the war, the Grand Army of the Republic and its Southern counterpart, the United Confederate Veterans, sponsored large annual conventions. In 1915 U.C.V. member Silas C. Buck (right) proudly displays the battle flag he carried 50 years earlier as colorbearer of the 10th Mississippi Cavalry.

thousands, as the graying soldiers recorded their versions of history for posterity. And as the literature grew, the depth of feeling that the writing veterans had for the men who fought with them and against them became widespread. No longer were the men on the other side the enemy. Now they were comrades who had shared the "incommunicable experience of war." "We believed in the principle that the Union is indissoluble; and that slavery had lasted long enough," wrote a Massachusetts soldier. "But we equally believed that those who stood against us held just as sacred convictions that were the opposite of ours, and we respected them as every man with a heart must respect those who give all for their belief." And former Confederate soldiers, while still honoring their dead, in time grew willing to admit the advantages of being united. In a versified address to a reunion of Federal soldiers, an old Confederate rhymed:

I clasp the hand that made my scars,
I cheer the flag my foemen bore,
I shout for joy to see the stars
All on our common shield once more.

Having known war, the old soldiers loved peace with a greater intensity and welcomed reconciliation. "We are willing to forget and forgive those who have wronged us," wrote a Tennessean. "We look up above and beyond all these petty groveling things and shake hands and forget the past." Up to a point. Because they were still prisoners of their past, and there was no escape. They had seen war's horror and known its terror, and as they reflected on those conflicted years and recalled what they had experienced, they could wonder, as one Southerner did, "Is it true that I have seen these things? Did I see those brave and noble countrymen of mine laid low in death and weltering in their own blood? Did I see our country laid waste and in ruins? Did I see soldiers marching, the earth trembling and jarring beneath their measured tread? Did I see the ruins of smouldering cities and deserted homes? Are these things real?"

Among the annual veterans conventions was the Grand Army of the Republic's "encampment" advertised by an enterprising railroad company in the souvenir program above. In 1903 former members of the 165th New York Zouaves (above left) march proudly down a Brooklyn street during a Memorial Day parade. The 165th maintained an active veterans association and fielded a uniformed honor guard well into the twentieth century. As late as the 1930s the Zouaves were a conspicuous sight in commemorative observances sponsored by the G.A.R., the Union's largest veterans organization.

NEW OPPORTUNITIES

During Reconstruction, two blacks were elected to the U.S. Senate: Hiram R. Revels (above) and Blanche K. Bruce. Revels, a Republican and a Methodist minister, was born a free black in Illinois and educated at the state's Knox College. Both he and Bruce represented Mississippi—Revels in 1870 and '71, and Bruce from 1875 to 1881—and both sought to improve not just the lot of blacks, but also white-black relations, which included working to end discrimination against former Confederates.

CELEBRATION OF FIFTEENTH AMENDMENT MAY 19th 1870.

THE FIFTEENTH AMENDMENT.

CELEBRATED MAY 19th 1870

FREEDOM'S REWARD

An elaborate patriotic lithograph (left) celebrates the passage in 1870 of the 15th Amendment to the Constitution, which enfranchised black Americans by eliminating "race, color or previous condition of servitude" as legal barriers to voting. In addition to showing idealized scenes of blacks enjoying their newfound freedom, the print pays homage to noted civil rights leaders, including Frederick Douglass, John Brown, and Abraham Lincoln.

EMPOWERED BY WORDS

Photographed with two of her students in 1862, Kate Foote (above) was among a cadre of volunteer teachers who served with the New England Freedmen's Aid Society and tutored former slaves at Beaufort, South Carolina. New York and Pennsylvania sponsored similar wartime educational efforts, as did a number of religious organizations. The slaves, one instructor recalled, "had seen the magic of a scrap of writing and were eager to share such power." In March 1865 Congress established the Freedmen's Bureau to oversee the creation of schools, colleges, and universities for newly enfranchised black citizens.

DARING TO LEARN
A Northern teacher stands before her young students outside a rustic Freedmen's School (left) in North Carolina. By 1866 the Freedmen's Bureau was operating 965 schools for 90,778 pupils in the former Confederate states, an undertaking that enraged many white Southerners. "The opposition to Negro education was bitter in the South," wrote noted black educator and philosopher W. E. B. DuBois, "for the South believed an educated Negro to be a dangerous Negro."

THE LEGACY OF THE WAR

TOILING STILL

A decade after emancipation, only 5 percent of former slaves owned their own land, and with the abandonment of Reconstruction policies in 1877, many Southern blacks, like the Florida plantation workers above, photographed in 1879, found themselves scarcely better off than they had been before the war.

THE IRONIES OF FREEDOM

Supervised by a black foreman, laborers (opposite) bring in the day's pickings from a South Carolina cotton plantation. In order to survive in the postwar South, thousands of freed slaves continued to work for their former masters, earning menial wages that relegated them to a social class beneath even the most impoverished whites. As one former slave put it, "Freedom wasn't no difference I knows of."

A NATIONAL CEMETERY

Federal soldiers stand guard in front of the columned portico of Arlington House (left), the prewar residence of Robert E. Lee that overlooked the Potomac River and Washington. Union troops occupied the house in 1861 and used the 1,100-acre estate for encampments and a "freedmen's village" for escaped slaves. On June 15, 1864, General Montgomery Meigs suggested that the grounds surrounding the mansion be made into "a National Military Cemetery." Secretary of War Stanton immediately sanctioned the proposal. Some of the first burials were in Mrs. Lee's former rose garden.

BIVOUAC OF THE DEAD

Denied interment in U.S. national cemeteries, the bodies of Confederate soldiers often remained on the fields where the men had died, or were laid to rest beneath crude wooden headboards in private burial grounds like Richmond's Hollywood Cemetery (opposite). Ultimately some 18,000 Confederate soldiers were buried at Hollywood, including more than 2,000 dead recovered from the Gettysburg battlefield.

A CHERISHED HERITAGE

Clad in the uniforms they wore at Appomattox 32 years earlier, members of the Old Guard of Richmond (above)—an affiliate of the United Confederate Veterans organization—gather at the Virginia Soldiers Home in 1897 to raise funds for a monument to General J. E. B. Stuart. Rather than foster sectional differences, Southern veneration of the "Lost Cause" over time became linked with national reconciliation. "It is all the better that the war was fought, even though our cause went down in defeat," Colonel N. E. Harris remarked at a 1912 U.C.V. reunion. "The struggle has left a heritage of brave deeds, a history of heroic endurance, of fidelity to country and home and fireside for the whole American nation, North and South, to cherish."

MEMORIALS TO VALOR

On June 10, 1865, soldiers, veterans, and civilians gathered on the field of Bull Run (right) to dedicate a monument on the site of the war's first great engagement. Constructed of native sandstone and decorated with 100-pound artillery shells, the commemorative shaft was one of the earliest Civil War memorials, thousands of which would eventually be erected on town squares, courthouse lawns, and battlefields. "These monuments shall last," former Confederate General William Bate declared at a dedication ceremony in Chattanooga, Tennessee, "and through all the coming years shall inspire our remotest descendants with that loyalty to conviction which these fields illustrate."

PROGRAM

GETTYSBURG

BLUE AND GRAY REUNION

75TH ANNIVERSARY BATTLE of GETTYSBURG 1938

A LAST REUNION

Participants in the 75th anniversary commemoration of the Battle of Gettysburg were given a program (above) that emphasized the common heritage of the Union and Confederate soldiers. Only about 1,800 veterans, most of them in their 90s and some confined to wheelchairs, attended the last great reunion. At the event, more than 250,000 spectators heard President Franklin D. Roosevelt deliver an address at the dedication of a peace memorial, unveiled by representatives of the G.A.R. and U.C.V.

IN THE FOOTSTEPS OF HISTORY

On July 3, 1913—50 years to the day after a series of decisive Confederate victories ended at Gettysburg's Cemetery Ridge—a group of Confederate veterans (left), still spry and enthusiastic, re-create the dramatic charge of General George Pickett's division. More than 50,000 former Yanks and Rebs gathered that summer for a reunion on the war's most famous battlefield. They were quartered in vast tented encampments that brought back memories of their youth.

438

REUNIONS

SIX DECADES OF MEMORIES

Clad in Rebel gray, elderly Southern veterans (above), their
patriotism undiminished by the passage of decades, muster
for a 1922 parade in Richmond, Virginia. Addressing a gathering of old comrades, Confederate veteran Robert Stiles, noting
the men's shared pride, said, "If there is any part of your life
where you should have been, and did what you should have
done, it is the great Olympiad of '61 to '65. What have you felt
or looked on since that is not pitifully small in comparison?"

A COMMON HONOR

The culmination of the 50th anniversary observances at Gettysburg was a symbolic handshake (above) between Union veterans of the Philadelphia Brigade and Confederate veterans of Pickett's division. Where they had once locked in battle on Cemetery Ridge, they now greeted one another in friendship and with a common honor. "Your last memories of this field will overlay the earlier ones," a speaker told them. "It will no longer picture itself as a field of carnage and suffering, but a field of smiling faces and happy hearts."

PRESERVING THE PAST

Former Union generals (right, from left) Lawrence P. Graham, Daniel E. Sickles, and Eugene A. Carr tour Gettysburg in 1886. Sickles, a controversial corps commander who lost his leg to a Confederate shell on the second day of the battle, was a fervent supporter of battlefield preservation and a leader in the movement to establish Gettysburg as a national shrine. In the years following the war, state-sponsored veterans groups acquired areas of the field, and in 1895 Congress designated 6,000 acres a National Military Park.

Photography

DARKROOM ON WHEELS

One of the Civil War's most accomplished photographers, Alexander Gardner headed west after the war to record the construction of the railroads. The 1867 image at left shows him seated beside his portable darkroom and conferring with an assistant near Fort Riley, Kansas. Civil War soldiers dubbed these vehicles "what is it?" wagons. Inside were the chemicals and glass-plate negatives used to record and fix images taken with bulky wooden cameras like the one below.

The vast photographic legacy of the Civil War opens a window onto the past, permitting us to witness the aftermath of terrible battles, the boredom and humor of camp life, and the pride of youthful warriors.

THE CAMERA AT WAR

Some Civil War photographers applied their skills in support of military operations. During the siege of Petersburg, the large bellows camera at left, mounted on a table and equipped with a special lens, was used to photograph maps prepared by U.S. topographical engineers. The copies were then distributed to officers in the field.

PHOTOGRAPHER

Alexander Gardner (left), unable to earn a profitable livelihood as a photographer in his native Scotland, emigrated to New York in 1856 and found employment in Mathew Brady's Manhattan gallery. Gardner's success as a war photographer prompted him to leave Brady's employ in late 1862 and open his own studio in Washington, D.C.

VISIONARY

By 1861 Mathew Brady (right) was considered America's most successful photographer, though his role after nearly two decades in the trade was that of entrepreneurial business manager, not cameraman. His studios attracted well-known people eager to have their portrait recorded by Brady's talented staff. While he made few, if any, wartime photos himself, it was Brady who thought of dispatching photographers to the field in order to assemble a visual record of the conflict.

A DIFFICULT ART

Shot by a Brady photographer in 1864, this view (right) of the Federal supply base at Port Royal, Virginia, includes the portable darkroom (lower right) that was an essential part of the field artist's equipment. An exposure took almost a minute, and then the glass negative, with its sensitive collodion emulsion, had to be carried to the darkroom, where it was bathed in a solution that "fixed" the image for later printing on albumen paper.

Battle Summaries by State

Of the Civil War's more than 10,000 armed conflicts fought in 26 states, 384 are considered principal battles and have been ranked A, B, C, or D, depending on their influence on the outcome of a particular campaign. The 149 battles below, all classified as A or B, represent the major strategic operations of the war.

BATTLE	LOCATION	DATE	FORCES ENGAGED	ESTIMATED CASUALTIES	RESULT
Alabama					
FORT BLAKELY	*Baldwin County*	4/2-9/65	13th and 16th Corps [US]; Fort Blakely Garrison [CS]	**US 629; CS 2,900**	*Union victory*
MOBILE BAY	*Mobile and Baldwin Counties*	8/2-23/64	Farragut's Fleet and U.S. army forces near Mobile [US]; Buchanan's Flotilla, Fort Morgan Garrison, Fort Gaines Garrison, and Fort Powell Garrison [CS]	**US 322; CS 1,500**	*Union victory*
SELMA	*Dallas County*	4/2/65	Two calvary divisions [US]; troops in city [CS]	**US 319; CS 2,700**	*Union victory*
SPANISH FORT	*Baldwin County*	3/27-4/28/65	16th and 13th Corps [US]; Spanish Fort Garrison [CS]	**US 657; CS 744**	*Union victory*
Arkansas					
BAYOU FOURCHE	*Pulaski County*	9/10/63	Calvary Division, Army of Arkansas, Arkansas Expedition [US]; District of Arkansas [CS]	**US 72; CS unknown**	*Union victory*
HELENA	*Phillips County*	7/4/63	District of Eastern Arkansas [US]; District of Arkansas [CS]	**US 206; CS 1,636**	*Union victory*
PEA RIDGE	*Benton County*	3/6-8/62	Army of the Southwest [US]; Army of the West [CS]	**US 1,349; CS 4,600**	*Union victory*
PRAIRIE D'ANE	*Nevada County*	4/9-13/64	Department of Arkansas [US]; District of Arkansas [CS]	**Unknown**	*Union victory*
PRAIRIE GROVE	*Washington County*	12/7/62	Army of the Frontier [US]; 1st Corps, Trans-Mississippi Army [CS]	**US 1,251; CS 1,317**	*Union strategic victory*
Colorado					
SAND CREEK	*Kiowa Country*	11/29-30/64	Third Colorado Regiment [US]; 500 Cheyennes and a few Arapahos [Native American]	**US unknown; Native American 200**	*Union victory (massacre)*
District of Columbia					
FORT STEVENS	*District of Colombia*	7/11-12/64	Divisions	**874 total**	*Union victory*
Florida					
OLUSTEE	*Baker County*	2/20/64	Division [US]; District of East Florida [CS]	**US 1,860; CS 946**	*Confederate victory*
Georgia					
ALLATOONA	*Bartow County*	10/5/64	One brigade [US]; one division [CS]	**US 706, CS 799**	*Union victory*
ATLANTA	*Fulton County*	7/22/64	Military Division of the Mississippi [US]; Army of Tennessee [CS]	**US 3,641; CS 8,499**	*Union victory*
CHICKAMAUGA	*Catoosa and Walker Counties*	9/18-20/63	The Army of the Cumberland [US]; Army of Tennessee [CS]	**US 16,170; CS 18,454**	*Confederate victory*
EZRA CHURCH	*Fulton County*	7/28/64	Army of the Tennessee [US]; two corps of Army of Tennessee [CS]	**US 562; CS 3,000**	*Union victory*
FORT MCALLISTER II	*Bryan County*	12/13/64	2nd Division, 15th Corps, Army of the Tennessee [US]; Fort McAllister Garrison [CS]	**US 134; CS 71**	*Union victory*

This appendix was prepared using the Civil War Sites Advisory Commission's 1998 Report on the Nation's Civil War Battlefields, Technical Volume II: Battle Summaries.

BATTLE	LOCATION	DATE	FORCES ENGAGED	ESTIMATED CASUALTIES	RESULT
Georgia (cont.)					
FORT PULASKI	*Chatham County*	4/10–11/62	Port Royal Expeditionary Force's Fort Pulaski investment troops [US]; Fort Pulaski Garrison [CS]	**US 1; CS 364**	*Union victory*
GRISWOLDVILLE	*Jones and Twiggs Counties*	11/22/64	2nd Brigade, 1st Division, 15th Corps, Army of the Tennessee and two regiments of cavalry [US];1st Division Georgia Militia and Cavalry Corps, Department of South Carolina Georgia, and Florida [CS]	**US 62; CS 650**	*Union victory*
JONESBOROUGH	*Clayton County*	8/31–9/1/64	Six corps [US]; Two corps [CS]	**US 1,149; CS 2,000**	*Union victory*
KENNESAW MT.	*Cobb Country*	6/27/64	Military Division of the Mississippi [US]; Army of Tennessee [CS]	**US 3,000; CS 1,000**	*Confederate victory*
MARIETTA	*Cobb County*	6/9–7/3/64	Military Division of the Mississippi [US]; Army of Tennessee [CS]	**Unknown**	*Union victory*
PEACHTREE CREEK	*Fulton County*	7/20/64	Army of the Cumberland [US]; Army of Tennessee [CS]	**US 1,710; CS 4,796**	*Union victory*
RINGGOLD GAP	*Cartoosa County*	11/27/63	Three divisions [US]; one division [CS]	**US 432; CS 480**	*Confederate victory*
Kentucky					
MILL SPRINGS	*Pulaski and Wayne Counties*	1/19/62	1st Division, Army of the Ohio, and Brig. Gen A. Scheopf's Brigade [US]; division of two brigades [CS]	**US 232; CS 439**	*Union victory*
MUNFORDVILLE	*Hart County*	9/14–17/62	Union garrison [US]; Army of the Mississippi [CS]	**US 4,148; CS 714**	*Confederate victory*
PERRYVILLE	*Boyle County*	10/8/62	Army of the Ohio [US]; Army of the Mississippi [CS]	**US 4,211; CS 3,196**	*Union strategic victory*
RICHMOND	*Madison County*	8/29–30/62	1st and 2nd Brigades, Army of Kentucky [US]; Army of Kentucky [CS]	**US 4,900; CS 750**	*Confederate victory*
Louisiana					
BATON ROUGE	*East Baton Rouge Parish*	8/5/62	2nd Brigade, Department of the Gulf [US]; Breckinridge's Corps [CS]	**US 371; CS 478**	*Union victory*
FORT DERUSSY	*Avoyelles Parish*	3/14/64	3rd Division, 14th Army Corps [US]; Fort DeRussy Garrison [CS]	**US 48; CS 269**	*Union victory*
FORTS JACKSON AND ST. PHILIP	*Plaquemines Parish*	3/16–28/62	West Gulf Blockading Squadron [US]; garrisons of Fort Jackson and St. Philip and the crews of various ships [CS]	**US 229; CS 782**	*Union victory*
MANSFIELD	*DeSoto Parish*	4/8/64	Bank's Red River Expeditionary Force [US]; District of West Louisiana [CS]	**US 2,900; CS 1,500**	*Confederate victory*
NEW ORLEANS	*Orleans and St. Bernard Parishes*	4/25–5/1/62	Department of the Gulf [US]; Department No. 1 [CS]	**None**	*Union victory*
PLEASANT HILL	*DeSoro and Sabine Parishes*	4/9/64	Red River Expeditionary Force [US]; District of West Louisiana [CS]	**US 1,100; CS 2,000**	*Union victory*
PORT HUDSON	*East Baton Rouge and East Feliciana Parishes*	5/21–6/9/63	19th Army Corps, Army of the Gulf [US]; Confederate forces, 3rd District, Department of Mississippi and East Lousiana, Port Hudson [CS]	**US 5,000; CS 7,208**	*Union victory*
Maryland					
ANTIETAM	*Washington County*	9/16–18/62	Armies	**23,100 total**	*Inconclusive*
MONOCACY	*Frederick County*	7/9/64	Corps	**2,359 total**	*Confederate victory*
SOUTH MOUNTAIN	*Frederick and Washington Counties*	9/14/62	Corps	**4,500 total**	*Union victory*

BATTLE	LOCATION	DATE	FORCES ENGAGED	ESTIMATED CASUALTIES	RESULT
Mississippi					
BIG BLACK RIVER BRIDGE	Hinds and Warren Counties	5/17/63	13th Army Corps, Army of the Tennessee [US]; Bridgehead Defense Force [CS]	US 273; CS 2,000	Union victory
BRICE CROSS ROADS	Prentiss and Union Counties	6/10/64	Three-brigade division of infantry and a division of cavalry [US]; cavalry corps [CS]	US 2,610; CS 495	Confederate victory
CHAMPION HILL	Hinds County	5/16/63	Army of the Tennessee [US]; Department of Mississippi and East Louisiana [CS]	US 2,457; CS 4,300	Union victory
CHICKASAW BAYOU	Warren County	12/26-29/62	Right Wing, 13th Army Corps [US]; Department of Mississippi and East Louisiana [CS]	US 1,776; CS 207	Confederate victory
CORINTH	Alcorn County	10/3-4/62	Army of the Mississippi [US]; Army of the West Tennessee [CS]	US 2,359; CS 4,838	Union victory
CORINTH	Hardin and McNairy Counties, Tennessee; Alcorn and Toshimingo Counties, Mississippi	4/29-6/10/62	Department of the Mississippi [US]; Department No. 2 [CS]	Unknown	Union victory
JACKSON	Hinds and Jackson Counties	5/14/63	Army of the Tennessee [US]; Jackson Garrison [CS]	US 286; CS 850	Union victory
OKOLONA	Chicasaw County	2/22/64	Cavalry force [US]; Forrest's Cavalry Corps [CS]	US 100; CS 50	Confederate victory
PORT GIBSON	Claiborne County	5/1/63	Army of the Tennessee [US]; Confederate forces in the area [CS]	US 861; CS 787	Union victory
RAYMOND	Hinds County	5/12/63	17th Army Corps, Army of the Tennessee [US]; Gregg's Task Force [CS]	US 442; CS 569	Union victory
TUPELO	Pontotoc County	7/14-15/64	1st and 3rd Infantry Division and Cavalry Division, 16th Army Corps, and 1st Brigade, U.S. Colored Troops [US]; Department of Alabama, Mississippi, and East Louisiana [CS]	US 648; CS 1,300	Union victory
VICKSBURG	Warren County	5/18-7/4/63	Army of the Tennessee [US]; Army of Vicksburg [CS]	US 4,550; CS 31,275	Union victory
Missouri					
BYRAM'S FORD	Jackson County	10/22-23/64	1st Division, Army of the Border and provisional cavalry division [US]; Shelby's and Marmaduke's divisions [CS]	Unknown	Union victory
FORT DAVISON	Iron Country	9/27/64	Garrison [US]; Army of Missouri [CS]	US 184; CS 1,500	Union victory
NEW MADRID/ ISLAND NO. 10	City of New Madrid, Missouri; Lake County, Tennessee	2/28-4/8/62	Army of the Mississippi [US]; garrisons of New Madrid and Island No. 10 [CS]	Unknown	Union victory
NEWTONIA	Newton County	10/28/64	Five brigades [US]; remnants of Price's Army of Missouri [CS]	US 400; CS 250	Union victory
WESTPORT	Jackson County	10/23/64	Army of the Border [US]; Army of Missouri [CS]	US 1,500; CS 1,500	Union victory
WILSON'S CREEK	Greene and Christian Counties	8/10/61	Army of the West [US]; Missouri State Guard and McCulloch's Brigade [CS]	US 1,235; CS 1,095	Confederate victory
New Mexico					
GLORIETA PASS	Santa Fe and San Miguel Counties	3/26-28/62	Northern Division, Army of New Mexico [US]; 4th, 5th, and 7th Texas Cavalry Regiment, artillery, and a company of independent volunteers [CS]	US 142; CS 189	Union victory
VALVERDE	Socorro County	2/20-21/62	Department of New Mexico [US]; Army of New Mexico [CS]	US 202; CS 187	Confederate victory
North Carolina					
BENTONVILLE	Johnston County	3/19-21/65	Sherman's Right Wing [US]; Johnston's Army [CS]	US 1,646; CS 3,092	Union victory

BATTLE	LOCATION	DATE	FORCES ENGAGED	ESTIMATED CASUALTIES	RESULT
North Carolina (cont.)					
FORT FISHER	*New Hanover County*	1/13-15/65	Expeditionary Corps, Army of the James [US]; Hoke's Division and Fort Fisher Garrison [CS]	**2,000 total**	*Union victory*
NEW BERNE	*Craven County*	3/14/62	Expeditionary Force and Foster's, Reno's, and Parke's brigades [US]; five regiments, militia [CS]	**1,080 total**	*Union victory*
ROANOKE ISLAND	*Dare County*	2/7-8/62	7,500 [US]; 3,000 [CS]	**US 264; CS 2,643**	*Union victory*
Oklahoma					
CHUSTENAHLAH	*Osage County*	12/26/61	Creek and Seminole [Native American]; McIntosh's and Douglas Cooper's brigades [CS]	**Unknown**	*Confederate victory*
HONEY SPRINGS	*Muskogee and McIntosh Counties*	7/17/63	District of the Frontier [US]; 1st Brigade and Native American troops [CS]	**US 79; CS 637**	*Union victory*
Pennsylvania					
GETTYSBURG	*Adams County*	7/1-3/63	83,289 [US]; 75,054 [CS]	**US 23,000; CS 28,000**	*Union victory*
South Carolina					
CHARLESTON HARBOR	*Charleston County*	9/7-8/61	Regiments	**US 117; CS unknown**	*Confederate victory*
FORT SUMTER	*Charleston County*	4/12-14/61	Regiments	**None**	*Confederate victory*
FORT SUMTER	*City of Charleston*	8/17-12/31/63	Morris Island Batteries [US]; Fort Sumter Garrison [CS]	**Unknown**	*Inconclusive*
FORT WAGNER/ MORRIS ISLAND	*City of Charleston*	7/18-9/7/63	5,000 [US]; 1,800 [CS]	**US 1,515; CS 174**	*Confederate victory*
SECESSIONVILLE	*City of Charleston*	6/16/62	6,600 [US]; 2,000 [CS]	**US 685; CS 204**	*Confederate victory*
Tennessee					
CHATTANOOGA	*Hamilton County, City of Chattanooga*	11/23-25/63	Military Division of the Mississippi [US]; Amy of Tennessee [CS]	**US 5,815; CS 6,670**	*Union victory*
FORT DONELSON	*Stewart County*	2/11-16/62	Army in the Field [US]; Fort Donelson Garrison [CS]	**US 2,331; CS 15,067**	*Union victory*
FORT HENRY	*Stewart and Henry Counties, Tennessee; Calloway County, Kentucky*	2/6/62	District of Cairo [US]; Fort Henry Garrison [CS]	**US 40; CS 79**	*Union victory*
FORT PILLOW	*Lauderdale County*	4/12/64	Detachments from three units [US]; Brig. Gen. James R. Chalmers's 1st Division, Forrest's Cavalry Corps [CS]	**US 574; CS 80**	*Confederate victory*
FORT SANDERS	*Knox County*	11/29/63	Department of the Ohio [US]; Confederate forces in East Tennessee [CS]	**US 100; CS 780**	*Union victory*
FRANKLIN	*Williamson County*	11/30/64	4th and 23rd Army Corps (Army of the Ohio and Cumberland) [US]; Army of Tennessee [CS]	**US 2,326; CS 6,261**	*Union victory*
JOHNSONVILLE	*Benton County*	11/4-5/64	Supply depot garrison [US]; Forrest's cavalry [CS]	**Unknown**	*Confederate victory*
MEMPHIS	*Shelby County*	6/6/62	Ironclads *Benton, Louisville, Carondelet, Cairo,* and *St. Louis;* army rams *Queen of the West* and *Monarch* [US]; navy rams *General Beauregard, General Bragg, General Price, General Van Dorn, General Thompson, Colonel Lovell, Sumter,* and *Rebel* [CS]	**US 1; CS 180**	*Union victory*

BATTLE	LOCATION	DATE	FORCES ENGAGED	ESTIMATED CASUALTIES	RESULT
Tennessee (cont.)					
NASHVILLE	*Davidson County*	12/15-16/64	4th Army Corps, 23rd Army Corps, Detachment of the Army of Tennessee, provisional detachment, and cavalry corps [US]; Army of Tennessee [CS]	**US 2,140; CS 4,462**	*Union victory*
SHILOH	*Hardin County*	4/6-7/62	Army of the Tennessee and Army of the Ohio [US]; Army of the Mississippi [CS]	**US 13,047; CS 10,699**	*Union victory*
SPRING HILL	*Maury County*	11/29/64	4th and 23rd Army Corps [US]; Army of Tennessee [CS]	**Unknown**	*Union victory*
STONES RIVER	*Rutherford County*	12/31/62-1/2/63	Army of the Cumberland [US]; Army of Tennessee [CS]	**US 13,249; CS 10,266**	*Union victory*
WAUHATCHIE	*Hamilton, Marion, and Dade Counties*	10/28-29/63	11th Army Corps and 2nd Division, 12th Army Corps [US]; Hood's Division [CS]	**US 420; CS 408**	*Union victory*
Texas					
GALVESTON	*Galveston County*	1/1/63	Companies D, G, and I, 42nd Massachusetts Volunteer Infantry Regiment and the blockading ships [US]; four Confederate gunboats and district of Texas, New Mexico, and Arizona troops [CS]	**US 600; CS 50**	*Confederate victory*
SABINE PASS II	*Jefferson County*	9/8/63	Four gunboats and seven transports loaded with troops [US]; Texas Davis Guards [CS]	**US 230; CS unknown**	*Confederate victory*
Virginia					
APPOMATTOX COURT HOUSE	*Appomattox*	4/9/65	Armies	**700 total**	*Union victory*
APPOMATTOX STATION	*Appomattox County*	4/8/65	Divisions	**Unknown**	*Union victory*
BALL'S BLUFF	*Loudoun County*	10/21/61	2,000 [US]; 1,600 [CS]	**US 921; CS 149**	*Confederate victory*
BEAVER DAM CREEK	*Hanover County*	6/26/62	15,631 [US]; 16,356 [CS]	**US 400; CS 1,300**	*Union victory*
BOYDTON PLANK ROAD	*Dinwiddie County*	10/27-28/64	Corps	**US 1,758; CS 1,300**	*Confederate victory*
BRANDY STATION	*Culpeper County*	6/9/63	Corps	**1,090 total**	*Inconclusive*
BRISTOE STATION	*Prince William County*	10/14/63	Corps	**1,980 total**	*Union victory*
CEDAR CREEK	*Frederick, Shenandoah, and Warren Counties*	10/19/64	31,945 [US]; 21,000 [CS]	**US 5,665; CS 2,910**	*Union victory*
CEDAR MOUNTAIN	*Culpeper County*	8/9/62	8,030 [US]; 16,868 [CS]	**US 1,400; CS 1,307**	*Confederate victory*
CHAFFIN'S FARM/ NEW MARKET HEIGHTS	*Henrico County*	9/29-30/64	Armies	**4,430 total**	*Union victory*
CHANCELLORSVILLE	*Spotsylvania County*	4/30-5/6/63	97,382 [US]; 57,352 [CS]	**US 14,000; CS 10,000**	*Confederate victory*
CHANTILLY	*Fairfax County*	9/1/62	Divisions	**US 1,300; CS 800**	*Inconclusive*
COLD HARBOR	*Hanover County*	5/31-6/12/64	108,000 [US]; 62,000 [CS]	**US 13,000; CS 2,500**	*Confederate victory*
THE CRATER	*Petersburg*	7/30/64	9th Corps [US]; elements of the Army of Northern Virginia [CS]	**5,300 total**	*Confederate victory*
CROSS KEYS	*Rockingham County*	6/8/62	11,500 [US]; 5,800 [CS]	**US 664; CS 287**	*Confederate victory*
DEEP BOTTOM II	*Henrico County*	8/13-20/64	Corps	**4,600 total**	*Confederate victory*

Virginia (cont.)

BATTLE	LOCATION	DATE	FORCES ENGAGED	ESTIMATED CASUALTIES	RESULT
DEWRY'S BLUFF	Chesterfield County	5/15/62	Five gunboats [US]; battery garrison [CS]	41 total	Confederate victory
FISHER'S HILL	Shenandoah County	9/21-22/64	29,444 [US]; 9,500 [CS]	US 528; CS 1,235	Union victory
FIVE FORKS	Dinwiddie County	4/1/65	Corps	6,030 total	Union victory
FORT STEDMAN	Petersburg	3/25/65	Corps	US 950; CS 2900	Union victory
FREDERICKSBURG I	Spotsylvania County and Fredericksburg	12/11-15/62	100,007 [US]; 72,497 [CS]	US 13,353; CS 4,576	Confederate victory
FREDERICKSBURG II	Fredericksburg	5/3/63	Corps	2,000 total	Union victory
GAINES MILL	Hanover County	6/27/62	34,214 [US]; 57,018 [CS]	US 6,800; CS 8,700	Confederate victory
GLENDALE	Henrico County	6/30/62	Armies	6,500 total	Inconclusive
GLOBE TAVERN	Dinwiddie County	8/18-21/64	Corps	US 4,279; CS 1,600	Union victory
HAMPTON ROADS	Hampton Roads	4/8-9/62	Four warships [US]; one warship [CS]	US 409; CS 24	Inconclusive
HATCHER'S RUN	Dinwiddie County	2/5-7/65	34,517 [US]; 13,835 [CS]	2,700 total	Union gained ground
JERUSALEM PLANK ROAD	Dinwiddie County and Petersburg	6/21-24/64	Corps	4,000 total	Union gained ground
KERNSTOWN, FIRST	Frederick County and Winchester	3/23/62	8,500 [US]; 3,800 [CS]	US 590; CS 718	Union victory
KERNSTOWN, SECOND	Frederick County and Winchester	7/24/64	10,000 [US]; 13,000 [CS]	US 1,200; CS 600	Confederate victory
LYNCHBURG	City of Lynchburg	6/17-18/64	Corps	900 total	Confederate victory
MALVERN HILL	Henrico County	7/1/62	Armies	8,500 total	Union victory
MANASSAS, FIRST	Fairfax and Prince William Counties	7/21/61	28,450 [US]; 32,230 [CS]	US 2,950; CS 1,750	Confederate victory
MANASSAS, SECOND	Prince William County	8/28-30/62	Armies	US 13,830; CS 3,850	Confederate victory
MANASSAS STATION OPERATIONS	Prince William County	8/25-27/62	Divisions	1,100 total	Confederate victory
MINE RUN	Orange County	11/27-12/2/63	69,643 [US]; 44,426 [CS]	US 1,272; CS 680	Inconclusive
NEW MARKET	Shenandoah County	5/15/64	6,275 [US]; 4,090 [CS]	US 840; CS 540	Confederate victory
NORTH ANNA	Caroline and Hanover Counties	5/23-26/64	Armies	4,000 total	Inconclusive
OPEQUON	Frederick County	9/19/64	39,240 [US]; 15,200 [CS]	US 5,020; CS 3,610	Union victory
PEEBLE'S FARM	Dinwiddie County	9/30-10/2/64	Corps	3,800 total	Union victory
PETERSBURG	City of Petersburg	6/15-18/64	62,000 [US]; 42,000 [CS]	US 8,150; CS 3,236	Confederate victory
PETERSBURG	City of Petersburg	4/2/65	Armies; 4,250 [CS]	US 3,500; CS 4,250	Union victory
PIEDMONT	Augusta County	6/5-6/64	8,500 [US]; 5,500 [CS]	US 875; CS 1,500	Union victory
PORT REPUBLIC	Rockingham County	6/9/62	Divisions	US 1,002; CS 816	Confederate victory

BATTLE	LOCATION	DATE	FORCES ENGAGED	ESTIMATED CASUALTIES	RESULT
Virginia (cont.)					
PROCTOR'S CREEK	*Chesterfield County*	5/12-16/64	30,000 [US]; 18,000 [CS]	**6,660 total**	*Confederate victory*
RAPPAHANNOCK STATION	*Fauquier and Culpeper Counties*	11/7/63	Corps	**2,537 total**	*Union victory*
REAM'S STATION	*Dinwiddie County*	8/25/64	Corps	**3,492 total**	*Confederate victory*
SALEM CHURCH	*Spotsylvania County*	5/3-4/63	Corps	**5,000 total**	*Confederate victory*
SAILOR'S CREEK	*Amelia, Prince Edward, and Nottoway Counties*	4/6/65	Corps	**9,980 total**	*Union victory*
SEVEN PINES	*Henrico County*	5/31-6/1/62	Armies	**US 5,739; CS 7,997**	*Inconclusive*
SPOTSYLVANIA COURT HOUSE	*Spotsylvania County*	5/8-21/64	100,000 [US]; 52,000 [CS]	**US 18,000; CS 12,000**	*Inconclusive*
TOTOPOTOMOY CREEK	*Hanover County*	5/28-30/64	Corps	**US 1,100; CS 1,100**	*Inconclusive*
TREVILIAN STATION	*Louisa County*	6/11-12/64	Divisions	**1,600 total**	*Confederate victory*
WAYNESBORO	*Augusta County*	3/2/65	2,500 [US]; 1,600 [CS]	**1,800 total**	*Union victory*
WHITE OAK ROAD	*Dinwiddie County*	3/31/65	Corps	**US 1,870; CS 800**	*Union gained ground*
WILDERNESS	*Spotsylvania County*	5/5-7/64	101,895 [US]; 61,025 [CS]	**US 18,400; CS 11,400**	*Inconclusive*
WILLIAMSBURG	*York County and Williamsburg*	5/5/62	40,768 [US]; 31,823 [CS]	**US 2,283; CS 1,560**	*Inconclusive*
YORKTOWN	*York County and Newport News*	4/5-5/4/62	Armies	**320 total**	*Inconclusive*
West Virginia					
CARNIFEX FERRY	*Nicholas County*	9/10/61	Brigades	**250 total**	*Union victory*
CHEAT MOUNTAIN	*Pocahontas County*	9/12-15/61	Brigades	**US 80; CS 90**	*Union victory*
HARPERS FERRY	*Jefferson County*	9/12-15/62	Corps	**US 12,636; CS 286**	*Confederate victory*
RICH MOUNTAIN	*Randolph County*	7/11/61	Brigades	**US 46; CS 300**	*Union victory*

National Park Battle Sites

The National Park Service operates more than 40 sites related to the Civil War. The sites are a combination of battlefields, military parks, monuments, and historic buildings, including Ford's Theater and the homes of Abraham Lincoln and Robert E. Lee. Major battles were fought at the 16 sites below.

ANTIETAM NATIONAL BATTLEFIELD
P.O. Box 158
Sharpsburg, MD 21782
(301) 432-5124
This Civil War site marks the end of General Robert E. Lee's first invasion of the North in September 1862. The battle claimed more than 23,000 men killed, wounded, and missing in a single day, September 17, 1862.
Battle of Antietam

APPOMATTOX COURT HOUSE NATIONAL HISTORIC PARK
P.O. Box 218
Appomattox, VA
(804) 352-8987
Where Lee, commanding general of the Army of Northern Virginia, surrendered to Ulysses Grant, general in chief of all Union armies, on April 9, 1865.
Site of Surrender Meeting and the Battles of Appomattox Station and Appomattox Court House

CHICKAMAUGA AND CHATTANOOGA NATIONAL MILITARY PARK
3370 LaFayette Road
Fort Oglethorpe, GA 30742
(706) 866-9241
Chickamauga was considered the last major Confederate victory in the western theater, but it was a hollow victory, since the Federals ultimately gained control of Chattanooga two months later, in November 1863.
Battles of Chickamauga, Chattanooga, and Lookout Mountain

FORT DONELSON NATIONAL BATTLEFIELD
P.O. Box 434
Dover, TN 37058
(931) 232-5348
On February 16, 1862, the Union Army in Tennessee, under General Grant, won its first major victory of the Civil War. The proposed terms of "unconditional surrender" were accepted by the defeated Confederates in the capture of Fort Donelson.
Battle of Fort Donelson

FORT SUMTER NATIONAL MONUMENT
1214 Middle Street
Sullivan's Island, SC 29482
(843) 883-3123
The first engagement of the Civil War took place at Fort Sumter on April 12 and 13, 1861. After 34 hours of fighting, the Union surrendered the fort to the Confederates.
Battle of Fort Sumter

FREDERICKSBURG AND SPOTSYLVANIA NATIONAL MILITARY PARK
120 Chatham Lane
Fredericksburg, VA 22405
(540) 373-6122
The years of 1863 and '64 saw approximately 110,000 casualties during the four major battles fought in the vicinity of Fredericksburg, Virginia, making it the bloodiest ground on the North American continent.
Battles of Fredericksburg, Chancellorsville, the Wilderness, and Spotsylvania Court House

GETTYSBURG NATIONAL MILITARY PARK
97 Taneytown Road
Gettysburg, PA 17325
(717) 334-1124
The small town of Gettysburg saw the Civil War's largest battle, which began July 1, 1863, and ended two days later with the tragic "Pickett's Charge." The Union won and successfully turned back the second invasion of the North by General Lee's Army of Northern Virginia. More than 51,000 soldiers were killed, wounded, or captured, making it the bloodiest battle of the war.
Battle of Gettysburg, Gettysburg Address

HARPERS FERRY NATIONAL HISTORIC PARK
P.O. Box 65
Harpers Ferry, WV 25425
(304) 535-6298
Stonewall Jackson took possession of Harpers Ferry in September 1862, then led most of his soldiers to join Lee at Sharpsburg.
Battle of Harpers Ferry

MANASSAS NATIONAL BATTLEFIELD PARK
6511 Sudley Road
Manassas, VA 22110
(703) 361-1339
The Civil War's First and Second Manassas (also called Bull Run) were fought here July 21, 1861, and August 28-30, 1862. The 1861 battle, during which Confederate general Thomas J. Jackson acquired his nickname, "Stonewall," was the first test of both armies' military prowess.
First and Second Manassas (the Battles of Bull Run)

MONOCACY NATIONAL BATTLEFIELD
4801 Urbana Pike
Frederick, MD 21704
(301) 662-3515
Known as the "Battle That Saved Washington," the battle of Monocacy was fought on July 9, 1864, between 18,000 Confederate and 5,800 Union forces. The Confederate raid was thwarted and the war taken to the South for the rest of the conflict.
Battle of Monocacy

PEA RIDGE NATIONAL MILITARY PARK
P.O. Box 700
Pea Ridge, AR 72751
(501) 451-8122
The battle that was fought here in March 1862 saved Missouri for the Union.
Battle of Pea Ridge

PETERSBURG NATIONAL BATTLEFIELD
1539 Hickory Hill Road
Petersburg, VA 23803
(804) 732-3531
Petersburg became the setting for the longest siege in American history when Grant failed to capture Richmond in the spring of 1864. On April 2, 1865, almost 10 months after the siege began, Lee evacuated Petersburg.
Battle of Petersburg

RICHMOND NATIONAL BATTLEFIELD PARK
3215 East Broad Street
Richmond, VA 23223
(804) 226-1981
Union armies repeatedly set out to capture the Confederate capital at Richmond and end the war. Three campaigns came within a few miles of the city; the park commemorates 11 sites associated with those campaigns.
Battles of Gaines' Mill, Malvern Hill, and Cold Harbor

SHILOH NATIONAL MILITARY PARK
Route 1 Box 9
Shiloh, TN 38376
(901) 689-5696
Shiloh, the first major battle in the West, was fought on April 6 and 7, 1862. It involved 65,000 Union and 44,000 Confederate troops and resulted in 24,000 killed, wounded, or missing. The battle allowed Federal forces to advance on and seize control of the Confederate railroad hub at Corinth, Mississippi.
Battle of Shiloh

STONES RIVER NATIONAL BATTLEFIELD
3501 Old Nashville Highway
Murfreesboro, TN 37129
(615) 893-9501
After fierce fighting here from December 31, 1862, to January 2, 1863, Southern forces withdrew, allowing the Federals to take middle Tennessee and providing the North with a much-needed boost after the horrendous loss at Fredericksburg.
Battle of Stones River

VICKSBURG NATIONAL MILITARY PARK
3201 Clay Street
Vicksburg, MS 39183
(601) 636-0583
In May and June of 1863, Grant's armies converged on Vicksburg, entrapping the city and the Confederate army under General John Pemberton. On July 4, Vicksburg surrendered after prolonged siege operations—one of the most brilliant military campaigns of the war.
Battle of Vicksburg

For information on all the Civil War–related sites in the National Park Service, call 202-208-6843 (Web address is www.nps.gov).

Photo credits

Credits from left to right are separated by semicolons; from top to bottom by dashes.

Abreviations
LC Library of Congress
USAMHI U.S. Army Military Historical Institute, Carlisle, PA
WPC Frank and Marie-Therese Wood Print Collection, Alexandria, Va
Photographs taken on assignment for Time Life Books by Larry Sherer of High Impact Photography are followed by an asterisk.

Front cover: Medford Historical Society / Corbis—Medford Historical Society. Spine: Stamatelos Brothers Collection, Cambridge*

Back cover: Chicago Historical Society [IF APPROVED]

Front endpaper: Harpers Ferry Center / National Park Service 2-3: (title page) National Archives, neg 111-B-292. 6-7: Harpers Ferry Center / National Park Service. 8-9: Museum of the Confederacy, photography by Katherine Wetzel. 10-11: Medford Historical Society 12: New Hampshire Historical Society. 13: Putnam County Historical Society, Cold Springs, NY; Minnesota Historical Society. 14: Merserve-Kunhardt Collection. 15: LC; USAMHI. 16: Louisiana State Museum; LC—Chicago Historical Society—New-York Historical Society. 17: Granger Collection. 18: LC; Washington & Lee University—Ohio Historical Society. 19: WPC. 20: Michigan Dept of State Archives. 21: New-York Historical Society, Bella C. Landauer Collection; WPC. 22: Library of Virginia, Richmond; Western Reserve Historical Society. 23: USAMHI (neg: Volume 118, p. 6081). 24: Vermont Historical Society. 25: British Library. 26: New-York Historical Society. 27: Peabody Museum, Harvard University; National Archives—The John Judkyn Memorial, Bath, England. 28: Sophia Smith Collection, Smith College—National Portrait Gallery, Smithsonian Institution / Art Resource—Schlesinger Library, Radcliffe College; LC. 29: Trustees of the Public Library of Boston—LC. 28-29 (BACKGROUND): British Library. 30: Smithsonian Institution, photo no. 64-107. 31: Chicago Historical Society—LC. 32: LC; Boston Athenaeum. 33: Chicago Historical Society; Museum of the Confederacy, photography by Katherine Wetzel. 34: The Genesis of the Civil War, by Samuel Wylie Crawford, published by Charles L. Webster & Company, New York, 1867—National Archives. 35: LC. 36: Chicago Historical Society. 37: LC. 38: LC. 39: LC—Culver Pictures. 40: WPC—South Caroliniana Library, Univ of South Carolina, Columbia. 41: Meserve-Kunhardt Collection; National Archives. 42: William Clements Library, University of Michigan, Ann Arbor. 43: Charleston Library Society—USAMHI. 44: New York Historical Association, Cooperstown. 45: Burton Historical Collection of the Detroit Public Library. 46: Charleston Confederate Museum, photographed by Michael Latil; LC; LC; LC; LC. 47: LC, #LC-B8184-4391; LC. 46-47 (BACKGROUND): LC. 48: Collection of C. Paul Loane* 49: LC, #LC-B8184-40477—National Archives. 50: LC—New-York Historical Society—Michigan Historical Collections, Bentley Historical Library, University of Michigan. 50-51: New-York Historical Society. 51: USAMHI. 52: USAMHI—US Military Academy, West Point. 53: US Military Academy, West Point—National Archives. 54: Valentine Museum. 55: West Virginia and Regional History Collection, West Virginia University Library—LC. 56: LC—US Military Academy, West Point. 57: US Military Academy, West Point. 58: General Sweeney's Museum, Republic, Mo. 58-59: USAMHI. 59: LC, #LC-B8184-10037. 60: LC. 61: Burton Historical Collection of the Detroit Public Library, Detroit, MI. 62: LC, #LC-B8184-4389. 62-63: Meserve-Kunhardt Collection. 64: George Barnard Erath Papers, CN08739, Center for American History, University of Texas, Austin; Kean Wilcox—Richard Bihari Jr* 65: First City Regiment*—First City Regiment*—Collection of Russ A. Pritchard*—Smithsonian Institution, National Museum of American History*—Dean S. Thomas Collection*; Courtesy Jerry Coates Collection*—Dean S. Thomas Collection* 64-65(BACKGROUND): LC. 66: United Daughters of the Confederacy, from collection on deposit at the Georgia Historical Society, Savannah, Georgia, photographed by Daniel Grantham. 67: The Lightfoot Collection—Museum of the Confederacy. 68: Museum of the Confederacy, photography by Katherine Wetzel (2). 68-69: Seventh Regiment Fund, Inc, photographed by Al Freni. 69: Brown Brothers. 70: Confederate Imprints Collection, the University of Georgia Libraries; John A Hess. 71: New-York Historical Society—Iowa State Historical Society, Iowa City. 72: WPC—State Historical Society of Wisconsin. 72-73: Western Reserve Historical Society. 74: Lightfoot Collection. 75: Anne S.K. Brown Military Collection, Brown Univ Library—Rare Book Department of Perkins Library, Duke University. 76: Illinois State Historical Society; Courtesy of Michael McAfee*; New York State Museum of Albany, NY* 77: LC; US Military Academy, West Point. 76-77(BACKGROUND): New-York Historical Society. 78: Museum of the Confederacy* 79: LC, #LC-B8184-4099—Boston Public Library, Print Department. 80: State Historical Society of Missouri, Columbia; LC. 80-81: Boston Athenaeum. 81: LC. 82: Dr. Larry Freeman, American Life Foundation, photographed by Lon Mattoon. 83: USAMHI; WPC—Museum of the Confederacy, photography by Katherine Wetzel. 84: WPC. 84-85: New York Public Library Print Collection, Miriam and Ira D. Wallach Division of Art, Prints and Photographs. 86: C. Fiske Harris Collection on the Civil War and Slavery, Providence Public Library; Museum of the City of New York, Harry T. Peters Collection—Mrs. Arthur Mourot, Library of Virginia, Richmond. 86-87: Meserve-Kunhardt Collection. 88: McClellan Lincoln Collection, John Hay Library, Brown University. 89: LC—LC. 90-91: National Archives, #111-B-6332. 91: LC; WPC. 92: LC. 92-93: Medford Historical Society. 94: Corbis. 95: Painting by J.R. Walker, courtesy Confederate Memorial Association, Washington, DC*; Louisiana State Museum Collections; Lee-Fendall House Museum, Alexandria, Virginia—Stonewall Jackson Foundation, Lexington, Virginia. 94-95: LC. 96-97: LC, #LC-B8184-4547A. 98: Gettysburg National Military Park Museum*; Gettysburg National Military Park Museum* 99: LC—National Archives, #111-B-4385. 100: LC—LC—National Portrait Gallery. 100-101: LC. 102-103: USAMHI. 103: LC—From The Armies of Europe by G.M. McClellan, published by J.B. Lippincott & Co., Philadelphia, 1861. 104-105: Medford Historical Society. 105: Collection of Brian Pohanka. 106: Prints Division, The New York Public Library—LC, #LC-B8184-4547A. 106-107: Philadelphia Museum of Art. 108-109: Kean Archives, Philadelphia. 109: LC. 110: LC. 111: LC. 112: White House Collection, Painting by A. Wordsworth Thompson—John M. Nielson Collection. 113: Valentine Museum, Richmond, Va; National Archives, #111-B-3804—Special Collections Division, The University of Georgia Libraries; New York Public Library Prints Division; Astor, Lenox & Tilden Foundations W #871. 112-113 (BACKGROUND): LC. 114: Museum of the Confederacy*—Vernon Floyd Moss III, Wilson, NC* 115: Chicago Historical Society—The New Jersey Historical Society, copied by Henry Groskinsky. 116: LC; The Samuel H. Lockett Papers in the Southern Historical Collection, the University of North Carolina—National Portrait Gallery; LC. 116-117: Williamson Art Gallery and Museum, Birkenhead, Merseyhead, England. 118: New York Public Library, General Research Division 118-119: From Le Monde Illustre, courtesy Musee de la Marine, Paris. 119: Samuel H. Lockett Papers, #432, Southern Historical Collection, Library of the University of North Carolina at Chapel Hill—Museum of the Confederacy* 120-121: WPC. 121: Franklin D. Roosevelt Library, Hyde Park, NY. 122: WPC. 122-123: USAMHI. 124: LC. 125: LC. 126-127: Western Reserve Historical Society. 127: New Hampshire Historical Society—Houghton Library, Harvard University, Cambridge, Massachusetts. 128: Corbis—Franklin D. Roosevelt Library, Hyde Park, NY. 128-129: Western Reserve Historical Society, Cleveland. 130-131: War Memorial of Virginia. 131: National Archives, #111-B-2802; U.S. Naval History Center, Department of the Navy. 132: The Mariners' Museum, Newport News, Va.—Museum of the City of New York, New York, NY, #60.122.7. 133: New-York Historical Society—USAMHI—The Chrysler Museum. 132-133 (BACKGROUND): National Maritime Museum, Greenwich, London, England. 134: Fort St. Joseph Museum, Niles, Michigan. 135: LC—Collection of Brian Pohanka. 136: LC—Mississippi State Historical Museum; a division of the Department of Archives and History. 136-137: Western Reserve Historical Society, Cleveland, OH. 138: Valentine Museum, Cook Collection. 138-139: Chicago Historical Society, Chicago, Ill. #P&S 1932.0027. 139: Courtesy the Historic New Orleans Collection, #OS47-4-L—Museum of the Confederacy. 140: National Archives, #165-C-702. 140-141: USAMHI. 141: New-York Historical Society. 142: USAMHI. 143: WPC—U.S. Naval Academy/ Beverly R. Robinson Collection. 144-145: WPC. 145: Smithsonian Institution, Washington DC, #48087—Kentucky Historical Society, Frankfort. 146: American Heritage Picture Collection—National Archives, #111-BH-1172. 146-147: State Historical Museum of Missouri. 148: WPC—LC. 148-149: USAMHI. 150-151: National Archives, #111-B-292. 151: Seventh Regiment Fund, photographed by Al Freni—Chicago Historical Society. 152: Vermont Historical Society. 152-153: LC. 154: LC, #LC-B8171-0377. 155: LC. 156: Smithsonian Institution, Washington DC, #CT-80-1290. 157: LC. 158: Collection of Jay P. Altmayer, copied by Larry Cantrell—Mariners Museum, Newport News, Va (US Navy Photo). 159 Mariners Museum, Newport News, Va. (10); LC—LC; Mariners Museum, Newport News, Va. 158-159: New-York Historical Society. 160: New Market Battlefield Park, Hall of Valor Museum* 161: Valentine Museum, Richmond, VA; From The Face of Robert E. Lee in Life and Legend copyright 1947 by Roy Meredith, published by Charles Scribner's Sons, New York—Courtesy Mrs. William Hunter deButts and the Virginia Historical Society, Richmond, Virginia—Arlington House, Robert E. Lee Memorial, National Park Service* 162: The Corcoran Gallery of Art, Gift of William Wilson Corcoran. 162-163: Library of Virginia. 163: Antietam National Battlefield Park* 164: LC, #LC-B8171-0489. 164-165: LC, #LC-B8171-431. 165: LC, Geography and Map Division No. 621. 166-167: National Archives #79-CWC-3F2. 167: WPC—USAMHI. 168-169: USAMHI. 169: Museum of the Confederacy. 170: LC, #LC-B8171-7383. 171: LC,. #LC-B8171-656. 172: WPC—LC. 173: American Heritage Picture Collection. 174-175: Michigan Historical Collection, Bentley Historical Library, University of Michigan. 175: USAMHI—Museum of the Confederacy* 176-177: Minnesota Historical Society. 177: LC, #LC-B8171-0468. 178: Minnesota Historical Society—Courtesy Ronn Palm. 178-179: LC. 180: LC, Geography and Map Division No. 566.2—Elkhart County Historical Museum, Bristol, Indiana. Collection on loan from D.W. Strauss. Photography courtesy Troyer Studios (2). 181: Elkhart County Historical Museum, Bristol, Indiana. Collection on loan from D.W. Strauss. Photography courtesy Troyer Studios—Stonewall Jackson's Headquarters Museum, Winchester-Frederick County Historical Society*—From Stonewall Jackson's Way by John W. Wayland, The McClure Col, Inc., Staunton, Va, 1940; Civil War Library and Museum, Philadelphia; Rensselaer Polytechnic Institute, Troy, New York; USAMHI. 180-181(BACKGROUND): LC, Geography and Map Division No. 436. 182: Division of Military and Naval Affairs, State of New York, photographed by Henry Groskinsky. 183: LC—Courtesy John F. Weaver, McClean, Va. 184: LC; Western Reserve Historical Society, Cleveland, Ohio. 185: Gilder Lehrman Collection, on deposit at the Pierpont Morgan Library #GLC 6106.14 / Art Resource—LC. 186: LC, Geography and Map Division No. 252. 186-187: By A.A. Lamb, National Gallery of Art, Gift of Edgar William and Bernice Chrysler Garbisch. 187: LC. 188-189: Western Reserve Historical Society, Cleveland, Ohio. 189: LC—Anne S. K. Brown Military Collection, Brown University, Providence, Rhode Island. 190: LC, #LC-B8171-0595—Old Court House Museum, Vicksburg, Mississippi. 190-191: Seventh Regiment Fund, photographed by Al Freni. 192-193: LC. 193: LC. 194-195: USAMHI. 195: LC. 196: LC. 196-197: National Archives, #111-B-4782. 198: National Archives #77-F-194-6-42—LC. 198-199: Medford Historical Society. 200: USAMHI. 200-201: LC. 202: Museum of the Confederacy*—National Archives, Military Archives Division*; From On Hazardous Service by William Gilmore Beymer, published by Harper & Brothers, New York, 1912; LC; Valentine Museum, Richmond, Va. 202-203: LC; Lloyd Ostendorf Collection—Museum of the Confederacy*; Francis Lord Collection, photographed by Harold Norvell. 202-203 (BACKGROUND): From The Spy of the Rebellion, by Allan Pinkerton, published by G.W. Dillingham, NY, 1888. 204: Smithsonian Institution, National Museum of American History, Washington, DC, photographed by Dane Penland. 205: Medford Historical Society / Corbis—Smithsonian Institution, National Museum of American History, Washington, DC, photographed by Steve Tuttle; Smithsonian Institution, National Museum of American History, Washington, DC, photographed by Dane Penland. 206: Louisa May Alcott Memorial Association. 206-207: LC. 207: Frederick Law Olmsted National Historic Site / National Park Service; US Military Academy, West Point, photographed by Henry Groskinsky. 208: Houghton Library, Harvard Univ—From The Embattled Confederacy, Vol. 3, The Image of War: 1861-1865, published by Doubleday & Company, Inc. 1982 (Courtesy Fanny U. Phillips)—American Antiquarian Society, Worcester, MA. 208-209: LC, #LC-B8184-740. 209: LC, #LC-B8171-7448—LC. 210: Museum of the City of New York, gift of Mrs. J. West Roosevelt. 211: Western Reserve Historical Society, Cleveland, OH—The Rhode Island Historical Society, #Rhi (X3)4885. 212:

Index